MAD LIBS®

GO BIG OR GO MAD LIBS

MAD LIBS

An imprint of Penguin Random House LLC, New York

Go Big or Go Mad Libs first published in the United States of America by Mad Libs,
an imprint of Penguin Random House LLC, New York, 2022

Mad Libs format and text copyright © 1996, 2001, 2012, 2014, 2015, 2016, 2017, 2018, 2022
by Penguin Random House LLC

Concept created by Roger Price & Leonard Stern

Cover illustration by Scott Brooks

Photo credits: *Dog Ate My Mad Libs*: Eric Isselée/Thinkstock, *History of the World Mad Libs*:
Niko Guido/Getty Images, *Meow Libs*: GlobalP/Thinkstock

Visit us online at penguinrandomhouse.com.

Printed in the United States of America

Go Big or Go Mad Libs ISBN 9780593521434
3 5 7 9 10 8 6 4 2
COMR

MAD LIBS®
FIELD TRIP MAD LIBS

by Mickie Matheis

MAD LIBS
FIRE STATION FUN

When I was a little _____, my favorite field trip was visiting the fire
NOUN

station!

Firefighter _____ showed my class the big _____ that the
        PERSON IN ROOM (MALE)   VEHICLE

firefighters drove. He turned on the flashing red _____ and even sounded
                                           PLURAL NOUN

the alarm. It was so _____ loud that I had to cover my
                      ADVERB

_____! Another firefighter came out dressed in their
PART OF THE BODY (PLURAL)

_____-fighting gear, which included boots, a smoke mask, rubber
NOUN

_____, and a protective _____. Afterward, Chief
PLURAL NOUN   ARTICLE OF CLOTHING

_____ took us on a tour of the fire station. We saw where the
CELEBRITY (MALE)

firefighters ate, slept, and _____. There was an exercise room
                              VERB (PAST TENSE)

for the firefighters to use to stay strong and _____ in order to climb up
                                     ADJECTIVE

_____ and haul the heavy hoses that spray _____. The chief
PLURAL NOUN   TYPE OF LIQUID

taught us to always make sure the _____ detectors in our houses worked
                              NOUN

and never play with a lighted _____. He also showed us how to stop, drop,
                          NOUN

and _____, because it's always better to be safe than _____!
    VERB   ADJECTIVE

MAD LIBS® is fun to play with friends, but you can also play it by yourself! To begin with, DO NOT look at the story on the page below. Fill in the blanks on this page with the words called for. Then, using the words you have selected, fill in the blank spaces in the story.

Now you've created your own hilarious MAD LIBS® game!

AFTER THE AQUARIUM: A FIELD TRIP ESSAY

PERSON IN ROOM _____

A PLACE _____

TYPE OF LIQUID _____

VERB _____

ADJECTIVE _____

ADVERB _____

NOUN _____

PLURAL NOUN _____

PLURAL NOUN _____

COLOR _____

TYPE OF LIQUID _____

NOUN _____

TYPE OF LIQUID _____

PLURAL NOUN _____

PLURAL NOUN _____

NOUN _____

ADJECTIVE _____

VERB _____

MAD ☺ LIBS®

INSTRUCTIONS

MAD LIBS® is a game for people who don't like games!
It can be played by one, two, three, four, or forty.

• RIDICULOUSLY SIMPLE DIRECTIONS

In this tablet you will find stories containing blank spaces where words are left out. One player, the READER, selects one of these stories. The READER does not tell anyone what the story is about. Instead, he/she asks the other players, the WRITERS, to give him/her words. These words are used to fill in the blank spaces in the story.

• TO PLAY

The READER asks each WRITER in turn to call out a word—an adjective or a noun or whatever the space calls for—and uses them to fill in the blank spaces in the story. The result is a MAD LIBS® game.

When the READER then reads the completed MAD LIBS® game to the other players, they will discover that they have written a story that is fantastic, screamingly funny, shocking, silly, crazy, or just plain dumb—depending upon which words each WRITER called out.

• EXAMPLE (*Before* and *After*)

"_____!" he said _____
       EXCLAMATION   ADVERB

as he jumped into his convertible _____ and
                          NOUN

drove off with his _____ wife.
          ADJECTIVE

"_____OUCH_____!" he said _____HAPPILY_____
       EXCLAMATION   ADVERB

as he jumped into his convertible _____CAT_____ and
                          NOUN

drove off with his _____BRAVE_____ wife.
          ADJECTIVE

MAD LIBS®

QUICK REVIEW

In case you have forgotten what adjectives, adverbs, nouns, and verbs are, here is a quick review:

An ADJECTIVE describes something or somebody. *Lumpy, soft, ugly, messy,* and *short* are adjectives.

An ADVERB tells how something is done. It modifies a verb and usually ends in "ly." *Modestly, stupidly, greedily,* and *carefully* are adverbs.

A NOUN is the name of a person, place, or thing. *Sidewalk, umbrella, bridle, bathtub,* and *nose* are nouns.

A VERB is an action word. *Run, pitch, jump,* and *swim* are verbs. Put the verbs in past tense if the directions say PAST TENSE. *Ran, pitched, jumped,* and *swam* are verbs in the past tense.

When we ask for A PLACE, we mean any sort of place: a country or city *(Spain, Cleveland)* or a room *(bathroom, kitchen)*.

An EXCLAMATION or SILLY WORD is any sort of funny sound, gasp, grunt, or outcry, like *Wow!, Ouch!, Whomp!, Ick!,* and *Gadzooks!*

When we ask for specific words, like a NUMBER, a COLOR, an ANIMAL, or a PART OF THE BODY, we mean a word that is one of those things, like *seven, blue, horse,* or *head.*

When we ask for a PLURAL, it means more than one. For example, *cat* pluralized is *cats.*

MAD LIBS® is fun to play with friends, but you can also play it by yourself! To begin with, DO NOT look at the story on the page below. Fill in the blanks on this page with the words called for. Then, using the words you have selected, fill in the blank spaces in the story.

Now you've created your own hilarious MAD LIBS® game!

I ♥ FIELD TRIPS

ADJECTIVE _____

A PLACE _____

VERB ENDING IN "ING" _____

NOUN _____

NOUN _____

PERSON IN ROOM _____

ADJECTIVE _____

NOUN _____

ANIMAL _____

VERB ENDING IN "ING" _____

NUMBER _____

PLURAL NOUN _____

VERB (PAST TENSE) _____

ADJECTIVE _____

PLURAL NOUN _____

ADJECTIVE _____

NOUN _____

I would rather go on a/an _____ field trip than go to school any day!
                          ADJECTIVE

Even just taking a trip to (the) _____ is better than being stuck
                                  A PLACE

_____ in the classroom all day. One of my favorite parts about
VERB ENDING IN "ING"

field trips is riding in a/an _____ to our destination. I always choose my
                              NOUN

best _____, _____, to be my seatmate. We like to pass the time
      NOUN   PERSON IN ROOM

playing a/an _____ game called Road Trip Scavenger Hunt. We make a
              ADJECTIVE

list of items to look for during the drive, such as a/an _____ riding a
                                                          NOUN

motorcycle or a/an _____ _____ along the roadside.
                    ANIMAL   VERB ENDING IN "ING"

Field trips are fun because they teach us more about things we have already

learned in school, like how there are _____ _____ in our solar
                                        NUMBER   PLURAL NOUN

system or how people cooked, farmed, and _____ back in the
                                            VERB (PAST TENSE)

_____ days. But the best part about taking field trips is that our
ADJECTIVE

_____ usually don't assign any _____ homework that day. If we
PLURAL NOUN   ADJECTIVE

could take field trips every day, I'd be the happiest _____ in the world!
                                                        NOUN

MAD LIBS® is fun to play with friends, but you can also play it by yourself! To begin with, DO NOT look at the story on the page below. Fill in the blanks on this page with the words called for. Then, using the words you have selected, fill in the blank spaces in the story.

Now you've created your own hilarious MAD LIBS® game!

RULES OF THE RIDE

CELEBRITY (MALE) _____

ADJECTIVE _____

NOUN _____

VERB ENDING IN "ING" _____

VERB _____

ADVERB _____

ADJECTIVE _____

PLURAL NOUN _____

PLURAL NOUN _____

NUMBER _____

ADJECTIVE _____

COLOR _____

PART OF THE BODY (PLURAL) _____

PLURAL NOUN _____

PART OF THE BODY _____

MAD LIBS®
RULES OF THE RIDE

Whenever our bus driver for field trips is _____, our class is in for
<u>CELEBRITY (MALE)</u>

a/an _____ time! This grumpy old _____ has strict rules to follow,
  <u>ADJECTIVE</u>   <u>NOUN</u>

such as these:

- No running or _____ up and down the aisles of the
           <u>VERB ENDING IN "ING"</u>

  bus.

- Do not scream, yell, or _____ too loudly because it is _____
                  <u>VERB</u>   <u>ADVERB</u>

  distracting for the driver. Use your _____ indoor voice.
                                   <u>ADJECTIVE</u>

- Eating any sort of _____ is expressly prohibited!
                 <u>PLURAL NOUN</u>

- Do not throw anything, including paper _____.
                               <u>PLURAL NOUN</u>

- Don't ask the bus driver every _____ minutes, "Are we _____
                            <u>NUMBER</u>   <u>ADJECTIVE</u>

  yet?" This habit will make him scream and turn a bright shade of

  _____!
  <u>COLOR</u>

- Most importantly, keep your _____ and _____
                          <u>PART OF THE BODY (PLURAL)</u>   <u>PLURAL NOUN</u>

  inside the bus at all times. Anyone caught sticking his or her

  _____ out the window will be immediately removed
     <u>PART OF THE BODY</u>

  from the bus.

MAD LIBS® is fun to play with friends, but you can also play it by yourself! To begin with, DO NOT look at the story on the page below. Fill in the blanks on this page with the words called for. Then, using the words you have selected, fill in the blank spaces in the story.

Now you've created your own hilarious MAD LIBS® game!

BUS BUDDY

ADJECTIVE_____

VERB ENDING IN "ING"_____

CELEBRITY_____

PART OF THE BODY_____

PLURAL NOUN_____

PLURAL NOUN_____

NOUN_____

VERB_____

ADJECTIVE_____

ANIMAL_____

ARTICLE OF CLOTHING_____

NOUN_____

A PLACE_____

VERB_____

PART OF THE BODY_____

MAD LIBS
BUS BUDDY

Having a/an _____ buddy _____ next to you on the bus
         ADJECTIVE   VERB ENDING IN "ING"

is a good way to have a great field trip! First of all, I require my bus buddy to

know all the lines from every _____ movie ever made so we can recite
                                  CELEBRITY

them throughout the entire bus ride, complete with random

_____ gestures. I also appreciate when my bus buddy packs
  PART OF THE BODY

snacks for the ride, especially things like chocolate-covered _____ and
                                               PLURAL NOUN

salted _____. Of course, we have to be careful that the _____
     PLURAL NOUN   NOUN

driver doesn't see us, as we're not supposed to _____ when we're on the
                                       VERB

bus! The best bus buddies also have _____ imaginations! We'll make up
                                  ADJECTIVE

stories about the flying _____ we wish we could have as a pet, or the
                           ANIMAL

sparkly _____ we'd wear as a superhero costume, or the giant
           ARTICLE OF CLOTHING

_____ we'd live in if we owned our own private island near
  NOUN

(the) _____. Perhaps the most important quality in a bus buddy is his/
      A PLACE

her size. After all, you don't want to _____ next to someone who has such
                           VERB

a ginormous _____ that you keep falling off the seat!
           PART OF THE BODY

MAD LIBS® is fun to play with friends, but you can also play it by yourself! To begin with, DO NOT look at the story on the page below. Fill in the blanks on this page with the words called for. Then, using the words you have selected, fill in the blank spaces in the story.

Now you've created your own hilarious MAD LIBS® game!

PERMISSION SLIP

ADJECTIVE _____

VERB ENDING IN "ING" _____

NUMBER _____

NOUN _____

ADJECTIVE _____

PLURAL NOUN _____

A PLACE _____

CELEBRITY _____

PLURAL NOUN _____

PART OF THE BODY (PLURAL) _____

VERB ENDING IN "ING" _____

ADJECTIVE _____

NOUN _____

TYPE OF LIQUID _____

PLURAL NOUN _____

PLURAL NOUN _____

CELEBRITY _____

PLURAL NOUN _____

MAD LIBS

PERMISSION SLIP

Dear Parents: Our class will be going on a/an _____ field trip to
<u>ADJECTIVE</u>

_____ Rivers State Park next Friday. The cost of the trip is
<u>VERB ENDING IN "ING"</u>

$_____, and we will be traveling to the park by _____. The purpose
<u>NUMBER</u>   <u>NOUN</u>

of this _____ trip is to support what we've been learning in science class
<u>ADJECTIVE</u>

about the flowers, wildlife, and _____ native to (the) _____.
<u>PLURAL NOUN</u>   <u>A PLACE</u>

The trip will include a guided tour of the park by park ranger _____. Be
<u>CELEBRITY</u>

sure to remind your child to wear comfortable _____ on his/her
<u>PLURAL NOUN</u>

_____ because he/she will be walking and
<u>PART OF THE BODY (PLURAL)</u>

_____ throughout the park the entire day. Also, please be sure
<u>VERB ENDING IN "ING"</u>

to pack a/an _____ lunch in a brown paper _____, including some
<u>ADJECTIVE</u>   <u>NOUN</u>

bottled _____. We are asking for several _____ to serve as
<u>TYPE OF LIQUID</u>   <u>PLURAL NOUN</u>

chaperones on this trip; you will oversee a group of six _____. If
<u>PLURAL NOUN</u>

interested, please call Principal _____ at the school. Thank you in
<u>CELEBRITY</u>

advance for encouraging your children to behave like young ladies and

_____.
<u>PLURAL NOUN</u>

MAD LIBS® is fun to play with friends, but you can also play it by yourself! To begin with, DO NOT look at the story on the page below. Fill in the blanks on this page with the words called for. Then, using the words you have selected, fill in the blank spaces in the story.

Now you've created your own hilarious MAD LIBS® game!

LET'S GROW TO THE FARM

NOUN _____

ANIMAL (PLURAL) _____

PERSON IN ROOM _____

EXCLAMATION _____

PART OF THE BODY _____

NOUN _____

CELEBRITY (MALE) _____

ADJECTIVE _____

NOUN _____

TYPE OF LIQUID _____

PLURAL NOUN _____

PLURAL NOUN _____

A PLACE _____

PLURAL NOUN _____

COLOR _____

PLURAL NOUN _____

NOUN _____

VERB ENDING IN "ING" _____

MAD LIBS®
LET'S GROW TO THE FARM

The moment I stepped onto the grass at Misty _____ Farm, I knew I was
NOUN

going to like it there. Just listening to the sounds of _____
ANIMAL (PLURAL)

mooing, _____ oinking, and sheep going "_____"
PERSON IN ROOM   EXCLAMATION

put a smile on my _____. The _____ who ran the place
PART OF THE BODY   NOUN

called himself Farmer _____.He showed my class how much
CELEBRITY (MALE)

_____ work was required to run a farm. The first thing we learned was
ADJECTIVE

how to milk a/an _____. It was amazing to see _____
NOUN   TYPE OF LIQUID

come out! Afterward, we visited the chicken coop and gathered up all the

_____ that the little feathered _____ had laid. Next, our class
PLURAL NOUN   PLURAL NOUN

climbed into a hay wagon and was pulled all around (the) _____ to check
A PLACE

out the wheat, corn, and other _____ growing on the farm. Lastly, the
PLURAL NOUN

farmer took us to his house, where we picked juicy _____ _____
COLOR   PLURAL NOUN

from a tree in his yard and had cold glasses of _____ cider. If I can't do
NOUN

_____ for a job someday, I'm going to farm!
VERB ENDING IN "ING"

MAD LIBS® is fun to play with friends, but you can also play it by yourself! To begin with, DO NOT look at the story on the page below. Fill in the blanks on this page with the words called for. Then, using the words you have selected, fill in the blank spaces in the story.

Now you've created your own hilarious MAD LIBS® game!

OVERNIGHT FIELD TRIPS

NUMBER _____

PLURAL NOUN _____

ADJECTIVE _____

PLURAL NOUN _____

VERB ENDING IN "ING" _____

ADJECTIVE _____

ADJECTIVE _____

PART OF THE BODY _____

NOUN _____

PLURAL NOUN _____

NOUN _____

NOUN _____

Taking _____ school-age _____ on the road to a
          NUMBER   PLURAL NOUN

far-off location for a class trip is no small feat! Unlike trips that are close to

school, there's a whole other set of _____ rules for "away" trips, including
                                        ADJECTIVE

these:

- Remember to pack enough clean _____ to wear each day. After
                                    PLURAL NOUN

  all, if you're going to be _____ in a bus for hours, you
                              VERB ENDING IN "ING"

  should look and smell _____!
                          ADJECTIVE

- Exhibit _____ manners at meals. Be sure to neatly spread your
            ADJECTIVE

  napkin on your _____, and use your fork, knife, and
                  PART OF THE BODY

  _____ properly.
    NOUN

- Don't ruin your hotel room by cramming furniture and _____
                                                         PLURAL NOUN

  in the bathroom.

- Don't try to leave your hotel room after "lights out." While there may

  not be an armed _____ stationed outside your door, an exhausted
                    NOUN

  mom or _____ will be just as scary!
           NOUN

MAD LIBS® is fun to play with friends, but you can also play it by yourself! To begin with, DO NOT look at the story on the page below. Fill in the blanks on this page with the words called for. Then, using the words you have selected, fill in the blank spaces in the story.

Now you've created your own hilarious MAD LIBS® game!

WANTED:
PARENT CHAPERONES

ADJECTIVE _____

NOUN _____

PLURAL NOUN _____

PART OF THE BODY _____

ADJECTIVE _____

ANIMAL (PLURAL) _____

PLURAL NOUN _____

VERB _____

A PLACE _____

ADJECTIVE _____

NUMBER _____

PLURAL NOUN _____

ADJECTIVE _____

PART OF THE BODY (PLURAL) _____

ADJECTIVE _____

PART OF THE BODY (PLURAL) _____

ADJECTIVE _____

VERB _____

MAD LIBS®
WANTED:
PARENT CHAPERONES

Are you daring, adventurous, and _____? Does the thought of driving in
_{ADJECTIVE}

a stuffy, cramped _____ with a bunch of loud, boisterous _____
_{NOUN} _{PLURAL NOUN}

make your _____ beat with excitement? Can you picture
_{PART OF THE BODY}

yourself herding rowdy, _____ children like a pack of pygmy
_{ADJECTIVE}

_____? If so, then *you* could be a field trip chaperone! Join our
_{ANIMAL (PLURAL)}

team of ultra-responsible adult _____ charged with making sure that
_{PLURAL NOUN}

students *walk*, not _____, around a zoo, a museum, (the) _____,
_{VERB} _{A PLACE}

or whatever location their _____ teacher has selected for the field trip.
_{ADJECTIVE}

While previous experience is not required, candidates who can manage up to

_____ _____ at any given time while maintaining a/an _____
_{NUMBER} _{PLURAL NOUN} _{ADJECTIVE}

sense of humor are preferred. Those with eyes in the back of their

_____ will be given top consideration. And while there's no
_{PART OF THE BODY (PLURAL)}

salary, the joy of seeing _____ expressions on the kids'
_{ADJECTIVE}

_____ as they learn something new will be reward enough!
_{PART OF THE BODY (PLURAL)}

If this sounds like a/an _____ job, _____today for an application!
_{ADJECTIVE} _{VERB}

MAD LIBS® is fun to play with friends, but you can also play it by yourself! To begin with, DO NOT look at the story on the page below. Fill in the blanks on this page with the words called for. Then, using the words you have selected, fill in the blank spaces in the story.

Now you've created your own hilarious MAD LIBS® game!

FORGETTABLE FIELD TRIPS

ADJECTIVE _____

PART OF THE BODY _____

ADJECTIVE _____

VERB _____

PLURAL NOUN _____

PLURAL NOUN _____

ADJECTIVE _____

PART OF THE BODY (PLURAL) _____

ADVERB _____

NOUN _____

CELEBRITY _____

VERB ENDING IN "ING" _____

ADVERB _____

VERB (PAST TENSE) _____

PLURAL NOUN _____

VERB ENDING IN "ING" _____

ADJECTIVE _____

ADJECTIVE _____

MAD LIBS®
FORGETTABLE FIELD TRIPS

Not all field trips are fun, _____ adventures. Some have left me shaking
                              ADJECTIVE

my _____ and wondering what in the world my _____
      PART OF THE BODY   ADJECTIVE

teacher was thinking. For example, one time my class had to _____ along
                                                                VERB

the highway, picking up crumpled _____, moldy _____, and
                                   PLURAL NOUN   PLURAL NOUN

other _____ garbage that made us turn up our _____ in
        ADJECTIVE   PART OF THE BODY (PLURAL)

disgust. It was _____ gross! Another time, we went to a/an _____
                  ADVERB   NOUN

hardware store where an employee wearing a name tag that said "Hi! My name

is _____" showed us pieces of wood, paint samples, and tools for
     CELEBRITY

building, gardening, and _____. It was _____ boring!
                          VERB ENDING IN "ING"   ADVERB

And another time, we _____ for hours at a local funeral home
                       VERB (PAST TENSE)

and learned how dead _____ were prepared for burial. I still have
                       PLURAL NOUN

nightmares where I wake up trembling and _____! The next
                                          VERB ENDING IN "ING"

time one of these _____ field trips is planned, I'll be calling in _____!
                    ADJECTIVE   ADJECTIVE

MAD LIBS® is fun to play with friends, but you can also play it by yourself! To begin with, DO NOT look at the story on the page below. Fill in the blanks on this page with the words called for. Then, using the words you have selected, fill in the blank spaces in the story.

Now you've created your own hilarious MAD LIBS® game!

BEST. FIELD TRIP. EVER.

A PLACE _____

CELEBRITY _____

VERB _____

PLURAL NOUN _____

PART OF THE BODY _____

TYPE OF LIQUID _____

NUMBER _____

SILLY WORD _____

PART OF THE BODY (PLURAL) _____

ADJECTIVE _____

NOUN _____

NOUN _____

PLURAL NOUN _____

ADJECTIVE _____

PERSON IN ROOM _____

SAME PERSON IN ROOM _____

PART OF THE BODY _____

SILLY WORD _____

ADJECTIVE _____

MAD LIBS®
BEST. FIELD TRIP. EVER.

Our class was visiting the Bank of (the) _____ to learn about money. As
A PLACE

we stood there, waiting for security guard _____ to unlock the door
CELEBRITY

to the vault so we could _____ inside, three masked _____ ran
VERB _PLURAL NOUN_

into the bank. They blasted the guard squarely in the _____
PART OF THE BODY

with _____ from a water gun and knocked him to the ground. Then
TYPE OF LIQUID

they ran into the vault and stuffed bags full of $_____ bills. "_____!
NUMBER _SILLY WORD_

Get down on your _____!" one of the _____ robbers
PART OF THE BODY (PLURAL) _ADJECTIVE_

yelled at us. Then they ran out the front door, jumped into a getaway

_____, and sped off. Back inside the bank, the security _____
NOUN _NOUN_

called the police to report the theft of thousands of _____. I could
PLURAL NOUN

hear the _____ sound of a police siren getting closer. "_____!
ADJECTIVE _PERSON IN ROOM_

_____!" a voice said into my _____. "We're
SAME PERSON IN ROOM _PART OF THE BODY_

here." _____, I had fallen asleep on the bus! The most exciting field trip
SILLY WORD

of my life had only been a/an _____ dream!
ADJECTIVE

MAD LIBS® is fun to play with friends, but you can also play it by yourself! To begin with, DO NOT look at the story on the page below. Fill in the blanks on this page with the words called for. Then, using the words you have selected, fill in the blank spaces in the story.

Now you've created your own hilarious MAD LIBS® game!

DREAM TRIPS

PERSON IN ROOM _____

PART OF THE BODY _____

ADJECTIVE _____

NOUN _____

A PLACE _____

NUMBER _____

CELEBRITY _____

VERB ENDING IN "ING" _____

PLURAL NOUN _____

TYPE OF LIQUID _____

NOUN _____

NOUN _____

A PLACE _____

TYPE OF FOOD _____

ANIMAL _____

A PLACE _____

TYPE OF FOOD _____

PLURAL NOUN _____

MAD LIBS
DREAM TRIPS

When the teacher asked for suggestions for class field trips, _____
PERSON IN ROOM
raised a/an _____ and proposed these far-fetched but
PART OF THE BODY
super-_____ ideas:
ADJECTIVE

- Charter a/an _____ to fly the class to (the) _____ for
  NOUN　　　　　　　　　　　　　_A PLACE_
  a/an _____-course meal prepared by _____.
  NUMBER　　　　　　　　　　　　_CELEBRITY_

- Go scuba-_____ with dolphins, stingrays, and other
  VERB ENDING IN "ING"
  undersea _____ in the crystal-clear _____ of the
  PLURAL NOUN　　　　　　　　　_TYPE OF LIQUID_
  _____ Ocean.
  NOUN

- Travel to a private _____ off the coast of (the) _____
  NOUN　　　　　　　　　　　　　　　　　_A PLACE_
  where students could Jet Ski, yacht, and sip _____-flavored
  TYPE OF FOOD
  lemonade all day.

- Go _____-back riding around the remote jungles of (the)
  ANIMAL
  _____.
  A PLACE

- Rent out the local ice-cream parlor and spend the afternoon eating
  _____-flavored ice cream with whipped _____ and
  TYPE OF FOOD　　　　　　　　　　　　　_PLURAL NOUN_
  sprinkles on top.

MAD LIBS® is fun to play with friends, but you can also play it by yourself! To begin with, DO NOT look at the story on the page below. Fill in the blanks on this page with the words called for. Then, using the words you have selected, fill in the blank spaces in the story.

Now you've created your own hilarious MAD LIBS® game!

BROWN BAG LUNCH SPECIAL

NOUN _____

NOUN _____

PLURAL NOUN _____

TYPE OF FOOD _____

TYPE OF LIQUID _____

VERB _____

PART OF THE BODY _____

PLURAL NOUN _____

NOUN _____

ADJECTIVE _____

PERSON IN ROOM _____

NOUN _____

NOUN _____

NOUN _____

CELEBRITY _____

TYPE OF FOOD _____

ADJECTIVE _____

PART OF THE BODY _____

Remember to pack lunches in a brown paper _____ when your child is
                                           NOUN

going on a field trip. One of the most popular bagged lunches is a peanut

butter and _____ sandwich, sliced _____, and
              NOUN   PLURAL NOUN

_____-chip cookies. A smart way to keep the lunch cold is to freeze a
   TYPE OF FOOD

bottle of _____ the night before the trip. It serves as an ice pack
             TYPE OF LIQUID

until it's time to _____. Don't forget to include a napkin so that your
                     VERB

child can wipe their _____. Some moms and _____
                        PART OF THE BODY   PLURAL NOUN

like to make a packed lunch special for their little _____. You could tuck a
                                                        NOUN

small note in the bag that says "Have a/an _____ day, _____—
                                             ADJECTIVE   PERSON IN ROOM

I love you with all my _____!" Or you could liven up the lunch by drawing
                          NOUN

games of tic-tac-_____ on the bag or creating a lunch-themed word search
                    NOUN

with words like "sandwich," "drink," "_____," and more! Or decorate
                                          NOUN

the bag with pictures of _____ or stuff _____-scented stickers
                              CELEBRITY   TYPE OF FOOD

inside. Any of these _____ ideas will bring a smile to your child's
                          ADJECTIVE

_____!
   PART OF THE BODY

MAD LIBS® is fun to play with friends, but you can also play it by yourself! To begin with, DO NOT look at the story on the page below. Fill in the blanks on this page with the words called for. Then, using the words you have selected, fill in the blank spaces in the story.

Now you've created your own hilarious MAD LIBS® game!

FIELD TRIP ETIQUETTE

ADJECTIVE _____

ADJECTIVE _____

PLURAL NOUN _____

VERB _____

NOUN _____

VERB ENDING IN "ING" _____

VERB _____

PART OF THE BODY _____

PLURAL NOUN _____

PART OF THE BODY (PLURAL) _____

NOUN _____

VERB _____

NOUN _____

NOUN _____

SILLY WORD _____

MAD LIBS®
FIELD TRIP ETIQUETTE

Students are expected to be on their most _____ behavior during a field
 ADJECTIVE

trip so a/an _____ time can be had by all. Our class rules are as follows:
 ADJECTIVE

- Stay with the other _____ in your group as well as your chaperone.
   PLURAL NOUN

  When using the "buddy system," make sure you always _____
   VERB

  with your _____.
   NOUN

- No talking or _____ when the tour guide is trying to
   VERB ENDING IN "ING"

  _____.
  VERB

- If you have a question, raise your _____.
   PART OF THE BODY

- Don't touch any _____ on display unless you are given
   PLURAL NOUN

  permission.

- Keep your hands and _____ to yourself.
   PART OF THE BODY (PLURAL)

- If you get separated from your _____, don't panic. Calmly
   NOUN

  _____ where you are until an adult _____ comes to find
  VERB NOUN

  you.

- Be courteous to the tour _____ and say things like "please," "thank
   NOUN

  you," and "_____."
   SILLY WORD

MAD LIBS® is fun to play with friends, but you can also play it by yourself! To begin with, DO NOT look at the story on the page below. Fill in the blanks on this page with the words called for. Then, using the words you have selected, fill in the blank spaces in the story.

Now you've created your own hilarious MAD LIBS® game!

THE NATURAL HISTORY MUSEUM

A PLACE _____

PLURAL NOUN _____

PLURAL NOUN _____

VERB ENDING IN "ING" _____

ANIMAL (PLURAL) _____

ADJECTIVE _____

PLURAL NOUN _____

ADJECTIVE _____

TYPE OF LIQUID _____

PART OF THE BODY _____

ANIMAL (PLURAL) _____

NUMBER _____

NOUN _____

A PLACE _____

PERSON IN ROOM _____

VERB _____

ADJECTIVE _____

VERB _____

MAD LIBS®
THE NATURAL
HISTORY MUSEUM

Teachers, one of the best places in all of (the) _____ to take your class on

A PLACE

a field trip is the Natural History Museum. The museum offers unique

experiences for _____ of all ages. Whether your students are learning

PLURAL NOUN

about the Earth, the solar system, dinosaurs, mammals, _____, or

PLURAL NOUN

_____ _____, the Natural History Museum

VERB ENDING IN "ING"   ANIMAL (PLURAL)

has _____ displays and interactive _____ to support your classroom

ADJECTIVE   PLURAL NOUN

teachings. It's a one-of-a-kind environment to explore and learn about the

_____ natural world and our place in it. New exhibits include an actual

ADJECTIVE

working volcano from which _____ erupts, a hands-on enclosure

TYPE OF LIQUID

where you can come face-to-_____ with live _____,

PART OF THE BODY   ANIMAL (PLURAL)

a/an _____-year-old fossilized _____ found on an archaeological dig

NUMBER   NOUN

in (the) _____, and _____, a skeleton of a three-million-year-

A PLACE   PERSON IN ROOM

old human ancestor. Come to explore, stay to _____! You'll have such

VERB

a/an _____ time visiting the Natural History Museum, you won't ever

ADJECTIVE

want to _____!

VERB

MAD LIBS® is fun to play with friends, but you can also play it by yourself! To begin with, DO NOT look at the story on the page below. Fill in the blanks on this page with the words called for. Then, using the words you have selected, fill in the blank spaces in the story.

Now you've created your own hilarious MAD LIBS® game!

THEATER ADVENTURES

ADJECTIVE _____

VERB ENDING IN "ING" _____

NOUN _____

NOUN _____

CELEBRITY (MALE) _____

NOUN _____

VERB _____

NUMBER _____

ADJECTIVE _____

ADJECTIVE _____

PART OF THE BODY (PLURAL) _____

VERB _____

NOUN _____

VERB (PAST TENSE) _____

PLURAL NOUN _____

VERB _____

PART OF THE BODY _____

ADJECTIVE _____

MAD LIBS
THEATER ADVENTURES

On the way to see the _____ stage musical _____ *in the*
                        ADJECTIVE   VERB ENDING IN "ING"

Rain at the Little _____ Playhouse, our _____ teacher, Mr.
                        NOUN   NOUN

_____, quizzed the class on theater terms:
CELEBRITY (MALE)

- To **audition** means to show the casting _____ how well you can
                                            NOUN

  _____. You'll recite up to _____ lines from a/an _____
    VERB   NUMBER   ADJECTIVE

  play while making _____ facial expressions and gesturing wildly
                    ADJECTIVE

  with your _____.
            PART OF THE BODY (PLURAL)

- A **callback** is the opportunity to _____ for the casting _____
                                       VERB   NOUN

  a second time because you _____ so well the first time.
                            VERB (PAST TENSE)

- A **curtain call** is when the _____ who acted in the play come
                                 PLURAL NOUN

  back out onto the stage and take bows while audience members clap and

  _____ with appreciation.
    VERB

- "**Break a/an** _____" is an odd but _____ way of saying
                  PART OF THE BODY   ADJECTIVE

  "good luck" to an actor.

MAD LIBS® is fun to play with friends, but you can also play it by yourself! To begin with, DO NOT look at the story on the page below. Fill in the blanks on this page with the words called for. Then, using the words you have selected, fill in the blank spaces in the story.

Now you've created your own hilarious MAD LIBS® game!

WELCOME TO WASHINGTON, DC

A PLACE _____

PLURAL NOUN _____

NOUN _____

ANIMAL (PLURAL) _____

NOUN _____

PLURAL NOUN _____

ADJECTIVE _____

CELEBRITY _____

VERB ENDING IN "ING" _____

PERSON IN ROOM _____

ADJECTIVE _____

NOUN _____

COLOR _____

PERSON IN ROOM _____

ADJECTIVE _____

VERB _____

PLURAL NOUN _____

MAD LIBS®
WELCOME TO
WASHINGTON, DC

Visiting (the) _____, the capital of the United States, is an amazing way
                    A PLACE

to teach students about our country! This bustling city is home to many national

monuments, memorials, museums, and other _____ of historical
                                            PLURAL NOUN

significance. Get ready to explore the National Air and _____ Museum,
                                                          NOUN

which highlights America's journey of sending _____ into space.
                                               ANIMAL (PLURAL)

Pay your respects at the _____ War Memorial, which remembers the
                          NOUN

_____ that served in that _____ conflict. Grab photos at the
PLURAL NOUN   ADJECTIVE

_____ Memorial, which honors the leader of the _____
CELEBRITY   VERB ENDING IN "ING"

movement, and the _____ Monument, which commemorates
                   PERSON IN ROOM

the pioneering works of this _____ _____. The grand finale is a
                             ADJECTIVE   NOUN

private tour of the _____ House, led by the head of the Secret Service,
                    COLOR

Agent _____. Previous students have called this part of the trip
      PERSON IN ROOM

"unforgettable," "once in a lifetime," and "_____." Who knows? Maybe
                                            ADJECTIVE

someday you'll return to Washington, DC, to _____ there—as president
                                             VERB

of the United _____!
              PLURAL NOUN

MAD LIBS® is fun to play with friends, but you can also play it by yourself! To begin with, DO NOT look at the story on the page below. Fill in the blanks on this page with the words called for. Then, using the words you have selected, fill in the blank spaces in the story.

Now you've created your own hilarious MAD LIBS® game!

INTERVIEW WITH
A ZOOKEEPER

PERSON IN ROOM (MALE) _____

PLURAL NOUN _____

PLURAL NOUN _____

NOUN _____

NOUN _____

COLOR _____

NOUN _____

CELEBRITY _____

NOUN _____

PLURAL NOUN _____

A PLACE _____

ADJECTIVE _____

NUMBER _____

PART OF THE BODY (PLURAL) _____

VERB _____

TYPE OF LIQUID _____

VERB _____

ADJECTIVE _____

MAD LIBS®
INTERVIEW WITH A ZOOKEEPER

This is Suzy Woods of ZOO-TV with _____, aka "Jungle
                                    PERSON IN ROOM (MALE)

Genius," here at the _____ of the Wild Animal Park. He teaches facts
                     PLURAL NOUN

to kids about the different mammals, reptiles, and _____ from around
                                                    PLURAL NOUN

the world. I asked him to tell me which _____ at the park he liked best.
                                         NOUN

Suzy: What's your favorite _____ here at the zoo?
                               NOUN

Genius: It's a two-ton _____ _____ named _____. It's a
                            COLOR   NOUN   CELEBRITY

rare species of _____ found only in the deepest, darkest _____ of
                NOUN   PLURAL NOUN

(the) _____.
      A PLACE

Suzy: What should we know about this _____ creature?
                                          ADJECTIVE

Genius: It has gills, _____ legs, and wings resembling
                           NUMBER

_____, meaning it can _____ in
PART OF THE BODY (PLURAL)   VERB

_____, walk on the ground, and _____ through the air!
TYPE OF LIQUID   VERB

Who needs a/an _____ dog or a cat when you can have one of these?
               ADJECTIVE

MAD LIBS® is fun to play with friends, but you can also play it by yourself! To begin with, DO NOT look at the story on the page below. Fill in the blanks on this page with the words called for. Then, using the words you have selected, fill in the blank spaces in the story.

Now you've created your own hilarious MAD LIBS® game!

FIRE STATION FUN

NOUN _____

PERSON IN ROOM (MALE) _____

VEHICLE _____

PLURAL NOUN _____

ADVERB _____

PART OF THE BODY (PLURAL) _____

NOUN _____

PLURAL NOUN _____

ARTICLE OF CLOTHING _____

CELEBRITY (MALE) _____

VERB (PAST TENSE) _____

ADJECTIVE _____

PLURAL NOUN _____

TYPE OF LIQUID _____

NOUN _____

NOUN _____

VERB _____

ADJECTIVE _____

MAD LIBS®
AFTER THE AQUARIUM: A FIELD TRIP ESSAY

Ocean Life, by _____
PERSON IN ROOM

Oceans cover more than 70 percent of (the) _____'s surface and contain
A PLACE

about 97 percent of the Earth's supply of _____. There are many
TYPE OF LIQUID

fascinating creatures that _____ in the oceans, with _____ features
VERB   ADJECTIVE

and _____ amazing abilities. For example, the blue whale is the largest
ADVERB

_____ ever to have lived and weighs close to two hundred tons, which is
NOUN

roughly the equivalent of fifty full-grown African _____. The octopus
PLURAL NOUN

has eight long _____, called tentacles, and can shoot out _____
PLURAL NOUN   COLOR

_____ when a predator threatens it. A puffer-_____ is a fish that
TYPE OF LIQUID   NOUN

can quickly swallow enough _____ to inflate its own body so large,
TYPE OF LIQUID

no other _____ can eat it. Crabs are very lucky sea-_____
PLURAL NOUN   PLURAL NOUN

because whenever they lose a claw, another _____ grows in its place.
NOUN

These are just some of the _____ facts I learned about ocean life during
ADJECTIVE

my trip to the aquarium. I can't wait to _____ there again!
VERB

MAD LIBS® is fun to play with friends, but you can also play it by yourself! To begin with, DO NOT look at the story on the page below. Fill in the blanks on this page with the words called for. Then, using the words you have selected, fill in the blank spaces in the story.

Now you've created your own hilarious MAD LIBS® game!

CHAPERONE SURVIVAL TIPS

NOUN _____

ADJECTIVE _____

PART OF THE BODY _____

VERB _____

PLURAL NOUN _____

PART OF THE BODY (PLURAL) _____

TYPE OF LIQUID _____

NOUN _____

PART OF THE BODY _____

NOUN _____

PART OF THE BODY _____

NUMBER _____

PART OF THE BODY _____

PERSON IN ROOM _____

NOUN _____

MAD LIBS®
CHAPERONE SURVIVAL TIPS

Any adult _____ who volunteers to chaperone a field trip is to be
          NOUN

congratulated for their _____ bravery. It's *not* a job for the faint of
                         ADJECTIVE

_____! Here are some tips from the pros to ensure you not only
PART OF THE BODY

survive, but _____!
              VERB

• Wear comfortable walking _____ on your
                              PLURAL NOUN

_____.
PART OF THE BODY (PLURAL)

• Stay hydrated with _____, and snack often.
                      TYPE OF LIQUID

• The bus ride will have the deafening noise level of a/an _____
                                                            NOUN

concert, and the seats will (literally) be a pain in your _____.
                                                           PART OF THE BODY

Take a headache pill in advance—or just plan to drive your own

_____.
  NOUN

• Do frequent _____-counts to ensure you start and
                PART OF THE BODY

finish with _____ kids.
             NUMBER

• Last but not least, keep a/an _____ on any student named
                                  PART OF THE BODY

_____. A/An _____ with that name *always* seems
PERSON IN ROOM   NOUN

to be trouble!

MAD LIBS® is fun to play with friends, but you can also play it by yourself! To begin with, DO NOT look at the story on the page below. Fill in the blanks on this page with the words called for. Then, using the words you have selected, fill in the blank spaces in the story.

Now you've created your own hilarious MAD LIBS® game!

CLASSIC FIELD TRIP MOVIES

PLURAL NOUN _____

NOUN _____

ADJECTIVE _____

NOUN _____

PLURAL NOUN _____

ADJECTIVE _____

PERSON IN ROOM _____

ADJECTIVE _____

NOUN _____

CELEBRITY _____

VERB ENDING IN "ING" _____

PERSON IN ROOM (MALE) _____

TYPE OF FOOD _____

NOUN _____

NOUN _____

ADJECTIVE _____

NOUN _____

LAST NAME _____

MAD LIBS®
CLASSIC FIELD TRIP MOVIES

Let's grab a bucket of buttered _____ and curl up on the _____
                                   PLURAL NOUN   NOUN

to watch these _____ field trip movies that every school-age _____
                 ADJECTIVE   NOUN

should see:

Prehistoric Park: A class of science-minded junior _____ visit an ancient
                                                         PLURAL NOUN

forest where _____ dinosaurs such as the _____-asaurus
              ADJECTIVE   PERSON IN ROOM

roam free.

Overnight at the _____ *Museum*: Students camp out at the Historical
                    ADJECTIVE

_____ Museum and discover that wax figures of famous historical people,
  NOUN

such as Pocahontas, Christopher Columbus, Roosevelt, and _____,
                                                            CELEBRITY

come back to life at night and spend hours singing, dancing, and

_____ throughout the museum.
VERB ENDING IN "ING"

_____ *and the* _____ *Factory*: A young _____ finds a
PERSON IN ROOM (MALE)   TYPE OF FOOD   NOUN

winning golden _____ that allows him and his class to tour the elusive,
                 NOUN

_____ factory owned by an eccentric _____ named
ADJECTIVE   NOUN

Mr. _____.
     LAST NAME

MAD LIBS® is fun to play with friends, but you can also play it by yourself! To begin with, DO NOT look at the story on the page below. Fill in the blanks on this page with the words called for. Then, using the words you have selected, fill in the blank spaces in the story.

Now you've created your own hilarious MAD LIBS® game!

FIELD TRIPPIN':
TEACHER FEEDBACK

PLURAL NOUN _____

VERB ENDING IN "ING" _____

PLURAL NOUN _____

PLURAL NOUN _____

NUMBER _____

ANIMAL (PLURAL) _____

TYPE OF FOOD (PLURAL) _____

NOUN _____

ADJECTIVE _____

VERB _____

NUMBER _____

TYPE OF LIQUID _____

PERSON IN ROOM _____

TYPE OF LIQUID _____

PART OF THE BODY _____

PLURAL NOUN _____

VERB ENDING "ING" _____

ADJECTIVE _____

Dear Parents:

I am sending home this note to tell you how proud I was of your _____
                                                                    PLURAL NOUN

today on our field trip to the Science Museum! I was particularly impressed

with them during the Imagine an Invention exhibit. They put on their

_____ caps and came up with some genius _____! One
VERB ENDING IN "ING"   PLURAL NOUN

student used a spool of _____, _____ miniature _____,
                          PLURAL NOUN   NUMBER   ANIMAL (PLURAL)

paper clips, and some day-old _____ to fashion a
                                 TYPE OF FOOD (PLURAL)

jet-propelled _____. And the students had a ton of _____ fun at
                NOUN   ADJECTIVE

the Ocean Exhibit, a giant tank where they could splash, play, and _____
                                                                      VERB

in over _____ gallons of _____. There was one minor
         NUMBER   TYPE OF LIQUID

mishap where _____ drenched the poor tour guide with
               PERSON IN ROOM

a/an _____ cannon and soaked her from head to _____!
      TYPE OF LIQUID   PART OF THE BODY

Be sure to ask your _____ about the trip tonight when you're
                      PLURAL NOUN

_____ around the dinner table. They had a/an _____
VERB ENDING IN "ING"   ADJECTIVE

time!

GRAB BAG MAD LIBS

MAD LIBS®

INSTRUCTIONS

MAD LIBS® is a game for people who don't like games!
It can be played by one, two, three, four, or forty.

•RIDICULOUSLY SIMPLE DIRECTIONS

In this tablet you will find stories containing blank spaces where words are left out. One player, the READER, selects one of these stories. The READER does not tell anyone what the story is about. Instead, he/she asks the other players, the WRITERS, to give him/her words. These words are used to fill in the blank spaces in the story.

•TO PLAY

The READER asks each WRITER in turn to call out a word—an adjective or a noun or whatever the space calls for—and uses them to fill in the blank spaces in the story. The result is a MAD LIBS® game.

When the READER then reads the completed MAD LIBS® game to the other players, they will discover that they have written a story that is fantastic, screamingly funny, shocking, silly, crazy, or just plain dumb—depending upon which words each WRITER called out.

•EXAMPLE (*Before* and *After*)

"_____!" he said _____
        EXCLAMATION   ADVERB

as he jumped into his convertible _____ and
                                        NOUN

drove off with his _____ wife.
                        ADJECTIVE

"_____OUCH_____!" he said _____HAPPILY_____
        EXCLAMATION   ADVERB

as he jumped into his convertible _____CAT_____ and
                                        NOUN

drove off with his _____BRAVE_____ wife.
                        ADJECTIVE

MAD LIBS®

QUICK REVIEW

In case you have forgotten what adjectives, adverbs, nouns, and verbs are, here is a quick review:

An ADJECTIVE describes something or somebody. *Lumpy, soft, ugly, messy,* and *short* are adjectives.

An ADVERB tells how something is done. It modifies a verb and usually ends in "ly." *Modestly, stupidly, greedily,* and *carefully* are adverbs.

A NOUN is the name of a person, place, or thing. *Sidewalk, umbrella, bridle, bathtub,* and *nose* are nouns.

A VERB is an action word. *Run, pitch, jump,* and *swim* are verbs. Put the verbs in past tense if the directions say PAST TENSE. *Ran, pitched, jumped,* and *swam* are verbs in the past tense.

When we ask for A PLACE, we mean any sort of place: a country or city *(Spain, Cleveland)* or a room *(bathroom, kitchen).*

An EXCLAMATION or SILLY WORD is any sort of funny sound, gasp, grunt, or outcry, like *Wow!, Ouch!, Whomp!, Ick!,* and *Gadzooks!*

When we ask for specific words, like a NUMBER, a COLOR, an ANIMAL, or a PART OF THE BODY, we mean a word that is one of those things, like *seven, blue, horse,* or *head.*

When we ask for a PLURAL, it means more than one. For example, *cat* pluralized is *cats.*

MAD LIBS® is fun to play with friends, but you can also play it by yourself! To begin with, DO NOT look at the story on the page below. Fill in the blanks on this page with the words called for. Then, using the words you have selected, fill in the blank spaces in the story.

Now you've created your own hilarious MAD LIBS® game!

INTERVIEW WITH A ROCK STAR

PLURAL NOUN _____

PLURAL NOUN _____

NOUN _____

COLOR _____

VERB _____

ADJECTIVE _____

NOUN _____

NOUN _____

ADJECTIVE _____

ADJECTIVE _____

NUMBER _____

ADJECTIVE _____

ADJECTIVE _____

ADJECTIVE _____

NOUN _____

VERB _____

MAD LIBS
INTERVIEW WITH
A ROCK STAR

QUESTION: Whatever made you choose the name "The Psycho_____"
PLURAL NOUN

for your group?

ANSWER: All the other good names like the "Rolling _____,"
PLURAL NOUN

"_____ Jam," and "_____ Floyd" were taken.
NOUN   COLOR

QUESTION: You not only _____ songs, but you play many
VERB

_____ instruments, don't you?
ADJECTIVE

ANSWER: Yes. I play the electric _____, the bass
NOUN

_____ , and the _____ keyboard.
NOUN   ADJECTIVE

QUESTION: You now have a/an _____ song that is number
ADJECTIVE

_____ on the _____ charts. What was the inspiration for
NUMBER   ADJECTIVE

this _____ song?
ADJECTIVE

ANSWER: Believe it or not, it was a/an _____ song that my mother
ADJECTIVE

used to sing to me when it was time for _____, and it never failed to
NOUN

_____ me to sleep.
VERB

MAD LIBS® is fun to play with friends, but you can also play it by yourself! To begin with, DO NOT look at the story on the page below. Fill in the blanks on this page with the words called for. Then, using the words you have selected, fill in the blank spaces in the story.

Now you've created your own hilarious MAD LIBS® game!

HAVE I GOT A GIRAFFE FOR YOU!

PLURAL NOUN _____

PLURAL NOUN _____

PART OF THE BODY _____

NUMBER _____

PLURAL NOUN _____

PART OF THE BODY _____

TYPE OF LIQUID _____

PART OF THE BODY (PLURAL) _____

PART OF THE BODY _____

ADJECTIVE _____

PLURAL NOUN _____

ADJECTIVE _____

ADJECTIVE _____

VERB ENDING IN "ING" _____

NOUN _____

PLURAL NOUN _____

NOUN _____

Giraffes have aroused the curiosity of _____ since earliest times. The
PLURAL NOUN

giraffe is the tallest of all living _____, but scientists are unable to
PLURAL NOUN

explain how it got its long _____. The giraffe's tremendous
PART OF THE BODY

height, which might reach _____ _____, comes mostly from
NUMBER   PLURAL NOUN

its legs and _____. If a giraffe wants to take a drink of
PART OF THE BODY

_____ from the ground, it has to spread its
TYPE OF LIQUID

_____ far apart in order to reach down and lap up the
PART OF THE BODY (PLURAL)

water with its huge _____. The giraffe has _____ ears
PART OF THE BODY   ADJECTIVE

that are sensitive to the faintest _____, and it has a/an _____
PLURAL NOUN   ADJECTIVE

sense of smell and sight. When attacked, a giraffe can put up a/an _____
ADJECTIVE

fight by _____ out with its hind legs and using its head like a
VERB ENDING IN "ING"

sledge _____. Finally, a giraffe can gallop at more than thirty
NOUN

_____ an hour when pursued and can outrun the fastest
PLURAL NOUN

_____.
NOUN

MAD LIBS® is fun to play with friends, but you can also play it by yourself! To begin with, DO NOT look at the story on the page below. Fill in the blanks on this page with the words called for. Then, using the words you have selected, fill in the blank spaces in the story.

Now you've created your own hilarious MAD LIBS® game!

THE OLYMPICS

NOUN _____

PLURAL NOUN _____

ADJECTIVE _____

PLURAL NOUN _____

PLURAL NOUN _____

NUMBER _____

ADJECTIVE _____

ADJECTIVE _____

NOUN _____

ADJECTIVE _____

VERB ENDING IN "S" _____

PART OF THE BODY _____

NOUN _____

ADJECTIVE _____

PLURAL NOUN _____

PLURAL NOUN _____

Every two years, countries from all over the _____ send their best
NOUN

_____ to compete in _____ games and win
PLURAL NOUN   ADJECTIVE

_____. These events are called the Olympic _____, and
PLURAL NOUN   PLURAL NOUN

they started _____ years ago in _____ Greece. When a
NUMBER   ADJECTIVE

winner receives their _____ medal at the games, the national
ADJECTIVE

_____ of their is played by a/an _____ band. As
NOUN   ADJECTIVE

the band _____, the citizens of that country put their
VERB ENDING IN "S"

_____ to their chest and join in the singing of their
PART OF THE BODY

national _____. Thanks to television, these _____ events
NOUN   ADJECTIVE

can now be watched by over a billion _____ throughout the world
PLURAL NOUN

every two _____.
PLURAL NOUN

MAD LIBS® is fun to play with friends, but you can also play it by yourself! To begin with, DO NOT look at the story on the page below. Fill in the blanks on this page with the words called for. Then, using the words you have selected, fill in the blank spaces in the story.

Now you've created your own hilarious MAD LIBS® game!

HOME SWEET HOME

NOUN _____

PART OF THE BODY _____

NUMBER _____

NOUN _____

COLOR _____

ADJECTIVE _____

NOUN _____

NOUN _____

PLURAL NOUN _____

NOUN _____

NOUN _____

ADJECTIVE _____

NOUN _____

ADVERB _____

PART OF THE BODY _____

VERB ENDING IN "ING" _____

ADJECTIVE _____

MAD LIBS
HOME SWEET HOME

Some people are fond of the saying "Home is where you hang your

_____." Others say, "Home is where the _____
      NOUN   PART OF THE BODY

is." As for me, even though my home is a rustic, _____-story
                                                         NUMBER

_____ home with a/an _____ picket fence surrounding it,
     NOUN   COLOR

I think of it as my _____ castle. Perched on a/an _____
                     ADJECTIVE   NOUN

overlooking a babbling _____ and surrounded by a forest of huge
                           NOUN

_____, my home offers me _____ and tranquility. Each
 PLURAL NOUN   NOUN

and every _____, I look forward to coming back to my _____
         NOUN   ADJECTIVE

home, where my faithful _____ will _____ greet me by
                     NOUN   ADVERB

wagging its _____ and _____ all over
        PART OF THE BODY   VERB ENDING IN "ING"

me. I just love my home _____ home.
                   ADJECTIVE

MAD LIBS® is fun to play with friends, but you can also play it by yourself! To begin with, DO NOT look at the story on the page below. Fill in the blanks on this page with the words called for. Then, using the words you have selected, fill in the blank spaces in the story.

Now you've created your own hilarious MAD LIBS® game!

INTERVIEW WITH A COMEDIAN

NOUN _____

ADJECTIVE _____

ADJECTIVE _____

NOUN _____

NUMBER _____

PLURAL NOUN _____

NOUN _____

VERB _____

VERB _____

PLURAL NOUN _____

PLURAL NOUN _____

ADJECTIVE _____

NOUN _____

MAD LIBS®
INTERVIEW WITH
A COMEDIAN

QUESTION: Were you always a stand-up _____?

NOUN

ANSWER: No. I had many _____ jobs in my _____

ADJECTIVE   ADJECTIVE

lifetime. I started out as a used _____ salesperson, and then for

NOUN

_____ years, I sold ladies' _____.

NUMBER   PLURAL NOUN

QUESTION: When did you discover you were a funny _____

NOUN

who could make people _____ out loud?

VERB

ANSWER: It was in school. The first time our teacher had us do show and

_____, I made the _____ in my class laugh so hard

VERB   PLURAL NOUN

they fell out of their _____.

PLURAL NOUN

QUESTION: How would you describe your _____ act?

ADJECTIVE

ANSWER: I am a thinking person's _____.

NOUN

MAD LIBS® is fun to play with friends, but you can also play it by yourself! To begin with, DO NOT look at the story on the page below. Fill in the blanks on this page with the words called for. Then, using the words you have selected, fill in the blank spaces in the story.

Now you've created your own hilarious MAD LIBS® game!

MOVIES SHOULD BE FUN

PLURAL NOUN _____

ADJECTIVE _____

PLURAL NOUN _____

NOUN _____

ADJECTIVE _____

NOUN _____

NOUN _____

LAST NAME _____

A PLACE _____

ADJECTIVE _____

PERSON IN ROOM _____

PERSON IN ROOM _____

ADJECTIVE _____

PLURAL NOUN _____

PART OF THE BODY (PLURAL) _____

MAD LIBS
MOVIES SHOULD BE FUN

In recent years, there have been too many disaster movies in which tall

_____ catch on fire, _____ dinosaurs come to life,
　　PLURAL NOUN　　　　　　　　　　　　ADJECTIVE

and huge _____ attack people in the ocean, making you afraid to
　　　　　　PLURAL NOUN

get out of your _____ in the morning. Movie fans ask why we
　　　　　　　　　NOUN

can't have more _____ pictures like *It's a Wonderful*
　　　　　　　　　　ADJECTIVE

_____, *Gone with the* _____, or *Mr.*
　　　NOUN　　　　　　　　　　　　　　　　　NOUN

_____ *Goes to (the)* _____. These films
　　LAST NAME　　　　　　　　　　　　　　A PLACE

made you feel _____ all over. These same fans also ask why we can't have
　　　　　　　ADJECTIVE

more funny films with comedians such as Laurel and _____,
　　　　　　　　　　　　　　　　　　　　　　　　　PERSON IN ROOM

and Abbott and _____. These _____
　　　　　　　PERSON IN ROOM　　　　　　　　　　　　ADJECTIVE

performers gave us great slapstick _____ that still makes our
　　　　　　　　　　　　　　　PLURAL NOUN

_____ ache from laughing.
　PART OF THE BODY (PLURAL)

MAD LIBS® is fun to play with friends, but you can also play it by yourself! To begin with, DO NOT look at the story on the page below. Fill in the blanks on this page with the words called for. Then, using the words you have selected, fill in the blank spaces in the story.

Now you've created your own hilarious MAD LIBS® game!

COOL IT

PLURAL NOUN _____

ADJECTIVE _____

NOUN _____

ADJECTIVE _____

NOUN _____

NOUN _____

NOUN _____

NOUN _____

ADJECTIVE _____

VERB ENDING IN "ING" _____

NOUN _____

ADJECTIVE _____

NOUN _____

VERB _____

MAD ⦿ LIBS®
COOL IT

Weather plays an important part in our daily _____. What is
                                              PLURAL NOUN

weather, anyway? According to _____ scientists, who are known as
                                  ADJECTIVE

meteorologists, weather is what the air is like at any time of the _____.
                                                                      NOUN

It doesn't matter if the air is cold, hot, or _____, it's all weather. Weather
                                                ADJECTIVE

changes from hour to _____, from day to _____, from
                        NOUN   NOUN

season to _____, and from year to _____. Daily changes in
             NOUN   NOUN

weather are caused by _____ storms _____
                          ADJECTIVE   VERB ENDING IN "ING"

across the Earth. Seasonal changes are from the Earth moving around the

_____. When the vapors in _____ clouds condense, we
   NOUN   ADJECTIVE

have _____ and snow. Whether you like it or not, weather is here to
        NOUN

_____.
   VERB

MAD LIBS® is fun to play with friends, but you can also play it by yourself! To begin with, DO NOT look at the story on the page below. Fill in the blanks on this page with the words called for. Then, using the words you have selected, fill in the blank spaces in the story.

Now you've created your own hilarious MAD LIBS® game!

GOING TO TOWN

LAST NAME _____

ADJECTIVE _____

PLURAL NOUN _____

ADJECTIVE _____

PERSON IN ROOM _____

PLURAL NOUN _____

PLURAL NOUN _____

ADJECTIVE _____

NOUN _____

NUMBER _____

VERB ENDING IN "ING" _____

ADJECTIVE _____

ADJECTIVE _____

ADJECTIVE _____

NOUN _____

NOUN _____

MAD LIBS®
GOING TO TOWN

THE ART SCENE

Today the _____ Gallery presents a series of _____
          LAST NAME   ADJECTIVE
landscape paintings and still-life _____ by the _____ artist
                                    PLURAL NOUN   ADJECTIVE
_____. These beautiful _____ will be on exhibition for
PERSON IN ROOM   PLURAL NOUN
the next three _____.
                PLURAL NOUN

MUSIC

Tonight marks the _____ debut of the all-_____ choir of
                    ADJECTIVE   NOUN
_____ great _____ voices. This _____
   NUMBER   VERB ENDING IN "ING"   ADJECTIVE
ensemble will present _____ renditions of such _____ children's
                        ADJECTIVE   ADJECTIVE
songs as "Twinkle, Twinkle, Little _____" and "Old MacDonald
                                      NOUN
Had a/an _____."
           NOUN

MAD LIBS® is fun to play with friends, but you can also play it by yourself! To begin with, DO NOT look at the story on the page below. Fill in the blanks on this page with the words called for. Then, using the words you have selected, fill in the blank spaces in the story.

Now you've created your own hilarious MAD LIBS® game!

THE THREE MUSKETEERS

ADJECTIVE _____

PLURAL NOUN _____

ADJECTIVE _____

NOUN _____

ADJECTIVE _____

NOUN _____

NOUN _____

PLURAL NOUN _____

NOUN _____

PERSON IN ROOM _____

PLURAL NOUN _____

ADJECTIVE _____

NOUN _____

NOUN _____

PLURAL NOUN _____

NOUN _____

MAD LIBS®
THE THREE MUSKETEERS

There is no more rousing story in _____ literature than *The*
_{ADJECTIVE}

Three _____. This _____ romance by the
_{PLURAL NOUN} _{ADJECTIVE}

great French _____, Alexandre Dumas, tells the story of
_{NOUN}

D'Artagnan, a/an _____ young _____ who
_{ADJECTIVE} _{NOUN}

arrives in 17th-century Paris riding a/an _____ with only three
_{NOUN}

_____ in his pocket. Determined to be in the service of the
_{PLURAL NOUN}

_____ who rules all of France, he duels with Athos, Porthos,
_{NOUN}

and _____, three of the king's best _____.
_{PERSON IN ROOM} _{PLURAL NOUN}

Eventually, these swordsmen and D'Artagnan save their _____
_{ADJECTIVE}

king from being overthrown and losing his _____. Over the years, *The*
_{NOUN}

Three Musketeers has been made into a stage _____, two
_{NOUN}

motion _____, and even a Broadway _____.
_{PLURAL NOUN} _{NOUN}

MAD LIBS® is fun to play with friends, but you can also play it by yourself! To begin with, DO NOT look at the story on the page below. Fill in the blanks on this page with the words called for. Then, using the words you have selected, fill in the blank spaces in the story.

Now you've created your own hilarious MAD LIBS® game!

SNOW WHITE

PLURAL NOUN _____

PLURAL NOUN _____

ADJECTIVE _____

ADJECTIVE _____

NOUN _____

NOUN _____

NOUN _____

ADJECTIVE _____

ADJECTIVE _____

PLURAL NOUN _____

NOUN _____

COLOR _____

NOUN _____

PART OF THE BODY _____

ADVERB _____

MAD LIBS
SNOW WHITE

One of the most popular fairy _____ of all time is *Snow White*

PLURAL NOUN

and the Seven _____. Snow White is a princess whose

PLURAL NOUN

_____ beauty threatens her stepmother, the queen, who wants to

ADJECTIVE

be known as the most _____ lady in the _____.

ADJECTIVE · NOUN

Snow White is forced to flee from the _____ in which she lives and

NOUN

hide in the nearby _____. Once there, she is discovered by

NOUN

_____ animals who guide her to the _____ cottage of

ADJECTIVE · ADJECTIVE

the seven dwarfs. The dwarfs come home from digging in their mine and

discover Snow White asleep in their _____. The dwarfs take care

PLURAL NOUN

of her until a prince, who traveled the four corners of the _____

NOUN

in search of Snow _____, arrives and gives her a magical

COLOR

_____ on her _____, which miraculously brings her

NOUN · PART OF THE BODY

back to life. Snow White and the prince live _____ ever after.

ADVERB

MAD LIBS® is fun to play with friends, but you can also play it by yourself! To begin with, DO NOT look at the story on the page below. Fill in the blanks on this page with the words called for. Then, using the words you have selected, fill in the blank spaces in the story.

Now you've created your own hilarious MAD LIBS® game!

MAGIC, ANYONE?

PLURAL NOUN _____

ADJECTIVE _____

ADJECTIVE _____

NOUN _____

NOUN _____

NOUN _____

NOUN _____

ADJECTIVE _____

PART OF THE BODY _____

PLURAL NOUN _____

ADJECTIVE _____

NOUN _____

ADJECTIVE _____

NOUN _____

PART OF THE BODY (PLURAL) _____

PART OF THE BODY _____

PLURAL NOUN _____

_____ of all ages enjoy watching _____ magicians
   PLURAL NOUN   ADJECTIVE

perform their _____ tricks. Every man, woman, and _____
            ADJECTIVE   NOUN

loves to see a magician pull a/an _____ out of a hat, saw a live
                            NOUN

_____ in half, or make a huge _____ disappear into
   NOUN   NOUN

_____ air. Audiences love when magicians perform sleight of
   ADJECTIVE

_____ with a deck of _____, a/an _____ coin, or a
  PART OF THE BODY   PLURAL NOUN   ADJECTIVE

silk _____. The greatest of all magicians was the _____
   NOUN   ADJECTIVE

Harry Houdini, who was able to escape from a locked _____ even
                                  NOUN

though his _____ were tied behind his _____
     PART OF THE BODY (PLURAL)   PART OF THE BODY

and his feet were wrapped in iron _____.
                          PLURAL NOUN

MAD LIBS® is fun to play with friends, but you can also play it by yourself! To begin with, DO NOT look at the story on the page below. Fill in the blanks on this page with the words called for. Then, using the words you have selected, fill in the blank spaces in the story.

Now you've created your own hilarious MAD LIBS® game!

THE BIG GAME

PLURAL NOUN _____

PERSON IN ROOM _____

NOUN _____

LAST NAME _____

PLURAL NOUN _____

A PLACE _____

PLURAL NOUN _____

A PLACE _____

PLURAL NOUN _____

NOUN _____

ADJECTIVE _____

ADJECTIVE _____

NOUN _____

NOUN _____

NOUN _____

VERB _____

ADJECTIVE _____

MAD LIBS®
THE BIG GAME

To be read with great enthusiasm!

Hello there, sports _____! This is _____,
              PLURAL NOUN   PERSON IN ROOM

talking to you from the press _____ in _____ Stadium,
                                  NOUN   LAST NAME

where 57,000 cheering _____ have gathered to watch (the)
                            PLURAL NOUN

_____ _____ take on (the) _____
   A PLACE   PLURAL NOUN   A PLACE

_____. Even though the _____ is shining, it's a/an
  PLURAL NOUN   NOUN

_____ cold day with the temperature in the _____ 20s. A
  ADJECTIVE   ADJECTIVE

strong _____ is blowing fiercely across the playing _____ that
          NOUN   NOUN

will definitely affect the passing _____. We'll be back for the opening
                                       NOUN

_____-off after a few words from our _____ sponsor.
   VERB   ADJECTIVE

MAD LIBS® is fun to play with friends, but you can also play it by yourself! To begin with, DO NOT look at the story on the page below. Fill in the blanks on this page with the words called for. Then, using the words you have selected, fill in the blank spaces in the story.

Now you've created your own hilarious MAD LIBS® game!

THINGS TO DO
THIS WEEKEND

LAST NAME _____

ADJECTIVE _____

PLURAL NOUN _____

PLURAL NOUN _____

NOUN _____

ADJECTIVE _____

NOUN _____

ADVERB _____

NOUN _____

ADJECTIVE _____

PLURAL NOUN _____

PERSON IN ROOM _____

ADJECTIVE _____

NOUN _____

ADJECTIVE _____

ADJECTIVE _____

NOUN _____

NOUN _____

ADJECTIVE _____

FILM

_____ Theaters offers a/an _____ program of foreign
LAST NAME   ADJECTIVE

_____ never before seen in American _____. The first film to
PLURAL NOUN   PLURAL NOUN

be shown will be _Henry and the_ _____. This is the _____
                                                NOUN   ADJECTIVE

love story of a man and his _____. It will be shown _____
                                          NOUN   ADVERB

until the end of the _____.
                                NOUN

STAGE

Appearing in our _____ theater for the next three
                                  ADJECTIVE

_____ is _____, that very _____
PLURAL NOUN   PERSON IN ROOM   ADJECTIVE

star of stage, screen, and _____. They will be appearing with
                                          NOUN

our _____ repertory company in nightly performances of
        ADJECTIVE

William Shakespeare's _____ comedy _A Midsummer Night's_
                                    ADJECTIVE

_____. Tickets can be purchased now at the _____
NOUN   NOUN

office by telephone, fax, or _____ card.
                                          ADJECTIVE

MAD LIBS® is fun to play with friends, but you can also play it by yourself! To begin with, DO NOT look at the story on the page below. Fill in the blanks on this page with the words called for. Then, using the words you have selected, fill in the blank spaces in the story.

Now you've created your own hilarious MAD LIBS® game!

SCENE FROM A HORROR PICTURE

ADJECTIVE _____

PART OF THE BODY _____

PLURAL NOUN _____

NOUN _____

ADJECTIVE _____

PLURAL NOUN _____

EXCLAMATION _____

NOUN _____

PART OF THE BODY _____

PERSON IN ROOM _____

NOUN _____

NOUN _____

PART OF THE BODY _____

ADJECTIVE _____

VERB _____

ADVERB _____

NOUN _____

NOUN _____

MAD LIBS®
SCENE FROM
A HORROR PICTURE

To be read aloud (preferably by live people):

Actor #1: Why did we have to come to this _____ old castle?
ADJECTIVE

This place sends shivers up and down my _____.
PART OF THE BODY

Actor #2: We had no choice. You know all the _____ in town
PLURAL NOUN

were filled because of the _____ convention.
NOUN

Actor #1: I'd have been happy to stay in a/an _____ motel.
ADJECTIVE

Actor #2: Relax. Here comes the bellboy for our _____.
PLURAL NOUN

Actor #1: _____! Look, he's all bent over and has a big
EXCLAMATION

_____ riding on his _____. He looks just like
NOUN   PART OF THE BODY

_____ from that horror flick *Frankenstein*.
PERSON IN ROOM

Actor #2: No. I think he's my old _____ teacher from _____
NOUN   NOUN

school.

Actor #1: I'm putting my _____ down! I'm not staying in this
PART OF THE BODY

_____ place. I'd rather _____ in the car!
ADJECTIVE   VERB

Actor #2: You're worrying _____.
ADVERB

Actor #1: Really? Look at the bellboy. He has my _____ in one hand,
NOUN

your _____ in the other, and his third hand . . . His *third* hand?
NOUN

Ahhhhh!

MAD LIBS® is fun to play with friends, but you can also play it by yourself! To begin with, DO NOT look at the story on the page below. Fill in the blanks on this page with the words called for. Then, using the words you have selected, fill in the blank spaces in the story.

Now you've created your own hilarious MAD LIBS® game!

IN THE GOOD OLD SUMMERTIME

PLURAL NOUN _____

PLURAL NOUN _____

ADVERB _____

VERB ENDING IN "ING" _____

ADJECTIVE _____

NUMBER _____

PART OF THE BODY _____

PLURAL NOUN _____

NOUN _____

PLURAL NOUN _____

TYPE OF LIQUID _____

NOUN _____

ADVERB _____

PLURAL NOUN _____

PLURAL NOUN _____

NOUN _____

NOUN _____

NOUN _____

NOUN _____

Many selective _____ prefer the Summer Olympics to the

PLURAL NOUN

Winter _____. They respond _____ to such swimming

PLURAL NOUN   ADVERB

and _____ events as the hundred-meter _____-style

VERB ENDING IN "ING"   ADJECTIVE

race, the _____-meter _____-stroke race, and, of

NUMBER   PART OF THE BODY

course, the diving contests in which _____ dive off a high

PLURAL NOUN

_____ and do triple _____ in the air before

NOUN   PLURAL NOUN

landing in the _____. Equally fascinating are the track and

TYPE OF LIQUID

_____ events in which _____ conditioned _____

NOUN   ADVERB   PLURAL NOUN

compete for gold _____. They compete in such exciting events as

PLURAL NOUN

the 1,500-_____ race, the hundred-_____ dash, the ever-

NOUN   NOUN

popular _____ vaulting, and, last but not least, throwing the hammer,

NOUN

the javelin, and the _____.

NOUN

MAD LIBS® is fun to play with friends, but you can also play it by yourself! To begin with, DO NOT look at the story on the page below. Fill in the blanks on this page with the words called for. Then, using the words you have selected, fill in the blank spaces in the story.

Now you've created your own hilarious MAD LIBS® game!

GOOD MANNERS

NOUN _____

NOUN _____

NOUN _____

VERB _____

PART OF THE BODY _____

ADVERB _____

NOUN _____

NOUN _____

NOUN _____

NOUN _____

PART OF THE BODY (PLURAL) _____

NOUN _____

ADJECTIVE _____

ADVERB _____

MAD LIBS®
GOOD MANNERS

1. When you receive a birthday _____ or a wedding
   _____ NOUN, you should always send a thank-you _____.
   NOUN   NOUN

2. When you _____ or burp out loud, be sure to cover
   VERB

   your _____ and say, "I'm _____ sorry."
   PART OF THE BODY   ADVERB

3. If you are a man and wearing a/an _____ on your head
   NOUN

   and a/an _____ approaches, it's always polite to tip your
   NOUN

   _____.
   NOUN

4. When you are at a friend's _____ for dinner, remember, it's
   NOUN

   not polite to eat with your _____, take food from
   PART OF THE BODY (PLURAL)

   anyone else's _____, or leave the table before everyone else.
   NOUN

5. When meeting your friend's parents, always try to make a/an

   _____ impression by greeting them _____.
   ADJECTIVE   ADVERB

MAD LIBS® is fun to play with friends, but you can also play it by yourself! To begin with, DO NOT look at the story on the page below. Fill in the blanks on this page with the words called for. Then, using the words you have selected, fill in the blank spaces in the story.

Now you've created your own hilarious MAD LIBS® game!

TV GUIDANCE
PICK OF THE WEEK

NOUN _____

ADJECTIVE _____

NUMBER _____

PLURAL NOUN _____

PLURAL NOUN _____

NOUN _____

PART OF THE BODY (PLURAL) _____

ADJECTIVE _____

PERSON IN ROOM _____

NOUN _____

PART OF THE BODY _____

PLURAL NOUN _____

ADJECTIVE _____

ADJECTIVE _____

PERSON IN ROOM _____

NOUN _____

NOUN _____

THURSDAY, 8:00 P.M. *My Adventures as a Foreign* _____.
NOUN

This is an exciting and _____ made-for-TV movie that takes place
ADJECTIVE

during the time of World War _____. We give it a rating of three
NUMBER

_____.
PLURAL NOUN

FRIDAY, 7:30 P.M. *Happy* _____.
PLURAL NOUN

When an old high-school _____ welcomes him with open
NOUN

_____ and throws him a/an _____ party, this puts
PART OF THE BODY (PLURAL)   ADJECTIVE

_____, his former _____ friend, into a bad state of
PERSON IN ROOM   NOUN

_____.
PART OF THE BODY

SATURDAY, 10:00 P.M. *Where Have All the* _____ *Gone?*
PLURAL NOUN

This _____ thriller, by the _____ director _____,
ADJECTIVE   ADJECTIVE   PERSON IN ROOM

is about a Manhattan _____ searching for a missing person in a
NOUN

small _____.
NOUN

MAD LIBS® is fun to play with friends, but you can also play it by yourself! To begin with, DO NOT look at the story on the page below. Fill in the blanks on this page with the words called for. Then, using the words you have selected, fill in the blank spaces in the story.

Now you've created your own hilarious MAD LIBS® game!

GOOD HEALTH TO ONE AND ALL

ADJECTIVE _____

ADJECTIVE _____

VERB ENDING IN "ING" _____

PART OF THE BODY (PLURAL) _____

PLURAL NOUN _____

PLURAL NOUN _____

NOUN _____

PLURAL NOUN _____

PLURAL NOUN _____

NOUN _____

PLURAL NOUN _____

PLURAL NOUN _____

ADJECTIVE _____

PLURAL NOUN _____

ADJECTIVE _____

ADJECTIVE _____

MAD LIBS®
GOOD HEALTH
TO ONE AND ALL

A/An _____ fitness revolution is taking place. Today, millions of
      ADJECTIVE

people are doing all kinds of _____ exercises such as jogging, walking,
                 ADJECTIVE

and _____ to get their _____ in shape and
  VERB ENDING IN "ING"   PART OF THE BODY (PLURAL)

develop their _____. Many go to gyms and health _____
         PLURAL NOUN   PLURAL NOUN

to work out by punching a/an _____, lifting _____, or
               NOUN   PLURAL NOUN

performing aerobic _____. In the past _____
            PLURAL NOUN   NOUN

people have become very weight conscious. They have learned what

_____ they should and should not eat. They know it's healthy to eat
PLURAL NOUN

green _____ and _____ fruit. They also know to avoid
     PLURAL NOUN   ADJECTIVE

foods high in _____ and _____ fats, especially if they
        PLURAL NOUN   ADJECTIVE

want to lead a long and _____ life.
             ADJECTIVE

MAD LIBS® is fun to play with friends, but you can also play it by yourself! To begin with, DO NOT look at the story on the page below. Fill in the blanks on this page with the words called for. Then, using the words you have selected, fill in the blank spaces in the story.

Now you've created your own hilarious MAD LIBS® game!

WHY DO SKUNKS SMELL?

NOUN _____

ADJECTIVE _____

PLURAL NOUN _____

A PLACE _____

PLURAL NOUN _____

ADJECTIVE _____

NOUN _____

VERB ENDING IN "ING" _____

PART OF THE BODY _____

PART OF THE BODY (PLURAL) _____

PART OF THE BODY (PLURAL) _____

ADVERB _____

COLOR _____

PART OF THE BODY _____

PART OF THE BODY _____

MAD LIBS
WHY DO SKUNKS SMELL?

Surprisingly, a skunk is a friendly _____ who can make a/an
                                    NOUN

_____ household pet. But what makes these _____
ADJECTIVE   PLURAL NOUN

smell to high (the) _____? The skunk has scent _____
                    A PLACE   PLURAL NOUN

that contain a/an _____-smelling fluid. When attacked, the skunk
                  ADJECTIVE

aims this smelly _____ at its enemies. But the skunk does give
                 NOUN

warning before _____. It raises its _____ first, or
               VERB ENDING IN "ING"   PART OF THE BODY

stamps its _____ so that you can run away as fast as your
           PART OF THE BODY (PLURAL)

_____ can carry you. The most _____ recognizable
PART OF THE BODY (PLURAL)   ADVERB

skunk is the one with a/an _____ line on its _____ and
                           COLOR   PART OF THE BODY

another one between its _____ and its ears.
                        PART OF THE BODY

MAD LIBS® is fun to play with friends, but you can also play it by yourself! To begin with, DO NOT look at the story on the page below. Fill in the blanks on this page with the words called for. Then, using the words you have selected, fill in the blank spaces in the story.

Now you've created your own hilarious MAD LIBS® game!

FAMOUS QUOTES FROM THE AMERICAN REVOLUTION

NOUN _____

NOUN _____

COLOR _____

PART OF THE BODY (PLURAL) _____

NOUN _____

PLURAL NOUN _____

VERB ENDING IN "ING" _____

NOUN _____

PLURAL NOUN _____

PLURAL NOUN _____

ADJECTIVE _____

NOUN _____

MAD LIBS®
FAMOUS QUOTES FROM
THE AMERICAN REVOLUTION

Nathan Hale said: "I regret that I have but one _____ to give for
                                                        NOUN

my _____."
       NOUN

William Prescott said: "Don't fire until you see the _____ of their
                                                            COLOR

_____."
PART OF THE BODY (PLURAL)

Patrick Henry said: "Give me liberty or give me _____."
                                                        NOUN

Paul Revere said: "The _____ are _____."
                            PLURAL NOUN   VERB ENDING IN "ING"

John Hancock said: "I wrote my _____ large so the king could read it
                                    NOUN

without his _____."
                PLURAL NOUN

Thomas Jefferson said: "All _____ are created equal. They are
                                  PLURAL NOUN

endowed by their creator with certain _____ rights and among these
                                            ADJECTIVE

are life, liberty, and the pursuit of _____."
                                            NOUN

MAD LIBS

INSTRUCTIONS

MAD LIBS® is a game for people who don't like games!
It can be played by one, two, three, four, or forty.

• RIDICULOUSLY SIMPLE DIRECTIONS

In this tablet you will find stories containing blank spaces where words are left out. One player, the READER, selects one of these stories. The READER does not tell anyone what the story is about. Instead, he/she asks the other players, the WRITERS, to give him/her words. These words are used to fill in the blank spaces in the story.

• TO PLAY

The READER asks each WRITER in turn to call out a word—an adjective or a noun or whatever the space calls for—and uses them to fill in the blank spaces in the story. The result is a MAD LIBS® game.

When the READER then reads the completed MAD LIBS® game to the other players, they will discover that they have written a story that is fantastic, screamingly funny, shocking, silly, crazy, or just plain dumb—depending upon which words each WRITER called out.

• EXAMPLE (*Before* and *After*)

"_____!" he said _____
        EXCLAMATION   ADVERB

as he jumped into his convertible _____ and
                                              NOUN

drove off with his _____ wife.
                          ADJECTIVE

"_____OUCH_____!" he said _____HAPPILY_____
        EXCLAMATION   ADVERB

as he jumped into his convertible _____CAT_____ and
                                              NOUN

drove off with his _____BRAVE_____ wife.
                          ADJECTIVE

MAD LIBS®

QUICK REVIEW

In case you have forgotten what adjectives, adverbs, nouns, and verbs are, here is a quick review:

An ADJECTIVE describes something or somebody. *Lumpy, soft, ugly, messy,* and *short* are adjectives.

An ADVERB tells how something is done. It modifies a verb and usually ends in "ly." *Modestly, stupidly, greedily,* and *carefully* are adverbs.

A NOUN is the name of a person, place, or thing. *Sidewalk, umbrella, bridle, bathtub,* and *nose* are nouns.

A VERB is an action word. *Run, pitch, jump,* and *swim* are verbs. Put the verbs in past tense if the directions say PAST TENSE. *Ran, pitched, jumped,* and *swam* are verbs in the past tense.

When we ask for A PLACE, we mean any sort of place: a country or city *(Spain, Cleveland)* or a room *(bathroom, kitchen).*

An EXCLAMATION or SILLY WORD is any sort of funny sound, gasp, grunt, or outcry, like *Wow!, Ouch!, Whomp!, Ick!,* and *Gadzooks!*

When we ask for specific words, like a NUMBER, a COLOR, an ANIMAL, or a PART OF THE BODY, we mean a word that is one of those things, like *seven, blue, horse,* or *head.*

When we ask for a PLURAL, it means more than one. For example, *cat* pluralized is *cats.*

MAD LIBS® is fun to play with friends, but you can also play it by yourself! To begin with, DO NOT look at the story on the page below. Fill in the blanks on this page with the words called for. Then, using the words you have selected, fill in the blank spaces in the story.

Now you've created your own hilarious MAD LIBS® game!

HOW TO GET MY LOOK
BY ALBERT EINSTEIN

OCCUPATION _____

ADVERB _____

ADJECTIVE _____

NOUN _____

ADJECTIVE _____

ADJECTIVE _____

COLOR _____

ADJECTIVE _____

PART OF THE BODY _____

NOUN _____

ARTICLE OF CLOTHING _____

OCCUPATION _____

Hallo. I am famous German ＿＿＿＿＿＿ Albert Einstein. Some people
　　　　　　　　　　　　　　　OCCUPATION

say I look ＿＿＿＿＿＿ strange. And zey are right, I do! But I am not
　　　　　　ADVERB

actually ＿＿＿＿＿＿. Zis is just how I like to look. If you would also like
　　　　　ADJECTIVE

to look like zis, use ze makeover tips I have outlined below.

- Never comb your ＿＿＿＿＿＿: It is supposed to look like zis! Ze
　　　　　　　　　　NOUN

  more ＿＿＿＿＿＿, the better, as I always say. It also helps if your
  　　　ADJECTIVE

  hair is a/an ＿＿＿＿＿＿ shade of ＿＿＿＿＿＿.
  　　　　　　ADJECTIVE　　　　　COLOR

- Make ＿＿＿＿＿＿ faces as often as possible. For example, stick out
  　　　ADJECTIVE

  your ＿＿＿＿＿＿ in pictures. Why? Because life is fun! Do zis when
  　　　PART OF THE BODY

  your eager ＿＿＿＿＿＿ students photograph you. Zey will love it!
  　　　　　　NOUN

- Always wear a white lab ＿＿＿＿＿＿＿＿＿. Zis way, you will
  　　　　　　　　　　　　ARTICLE OF CLOTHING

  look like a real ＿＿＿＿＿＿.
  　　　　　　　OCCUPATION

MAD LIBS® is fun to play with friends, but you can also play it by yourself! To begin with, DO NOT look at the story on the page below. Fill in the blanks on this page with the words called for. Then, using the words you have selected, fill in the blank spaces in the story.

Now you've created your own hilarious MAD LIBS® game!

THE BIOGRAPHY OF ALBERT EINSTEIN

A PLACE _____

NUMBER _____

OCCUPATION _____

ADJECTIVE _____

COLOR _____

ADJECTIVE _____

ADVERB _____

ADJECTIVE _____

PLURAL NOUN _____

PLURAL NOUN _____

VERB (PAST TENSE) _____

NOUN _____

NOUN _____

NOUN _____

PART OF THE BODY _____

A PLACE _____

MAD LIBS
THE BIOGRAPHY OF
ALBERT EINSTEIN

Albert Einstein was born in (the) _____ in Germany in the year
                                    A PLACE

18-_____. He grew up to be a genius _____ with a/an _____
      NUMBER   OCCUPATION   ADJECTIVE

_____ head of hair and a/an _____ sense of humor. Even
   COLOR   ADJECTIVE

though he was _____ smart, the people who knew him thought he acted
                 ADVERB

pretty _____. He was notorious for losing _____ and forgetting
         ADJECTIVE   PLURAL NOUN

the _____ in his equations. Einstein became famous for inventing
      PLURAL NOUN

things like E equals MC _____, the theory of _____,
                          VERB (PAST TENSE)   NOUN

and the quantum _____ of light. In 1921, he won the Nobel _____
                   NOUN   NOUN

in Physics. After his death in 1955, Einstein's _____ was
                                                  PART OF THE BODY

donated to (the) _____ Medical Center.
                   A PLACE

MAD LIBS® is fun to play with friends, but you can also play it by yourself! To begin with, DO NOT look at the story on the page below. Fill in the blanks on this page with the words called for. Then, using the words you have selected, fill in the blank spaces in the story.

Now you've created your own hilarious MAD LIBS® game!

QUIZ: ARE YOU A MAD SCIENTIST?

ADJECTIVE _____

ADJECTIVE _____

EXCLAMATION _____

ADJECTIVE _____

ADJECTIVE _____

VERB (PAST TENSE) _____

TYPE OF LIQUID _____

ANIMAL (PLURAL) _____

COLOR _____

ADJECTIVE _____

NOUN _____

NOUN _____

ADJECTIVE _____

ARTICLE OF CLOTHING _____

ADJECTIVE _____

OCCUPATION _____

MAD LIBS®
QUIZ: ARE YOU A
MAD SCIENTIST?

Are you crazy about science? Do you go nuts for _____ experiments?
                                                    ADJECTIVE

Take this _____ quiz to find out if you're a mad scientist.
              ADJECTIVE

1. Your favorite saying is: a) "Oh, _____! What did I do?",
                                        EXCLAMATION

   b) "It's _____!", c) "This _____ experiment went exactly as
              ADJECTIVE   ADJECTIVE

   _____."
       VERB (PAST TENSE)

2. Your lab always contains: a) test tubes filled with _____,
                                                          TYPE OF LIQUID

   b) _____ floating in jars, c) a few _____ mice in cages.
       ANIMAL (PLURAL)   COLOR

3. Your favorite thing to do at night is: a) go to bed and have _____
                                                                  ADJECTIVE

   dreams, b) laugh maniacally while bringing to life an evil _____,
                                                                NOUN

   c) plan tomorrow's _____-work.
                        NOUN

If you answered mostly *b*'s, guess what? You're a/an _____ scientist! Go
                                                        ADJECTIVE

put on your long white _____ and experiment in your
                          ARTICLE OF CLOTHING

_____ laboratory. If you answered mostly *a*'s and *c*'s, you're better off as
 ADJECTIVE

a/an _____!
        OCCUPATION

MAD LIBS® is fun to play with friends, but you can also play it by yourself! To begin with, DO NOT look at the story on the page below. Fill in the blanks on this page with the words called for. Then, using the words you have selected, fill in the blank spaces in the story.

Now you've created your own hilarious MAD LIBS® game!

LAB RAT ON THE LOOSE

SILLY WORD _____

ADJECTIVE _____

NUMBER _____

NOUN _____

VERB ENDING IN "ING" _____

NOUN _____

TYPE OF LIQUID _____

ADJECTIVE _____

PART OF THE BODY _____

ADJECTIVE _____

VERB ENDING IN "ING" _____

ADJECTIVE _____

ANIMAL _____

ADJECTIVE _____

MAD LIBS®
LAB RAT ON THE LOOSE

Uh-oh! Last night, _____ the lab rat escaped from his cage and ran amok
SILLY WORD

in the science lab. He was out to get revenge on the _____ scientists
ADJECTIVE

who'd held him captive for _____ weeks. First, he ran straight to the
NUMBER

_____ tubes and knocked them over, _____ glass all
NOUN   VERB ENDING IN "ING"

over the _____. Then he jumped into a vat of _____ and
NOUN   TYPE OF LIQUID

left _____ _____-prints all over the floor. Later on,
ADJECTIVE   PART OF THE BODY

the _____ rat finally got tired of _____ around and went
ADJECTIVE   VERB ENDING IN "ING"

to sleep under a/an _____-scope. Looks like that silly _____ is
ADJECTIVE   ANIMAL

finally done with all his _____ hijinks. For now, at least . . .
ADJECTIVE

MAD LIBS® is fun to play with friends, but you can also play it by yourself! To begin with, DO NOT look at the story on the page below. Fill in the blanks on this page with the words called for. Then, using the words you have selected, fill in the blank spaces in the story.

Now you've created your own hilarious MAD LIBS® game!

THE STORY OF FRANKENSTEIN

PERSON IN ROOM (MALE) _____

ADJECTIVE _____

NOUN _____

NOUN _____

A PLACE _____

PART OF THE BODY (PLURAL) _____

NUMBER _____

PLURAL NOUN _____

NOUN _____

ADJECTIVE _____

NOUN _____

ADJECTIVE _____

A PLACE _____

NOUN _____

NOUN _____

ADVERB _____

VERB (PAST TENSE) _____

MAD LIBS®
THE STORY OF FRANKENSTEIN

Mary Shelley wrote a science-fiction book about a villainous mad scientist

called _____ Frankenstein. Frankenstein was a/an
         PERSON IN ROOM (MALE)

_____ scientist from the nineteenth _____. His greatest wish was to
ADJECTIVE   NOUN

one day become a real _____. So he went to (the) _____ and took
                       NOUN   A PLACE

a brain, some _____, and _____ legs from several dead
              PART OF THE BODY (PLURAL)   NUMBER

_____. Once he had sewn the body parts together, Frankenstein used
PLURAL NOUN

electricity to make the hideous _____ come to life. Soon, in the middle
                                NOUN

of a/an _____ and stormy _____, the creature awoke! It was
        ADJECTIVE   NOUN

Frankenstein's greatest creation, and one of the most _____ beings to
                                                       ADJECTIVE

ever live—until it started terrorizing the citizens of (the) _____.
                                                            A PLACE

Frankenstein had to take action. He armed himself with a/an _____
                                                            NOUN

and went on a hunt for the _____ he'd created. After searching
                           NOUN

_____ for months, Frankenstein finally had to give up his search because
ADVERB

he _____ .
   VERB (PAST TENSE)

MAD LIBS® is fun to play with friends, but you can also play it by yourself! To begin with, DO NOT look at the story on the page below. Fill in the blanks on this page with the words called for. Then, using the words you have selected, fill in the blank spaces in the story.

Now you've created your own hilarious MAD LIBS® game!

ANNOUNCEMENT: THE SCIENCE FAIR WINNERS

CITY _____

ADVERB _____

ADJECTIVE _____

PERSON IN ROOM (FEMALE) _____

NOUN _____

SILLY WORD _____

PERSON IN ROOM (MALE) _____

ADJECTIVE _____

VERB (PAST TENSE) _____

PERSON IN ROOM _____

VERB ENDING IN "ING" _____

NUMBER _____

COLOR _____

ADJECTIVE _____

NOUN _____

ADJECTIVE _____

MAD LIBS®
ANNOUNCEMENT: THE
SCIENCE FAIR WINNERS

Thank you all for participating in the _____ Middle School Science Fair.
CITY

Everyone worked very _____ on their projects, and it shows. We will
ADVERB

now announce the first-, second-, and _____-place winners.
ADJECTIVE

_____ won first prize for her miniature erupting
PERSON IN ROOM (FEMALE)

_____, which was a model of the largest volcano in history, Mount
NOUN

_____.
SILLY WORD

_____ got second place for his super _____ miniature
PERSON IN ROOM (MALE)   ADJECTIVE

solar system, in which all the planets _____ in circles.
                                       VERB (PAST TENSE)

_____ was given a third-place ribbon for _____ an
PERSON IN ROOM   VERB ENDING IN "ING"

ant farm using sand and _____ tiny _____ ants.
                        NUMBER   COLOR

That's it for the _____ annual science fair. We'll see you next _____
ADJECTIVE   NOUN

for another round of _____ science experiments.
                     ADJECTIVE

MAD LIBS® is fun to play with friends, but you can also play it by yourself! To begin with, DO NOT look at the story on the page below. Fill in the blanks on this page with the words called for. Then, using the words you have selected, fill in the blank spaces in the story.

Now you've created your own hilarious MAD LIBS® game!

THE PERIODIC TABLE

PLURAL NOUN _____

NOUN _____

NOUN _____

ADJECTIVE _____

A PLACE _____

LAST NAME _____

PLURAL NOUN _____

NUMBER _____

NOUN _____

PLURAL NOUN _____

NOUN _____

LETTER OF THE ALPHABET _____

LETTER OF THE ALPHABET _____

PLURAL NOUN _____

VERB _____

MAD LIBS
THE PERIODIC TABLE

The periodic table of _____ hangs in classrooms and _____
                        PLURAL NOUN   NOUN

laboratories all around the _____. So what's this _____ chart
                             NOUN   ADJECTIVE

all about? Well, in the eighteenth century, a chemist from (the) _____
                                                                  A PLACE

named Dmitri _____ created the very first periodic table of
              LAST NAME

_____. There are more than _____ elements on the periodic table,
PLURAL NOUN   NUMBER

organized by atomic _____. The elements all have a certain number of
                     NOUN

protons, neutrons, and _____. Each element on the periodic
                        PLURAL NOUN

_____ has a symbol that is often the first two letters of the element's
NOUN

name. For example, helium's symbol is _____
                                        LETTER OF THE ALPHABET

_____. Some scientists say more _____ should be
LETTER OF THE ALPHABET   PLURAL NOUN

added to the table. Maybe someday you'll _____ one yourself!
                                          VERB

MAD LIBS® is fun to play with friends, but you can also play it by yourself! To begin with, DO NOT look at the story on the page below. Fill in the blanks on this page with the words called for. Then, using the words you have selected, fill in the blank spaces in the story.

Now you've created your own hilarious MAD LIBS® game!

DR. JEKYLL AND MR. HYDE

OCCUPATION _____

CITY _____

NOUN _____

ADJECTIVE _____

PLURAL NOUN _____

VERB (PAST TENSE) _____

ADJECTIVE _____

ADVERB _____

VERB _____

PLURAL NOUN _____

ADJECTIVE _____

OCCUPATION _____

NOUN _____

NOUN _____

ADJECTIVE _____

NOUN _____

ADJECTIVE _____

TYPE OF LIQUID _____

PART OF THE BODY _____

MAD LIBS®
DR. JEKYLL AND MR. HYDE

Dr. Jekyll was a friendly old _____ living in _____, England. Mr.

OCCUPATION   CITY

Hyde was an evil young _____ who did _____ things to every

NOUN   ADJECTIVE

person he met. But these two _____ were also a lot alike. They even

PLURAL NOUN

kind of _____ the same! But Hyde had a/an _____

VERB (PAST TENSE)   ADJECTIVE

power over the doctor, and became _____ evil as time went on. He was

ADVERB

willing to _____ anyone who got in his way, and even took _____

VERB   PLURAL NOUN

from the _____ townspeople. Then Hyde murdered a well-known

ADJECTIVE

_____! But what a surprise—it wasn't Hyde after all. It was Jekyll! They

OCCUPATION

were the same exact _____. Turns out, Jekyll had split-_____

NOUN   NOUN

disorder. To fix this, Jekyll did _____ experiments on himself so that

ADJECTIVE

Hyde would leave his _____ once and for all. But the experiments were

NOUN

too _____. The chemicals and _____ didn't work. In the

ADJECTIVE   TYPE OF LIQUID

end, Hyde took over Jekyll's _____, and Jekyll was never

PART OF THE BODY

seen again.

MAD LIBS® is fun to play with friends, but you can also play it by yourself! To begin with, DO NOT look at the story on the page below. Fill in the blanks on this page with the words called for. Then, using the words you have selected, fill in the blank spaces in the story.

Now you've created your own hilarious MAD LIBS® game!

LABORATORY SAFETY DOS AND DON'TS

PART OF THE BODY (PLURAL) _____

NOUN _____

ADVERB _____

VERB ENDING IN "ING" _____

NOUN _____

VERB _____

ADJECTIVE _____

PART OF THE BODY (PLURAL) _____

TYPE OF FOOD _____

ADJECTIVE _____

TYPE OF CONTAINER _____

ANIMAL (PLURAL) _____

Do wear safety goggles. They will protect your _____ .
<u>PART OF THE BODY (PLURAL)</u>

Don't light anything on fire. Always keep a/an _____ extinguisher handy
<u>NOUN</u>

in case you _____ set your laboratory aflame.
<u>ADVERB</u>

Do clean the lens of the microscope before _____ it. You
<u>VERB ENDING IN "ING"</u>

might think you're looking at a cell when really you're just looking at a piece of

_____ .
<u>NOUN</u>

Don't get too close to the test tubes after combining their contents. They might

_____ all over you!
<u>VERB</u>

Do clean up after yourself. Experiments can leave you with _____ hands
<u>ADJECTIVE</u>

and stinky _____ .
<u>PART OF THE BODY (PLURAL)</u>

Don't leave any experiments unattended. If you get hungry and want to grab

a/an _____ sandwich, stop! You need to stay put until the _____
<u>TYPE OF FOOD</u>   <u>ADJECTIVE</u>

chemicals in your beakers are done boiling and you've put them safely away in

a/an _____ .
<u>TYPE OF CONTAINER</u>

Do remember to feed your lab _____ . They're not only
<u>ANIMAL (PLURAL)</u>

your test subjects, they're your friends.

MAD LIBS® is fun to play with friends, but you can also play it by yourself! To begin with, DO NOT look at the story on the page below. Fill in the blanks on this page with the words called for. Then, using the words you have selected, fill in the blank spaces in the story.

Now you've created your own hilarious MAD LIBS® game!

I NEED A NEW LAB PARTNER!

FIRST NAME _____

ADJECTIVE _____

LAST NAME _____

PERSON IN ROOM _____

ADJECTIVE _____

VERB (PAST TENSE) _____

NOUN _____

ADJECTIVE _____

NOUN _____

ADJECTIVE _____

ADJECTIVE _____

PLURAL NOUN _____

ADJECTIVE _____

To Whom It May Concern:

Hi. My name is _____, and I am looking for a new,
　　　　　　　　FIRST NAME

_____ lab partner for Mrs. _____'s biology class. My
ADJECTIVE　　　　　　　　　　　　　　LAST NAME

last lab partner, _____, was really _____ and
　　　　　　　　　PERSON IN ROOM　　　　　　　　ADJECTIVE

never _____ our experiments on time. So I asked to
　　　　VERB (PAST TENSE)

switch, and the teacher said if I wanted another _____ partner,
　　　　　　　　　　　　　　　　　　　　　　　NOUN

I had to find one all by myself. If you are smart, _____ in school,
　　　　　　　　　　　　　　　　　　　　ADJECTIVE

and always turn your _____-work in on time, you'd be a/an
　　　　　　　　　NOUN

_____ lab partner for me. Please only contact me if you're
ADJECTIVE

_____ about science and love doing scientific
ADJECTIVE

_____. If this describes you, contact me at
PLURAL NOUN

scienceluvr1@-_____-mail.com, or just find me by my locker
　　　　　　　ADJECTIVE

after lunch.

MAD LIBS® is fun to play with friends, but you can also play it by yourself! To begin with, DO NOT look at the story on the page below. Fill in the blanks on this page with the words called for. Then, using the words you have selected, fill in the blank spaces in the story.

Now you've created your own hilarious MAD LIBS® game!

MY WACKY
CHEMISTRY TEACHER

LAST NAME _____

PART OF THE BODY (PLURAL) _____

NOUN _____

EXCLAMATION _____

PERSON IN ROOM _____

ADJECTIVE _____

NOUN _____

ADJECTIVE _____

NOUN _____

EXCLAMATION _____

VERB (PAST TENSE) _____

NOUN _____

ADJECTIVE _____

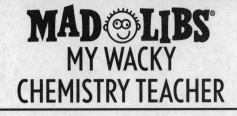

MY WACKY
CHEMISTRY TEACHER

There are a lot of rumors going around about Mr. _____ , our chemistry

                                             LAST NAME

teacher. He always has an odd look in his _____ . Sometimes,

                               PART OF THE BODY (PLURAL)

in the middle of a/an _____ lesson, he'll shout "_____!"

                    NOUN   EXCLAMATION

for no reason at all. My friend _____ told me that he acts

                               PERSON IN ROOM

_____ because one time during a/an _____-storm he was struck

ADJECTIVE   NOUN

by lightning in his classroom. Ouch! That would probably explain why he is

so _____ all the time and shakes whenever he writes on the

          ADJECTIVE

_____-board. Last week, while doing an experiment in class, he yelled,

NOUN

"_____! It's alive!" and then _____ around the

EXCLAMATION   VERB (PAST TENSE)

room holding a/an _____ full of mysterious bubbling liquid. Maybe the

                  NOUN

rumors are true; maybe my teacher really is _____!

                                       ADJECTIVE

MAD LIBS® is fun to play with friends, but you can also play it by yourself! To begin with, DO NOT look at the story on the page below. Fill in the blanks on this page with the words called for. Then, using the words you have selected, fill in the blank spaces in the story.

Now you've created your own hilarious MAD LIBS® game!

AT-HOME EXPERIMENT #1: FLOATING PAPER CLIPS!

NUMBER _____

ADJECTIVE _____

ADJECTIVE _____

TYPE OF LIQUID _____

ADJECTIVE _____

ADVERB _____

NOUN _____

VERB ENDING IN "S" _____

VERB _____

PART OF THE BODY (PLURAL) _____

MAD LIBS®
AT-HOME EXPERIMENT #1:
FLOATING PAPER CLIPS!

Materials:

_____ paper clips
<u>NUMBER</u>

A piece of _____ paper
       <u>ADJECTIVE</u>

A see-through _____-size bowl
       <u>ADJECTIVE</u>

A pencil

Instructions:

1. Fill the bowl with _____ .
       <u>TYPE OF LIQUID</u>

2. Rip a/an _____ piece of tissue paper and _____ drop it
    <u>ADJECTIVE</u>   <u>ADVERB</u>

   onto the water.

3. Drop one of the _____ clips onto the tissue paper.
       <u>NOUN</u>

4. Use the pencil to gently nudge the tissue paper until the paper clip

   _____ .
    <u>VERB ENDING IN "S"</u>

5. If you do this just right, the paper clip will start to _____ in
                 <u>VERB</u>

   front of your very _____ !
    <u>PART OF THE BODY (PLURAL)</u>

MAD LIBS® is fun to play with friends, but you can also play it by yourself! To begin with, DO NOT look at the story on the page below. Fill in the blanks on this page with the words called for. Then, using the words you have selected, fill in the blank spaces in the story.

Now you've created your own hilarious MAD LIBS® game!

FAMOUS SCIENTISTS

PLURAL NOUN _____

ADJECTIVE _____

NOUN _____

ADJECTIVE _____

VERB _____

NOUN _____

ADJECTIVE _____

SILLY WORD _____

PLURAL NOUN _____

ADJECTIVE _____

VERB (PAST TENSE) _____

ADVERB _____

ANIMAL _____

PLURAL NOUN _____

MAD LIBS®
FAMOUS SCIENTISTS

Over the years, many famous _____ have developed _____
                                PLURAL NOUN   ADJECTIVE
theories, inventions, and ideas that have contributed to the evolution of

_____-kind. Below are some of the most _____ scientists to ever
    NOUN   ADJECTIVE

_____.
    VERB

Galileo Galilei was an Italian _____ who invented telescopes and found
                                      NOUN

out a lot of information about the _____Way Galaxy, the solar system,
                                      ADJECTIVE

and planets like Jupiter and _____.
                               SILLY WORD

Sir Isaac Newton discovered most of what we now know about gravity. He

also wrote scientific _____ called the First Law of Motion, the Second
                         PLURAL NOUN

Law of Motion, and the _____ Law of Motion.
                          ADJECTIVE

Charles Darwin invented theories about natural selection, which proved how

different species _____ over hundreds of years on Earth.
                     VERB (PAST TENSE)

He _____ studied several species of _____ on the Galapagos
      ADVERB   ANIMAL

_____.
  PLURAL NOUN

MAD LIBS® is fun to play with friends, but you can also play it by yourself! To begin with, DO NOT look at the story on the page below. Fill in the blanks on this page with the words called for. Then, using the words you have selected, fill in the blank spaces in the story.

Now you've created your own hilarious MAD LIBS® game!

TURN YOUR BEDROOM INTO A SECRET LAB

ADJECTIVE _____

ADJECTIVE _____

VERB ENDING IN "ING" _____

NOUN _____

VERB _____

PLURAL NOUN _____

NOUN _____

ADJECTIVE _____

TYPE OF CONTAINER (PLURAL) _____

TYPE OF LIQUID _____

ADVERB _____

ADJECTIVE _____

VERB ENDING IN "ING" _____

Follow these _____ steps to turn your boring, _____ bedroom into
ADJECTIVE _ADJECTIVE_

a fully _____ science lab! First, put a big _____ on your
VERB ENDING IN "ING" _NOUN_

bedroom door that reads KEEP OUT! Scientists need to _____ in silence
VERB

without any annoying _____ interrupting them. Then clear off your
PLURAL NOUN

_____. You'll need it to hold all your oozy, _____ chemicals. Gather
NOUN _ADJECTIVE_

a bunch of _____ and put them all over your desk.
TYPE OF CONTAINER (PLURAL)

Connect them with tubing so you can watch all the _____ run
TYPE OF LIQUID

through them—_____ cool! Finally, pull your curtains shut—you don't
ADVERB

want anyone to see what kind of _____ concoctions you're
ADJECTIVE

_____!
VERB ENDING IN "ING"

MAD LIBS® is fun to play with friends, but you can also play it by yourself! To begin with, DO NOT look at the story on the page below. Fill in the blanks on this page with the words called for. Then, using the words you have selected, fill in the blank spaces in the story.

Now you've created your own hilarious MAD LIBS® game!

THE MAD SCIENTIST'S SHOPPING LIST

PLURAL NOUN _____

PART OF THE BODY _____

ARTICLE OF CLOTHING _____

VERB ENDING IN "ING" _____

ANIMAL (PLURAL) _____

PLURAL NOUN _____

NOUN _____

ADJECTIVE _____

VERB _____

NOUN _____

- Long, rubbery black _____ to wear on your hands
  PLURAL NOUN

- Giant round _____-glasses with black frames
  PART OF THE BODY

- Long white lab _____
  ARTICLE OF CLOTHING

- Two beakers—one to hold in each hand while _____
  VERB ENDING IN "ING"

  maniacally

- Several cages for all your lab _____
  ANIMAL (PLURAL)

- Assorted _____ floating in formaldehyde to add to your
  PLURAL NOUN

  collection

- A chalkboard and a piece of _____ to write down your
  NOUN

  _____ hypotheses and equations
  ADJECTIVE

- A giant electrical power switch to turn on when you need to

  _____ something to life
  VERB

- A Bunsen burner to light every _____ on fire!
  NOUN

MAD LIBS® is fun to play with friends, but you can also play it by yourself! To begin with, DO NOT look at the story on the page below. Fill in the blanks on this page with the words called for. Then, using the words you have selected, fill in the blank spaces in the story.

Now you've created your own hilarious MAD LIBS® game!

MORE FAMOUS SCIENTISTS

ADJECTIVE _____

ADJECTIVE _____

NOUN _____

PLURAL NOUN _____

FIRST NAME _____

OCCUPATION _____

NOUN _____

VERB _____

NOUN _____

PLURAL NOUN _____

COLOR _____

NOUN _____

MAD LIBS
MORE FAMOUS SCIENTISTS

Here are a few more _____ scientists!
ADJECTIVE

Nikola Tesla was born in Croatia. Later, he moved to the _____ States
ADJECTIVE

of America and became an inventor. He helped create fluorescent

_____-bulbs so that people wouldn't have to use _____ to light
NOUN   *PLURAL NOUN*

their homes. Tesla also invented radio and worked with _____
FIRST NAME

Edison to invent things that helped electricity work.

Alexander Graham Bell was a/an _____ from the nineteenth
OCCUPATION

century. His mother was deaf, as was his _____. Because of this, Bell was
NOUN

interested in speech and hearing. He decided to create something that would

help people _____ each other, no matter where they were. He invented
VERB

the tele-_____ so that people could talk to one another.
NOUN

Stephen Hawking was a British physicist who studied galaxies and solar

_____. He discovered a lot about _____ holes. His most famous
PLURAL NOUN   *COLOR*

book is called *A Brief History of* _____.
NOUN

MAD LIBS® is fun to play with friends, but you can also play it by yourself! To begin with, DO NOT look at the story on the page below. Fill in the blanks on this page with the words called for. Then, using the words you have selected, fill in the blank spaces in the story.

Now you've created your own hilarious MAD LIBS® game!

FRANKENSTEIN'S MONSTER

NUMBER _____

NOUN _____

ADJECTIVE _____

COLOR _____

NOUN _____

PLURAL NOUN _____

PART OF THE BODY _____

PART OF THE BODY _____

ADJECTIVE _____

VERB (PAST TENSE) _____

ARTICLE OF CLOTHING _____

ADJECTIVE _____

ADJECTIVE _____

NOUN _____

MAD LIBS®
FRANKENSTEIN'S MONSTER

Frankenstein's monster was a hideous, _____-foot-tall _____.
                                        NUMBER   NOUN

His skin was a/an _____ shade of _____, his head was shaped like
                   ADJECTIVE   COLOR

a/an _____, and he had _____ sticking out of both sides of his
      NOUN   PLURAL NOUN

neck. Frankenstein's monster also had black lips and spiky black hair on his

_____, and his _____ was filled with big
    PART OF THE BODY   PART OF THE BODY

white teeth. His _____ arms stuck straight out whenever he
                  ADJECTIVE

_____ down the street, because the black shirt and
    VERB (PAST TENSE)

_____ he always wore were too small on his grotesque,
   ARTICLE OF CLOTHING

_____ body. What a/an _____-looking _____ he was!
 ADJECTIVE   ADJECTIVE   NOUN

MAD LIBS® is fun to play with friends, but you can also play it by yourself! To begin with, DO NOT look at the story on the page below. Fill in the blanks on this page with the words called for. Then, using the words you have selected, fill in the blank spaces in the story.

Now you've created your own hilarious MAD LIBS® game!

AT-HOME EXPERIMENT #2: ERUPTING VOLCANO!

NOUN _____

ADJECTIVE _____

COLOR _____

VERB ENDING IN "ING" _____

TYPE OF LIQUID _____

ADJECTIVE _____

NOUN _____

PLURAL NOUN _____

ADJECTIVE _____

NUMBER _____

VERB _____

Materials:

A homemade volcano made out of plaster or _____-mâché
                                          NOUN

A small _____ container
         ADJECTIVE

_____ or yellow food coloring
  COLOR

_____ soda
VERB ENDING IN "ING"

_____
  TYPE OF LIQUID

Dish soap

Instructions:

1. Put the _____ container at the top of your volcano.
            ADJECTIVE

2. Pour in a little bit of baking soda and some dish _____.
                                                      NOUN

3. Add a few _____ of _____ food coloring.
              PLURAL NOUN   ADJECTIVE

4. Pour in _____ ounces of vinegar.
            NUMBER

5. Watch your volcano _____ with lava!
                       VERB

MAD LIBS® is fun to play with friends, but you can also play it by yourself! To begin with, DO NOT look at the story on the page below. Fill in the blanks on this page with the words called for. Then, using the words you have selected, fill in the blank spaces in the story.

Now you've created your own hilarious MAD LIBS® game!

THE WORST SCI-FI NIGHTMARE I EVER HAD

OCCUPATION _____

PART OF THE BODY _____

ADJECTIVE _____

PLURAL NOUN _____

VERB _____

ADJECTIVE _____

NOUN _____

PART OF THE BODY (PLURAL) _____

VERB _____

COLOR _____

TYPE OF LIQUID _____

NOUN _____

ADJECTIVE _____

I had a dream last night that a crazy _____ was trying to perform
OCCUPATION

experiments on me. He took a strand of my _____ and looked
PART OF THE BODY

at it under a microscope. Then he told me to sit in his _____
ADJECTIVE

chair. But I was scared—there were a bunch of electrical _____
PLURAL NOUN

tied to it, and I was afraid he was going to _____ me in it! I
VERB

said, "No, thanks, you _____ scientist—I'm getting the
ADJECTIVE

_____ out of here." He looked me right in the
NOUN

_____ and said, "Don't you dare try to leave my dungeon!
PART OF THE BODY (PLURAL)

You can't _____—the door's locked!" Suddenly, he pounced on
VERB

me, and everything turned to _____. I woke up with
COLOR

_____ running down my temples. Thank _____ that
TYPE OF LIQUID   NOUN

nightmare is over. I hope I never see that _____ scientist again!
ADJECTIVE

MAD LIBS® is fun to play with friends, but you can also play it by yourself! To begin with, DO NOT look at the story on the page below. Fill in the blanks on this page with the words called for. Then, using the words you have selected, fill in the blank spaces in the story.

Now you've created your own hilarious MAD LIBS® game!

AT-HOME EXPERIMENT #3: TORNADO IN A BOTTLE!

NOUN _____

VERB ENDING IN "ING" _____

VERB _____

ADJECTIVE _____

ADJECTIVE _____

VERB _____

NOUN _____

ADJECTIVE _____

NOUN _____

ADJECTIVE _____

NOUN _____

ADJECTIVE _____

VERB (PAST TENSE) _____

Materials:

Water

A see-through plastic soda _____ with a cap
NOUN

Glitter, to see debris _____ in the bottle
VERB ENDING IN "ING"

Dish soap to make your tornado _____
VERB

Instructions:

1. Fill the entire _____ bottle with water until it is almost all the
ADJECTIVE

   way _____.
   ADJECTIVE

2. _____ a few drops of dish _____ into the bottle. Add the
VERB   NOUN

   _____ glitter.
   ADJECTIVE

3. Screw the _____ onto the top of the bottle.
NOUN

4. Turn the bottle upside _____ and hold it near the cap.
ADJECTIVE

5. Spin the bottle in a/an _____-wise rotation.
NOUN

6. Stop spinning the bottle and admire the _____ tornado you
ADJECTIVE

   _____!
   VERB (PAST TENSE)

MAD LIBS® is fun to play with friends, but you can also play it by yourself! To begin with, DO NOT look at the story on the page below. Fill in the blanks on this page with the words called for. Then, using the words you have selected, fill in the blank spaces in the story.

Now you've created your own hilarious MAD LIBS® game!

THE FIRST WEEK OF SCIENCE CLASS

ADJECTIVE _____

LAST NAME _____

PLURAL NOUN _____

PLURAL NOUN _____

NOUN _____

NOUN _____

ANIMAL (PLURAL) _____

PERSON IN ROOM _____

ADJECTIVE _____

VERB _____

MAD LIBS
THE FIRST WEEK OF
SCIENCE CLASS

My first few days of science class were so _____! Our teacher, Ms.
                                          ADJECTIVE

_____, taught us all about matter and energy, atoms and
        LAST NAME

_____, and the difference between solids, _____, and gases. We
PLURAL NOUN   PLURAL NOUN

even got to watch a video about gravity and why things in outer _____
                                                                 NOUN

float but things on Earth fall to the _____! Our teacher says that next
                                       NOUN

week we're going to do our first experiment and that, if we want, some day this

year we can even dissect _____! My friend _____
                          ANIMAL (PLURAL)   PERSON IN ROOM

thought dissecting sounded gross, but I think it sounds really _____!
                                                               ADJECTIVE

I can't wait to _____ more about science next week.
                 VERB

MAD LIBS®

HISTORY OF THE WORLD
MAD LIBS

MAD LIBS®

INSTRUCTIONS

MAD LIBS® is a game for people who don't like games!
It can be played by one, two, three, four, or forty.

• RIDICULOUSLY SIMPLE DIRECTIONS

In this tablet you will find stories containing blank spaces where words are left out. One player, the READER, selects one of these stories. The READER does not tell anyone what the story is about. Instead, he/she asks the other players, the WRITERS, to give him/her words. These words are used to fill in the blank spaces in the story.

• TO PLAY

The READER asks each WRITER in turn to call out a word—an adjective or a noun or whatever the space calls for—and uses them to fill in the blank spaces in the story. The result is a MAD LIBS® game.

When the READER then reads the completed MAD LIBS® game to the other players, they will discover that they have written a story that is fantastic, screamingly funny, shocking, silly, crazy, or just plain dumb—depending upon which words each WRITER called out.

• EXAMPLE (*Before* and *After*)

"_____!" he said _____
    EXCLAMATION   ADVERB

as he jumped into his convertible _____ and
                     NOUN

drove off with his _____ wife.
         ADJECTIVE

"_____OUCH_____!" he said _____HAPPILY_____
    EXCLAMATION   ADVERB

as he jumped into his convertible _____CAT_____ and
                     NOUN

drove off with his _____BRAVE_____ wife.
         ADJECTIVE

MAD LIBS®

QUICK REVIEW

In case you have forgotten what adjectives, adverbs, nouns, and verbs are, here is a quick review:

An ADJECTIVE describes something or somebody. *Lumpy, soft, ugly, messy,* and *short* are adjectives.

An ADVERB tells how something is done. It modifies a verb and usually ends in "ly." *Modestly, stupidly, greedily,* and *carefully* are adverbs.

A NOUN is the name of a person, place, or thing. *Sidewalk, umbrella, bridle, bathtub,* and *nose* are nouns.

A VERB is an action word. *Run, pitch, jump,* and *swim* are verbs. Put the verbs in past tense if the directions say PAST TENSE. *Ran, pitched, jumped,* and *swam* are verbs in the past tense.

When we ask for A PLACE, we mean any sort of place: a country or city *(Spain, Cleveland)* or a room *(bathroom, kitchen).*

An EXCLAMATION or SILLY WORD is any sort of funny sound, gasp, grunt, or outcry, like *Wow!, Ouch!, Whomp!, Ick!,* and *Gadzooks!*

When we ask for specific words, like a NUMBER, a COLOR, an ANIMAL, or a PART OF THE BODY, we mean a word that is one of those things, like *seven, blue, horse,* or *head.*

When we ask for a PLURAL, it means more than one. For example, *cat* pluralized is *cats.*

MAD LIBS® is fun to play with friends, but you can also play it by yourself! To begin with, DO NOT look at the story on the page below. Fill in the blanks on this page with the words called for. Then, using the words you have selected, fill in the blank spaces in the story.

Now you've created your own hilarious MAD LIBS® game!

LIGHT MY FIRE

PART OF THE BODY (PLURAL) _____

ADJECTIVE _____

ADJECTIVE _____

ADJECTIVE _____

A PLACE _____

ANIMAL _____

PART OF THE BODY _____

NOUN _____

ADJECTIVE _____

ADVERB _____

EXCLAMATION _____

ADJECTIVE _____

PERSON IN ROOM _____

NOUN _____

MAD LIBS®
LIGHT MY FIRE

At one time man walked on four _____, spoke in
<u>PART OF THE BODY (PLURAL)</u>

_____ grunts, and did not know how to make a/an _____ fire.
<u>ADJECTIVE</u>   <u>ADJECTIVE</u>

Here is the story of the day that changed mankind forever (translated from the

_____ cave-speak):
<u>ADJECTIVE</u>

Caveman #1: It's colder than (the) _____ in this cave. Even my
<u>A PLACE</u>

warmest _____ fur won't keep my _____ from
<u>ANIMAL</u>   <u>PART OF THE BODY</u>

shivering.

Caveman #2: If only there was a way to make the cold _____
<u>NOUN</u>

warmer.

Caveman #1: I'm bored. I think I'll play with these _____ sticks
<u>ADJECTIVE</u>

of wood.

Caveman #2: Why don't you rub them _____ together and see
<u>ADVERB</u>

what happens?

Caveman #1: _____! There's smoke coming off these
<u>EXCLAMATION</u>

_____ sticks!
<u>ADJECTIVE</u>

Caveman #2: Ouch! It's hot! In the name of _____ —we made
<u>PERSON IN ROOM</u>

heat!

Caveman #1: We shall call this magical flaming _____ *fire*.
<u>NOUN</u>

MAD LIBS® is fun to play with friends, but you can also play it by yourself! To begin with, DO NOT look at the story on the page below. Fill in the blanks on this page with the words called for. Then, using the words you have selected, fill in the blank spaces in the story.

Now you've created your own hilarious MAD LIBS® game!

EUREKA!

PLURAL NOUN _____

OCCUPATION (PLURAL) _____

NOUN _____

PLURAL NOUN _____

PLURAL NOUN _____

NOUN _____

NOUN _____

PLURAL NOUN _____

PLURAL NOUN _____

ADJECTIVE _____

NOUN _____

NOUN _____

NOUN _____

Throughout history, inventors have been responsible for everyday things like

computers, cars, and _____. These are some of the most famous
<u>PLURAL NOUN</u>

_____ in history:
<u>OCCUPATION (PLURAL)</u>

Benjamin Franklin was not only a founding _____ of the United
<u>NOUN</u>

States, he also invented many things, including bifocal glasses, which allow

people to see _____ near and far. He also invented the lightning rod,
<u>PLURAL NOUN</u>

which protects _____ from electric bolts of _____.
<u>PLURAL NOUN</u> <u>NOUN</u>

Johannes Gutenberg was a German _____ who invented the printing
<u>NOUN</u>

press, a machine that could print words and _____ to make books,
<u>PLURAL NOUN</u>

newspapers, and _____.
<u>PLURAL NOUN</u>

Thomas Edison was a/an _____ inventor perhaps best known for
<u>ADJECTIVE</u>

making a light bulb that the average _____ could use. He also invented
<u>NOUN</u>

the phonograph, which was the first _____ to be able to record the
<u>NOUN</u>

human _____ and then play it back.
<u>NOUN</u>

MAD LIBS® is fun to play with friends, but you can also play it by yourself! To begin with, DO NOT look at the story on the page below. Fill in the blanks on this page with the words called for. Then, using the words you have selected, fill in the blank spaces in the story.

Now you've created your own hilarious MAD LIBS® game!

NEWS FLASH!: WORLD NOT FLAT

ADJECTIVE _____

ADJECTIVE _____

NOUN _____

TYPE OF FOOD _____

PLURAL NOUN _____

VERB (PAST TENSE) _____

NOUN _____

PLURAL NOUN _____

ADJECTIVE _____

SILLY WORD _____

ADJECTIVE _____

PERSON IN ROOM _____

ADJECTIVE _____

MAD LIBS
NEWS FLASH!: WORLD NOT FLAT

In _____ news for explorers everywhere, it has recently been discovered
ADJECTIVE

that the Earth is round. That's right: Earth is shaped like a/an _____
ADJECTIVE

ball! For as long as any _____ can remember, it has been widely believed
NOUN

that the Earth is as flat as a/an _____. Many _____
TYPE OF FOOD   PLURAL NOUN

believed that if you _____ too far, you would fall off the edge of
VERB (PAST TENSE)

the _____. Now, some _____ are trying to prove that the
NOUN   PLURAL NOUN

_____ Earth rotates around the sun, though most people think this is a
ADJECTIVE

bunch of _____! We will keep you updated as this _____
SILLY WORD   ADJECTIVE

story develops. In the meantime, back to you, _____, with the
PERSON IN ROOM

day's _____ stories.
ADJECTIVE

MAD LIBS® is fun to play with friends, but you can also play it by yourself! To begin with, DO NOT look at the story on the page below. Fill in the blanks on this page with the words called for. Then, using the words you have selected, fill in the blank spaces in the story.

Now you've created your own hilarious MAD LIBS® game!

CAT FANCY

ADJECTIVE _____

PLURAL NOUN _____

ADJECTIVE _____

PLURAL NOUN _____

ADJECTIVE _____

ADJECTIVE _____

PLURAL NOUN _____

ADJECTIVE _____

NOUN _____

ADVERB _____

PART OF THE BODY (PLURAL) _____

NOUN _____

PLURAL NOUN _____

ADJECTIVE _____

MAD LIBS®
CAT FANCY

You might say the ancient Egyptians were _____ cat people. After
                                             ADJECTIVE

all, they built an entire religion around worshipping their feline _____!
                                                                PLURAL NOUN

Cats were well liked by Egyptians for their ability to kill _____ vermin
                                                   ADJECTIVE

like rodents and wild _____. Cats were thought to be graceful and
                          PLURAL NOUN

_____ creatures. Some _____ cats were mummified and buried in
ADJECTIVE   ADJECTIVE

_____ along with their _____ owners. Harming a cat was
PLURAL NOUN   ADJECTIVE

a crime punishable by _____. And when a cat died, its family would
                        NOUN

mourn _____, shaving their _____ as a symbol of
          ADVERB   PART OF THE BODY (PLURAL)

their _____. So maybe it's a little funny that ancient _____
      NOUN   PLURAL NOUN

worshipped cats. But, then again, so does the _____ Internet!
                                   ADJECTIVE

MAD LIBS® is fun to play with friends, but you can also play it by yourself! To begin with, DO NOT look at the story on the page below. Fill in the blanks on this page with the words called for. Then, using the words you have selected, fill in the blank spaces in the story.

Now you've created your own hilarious MAD LIBS® game!

THE CODE OF THE SAMURAI

ADJECTIVE _____

ADJECTIVE _____

PLURAL NOUN _____

ADJECTIVE _____

PLURAL NOUN _____

VERB _____

PLURAL NOUN _____

PLURAL NOUN _____

NOUN _____

PLURAL NOUN _____

VERB _____

PLURAL NOUN _____

NOUN _____

Samurai were ancient, _____ Japanese warriors who followed a/an

ADJECTIVE

_____ code of virtue, which contained these eight _____:

ADJECTIVE   PLURAL NOUN

1. Samurai believed **justice** was the most _____ virtue.

                                                 ADJECTIVE

2. They always showed **courage** in the face of _____.

                                                        PLURAL NOUN

3. Samurai may have had the power to _____, but they also needed to

                                                   VERB

   show **mercy** toward all _____.

                               PLURAL NOUN

4. It was important to be **polite** and considerate of other people's _____.

                                                                                   PLURAL NOUN

5. Samurai also thought **honesty** was the best _____.

                                                       NOUN

6. _____ were not an option for the Samurai, who tried to _____

     PLURAL NOUN   VERB

   with **honor**.

7. Samurai were **loyal** to their fellow _____.

                                                PLURAL NOUN

8. And, finally, they had to show **character** and that they knew the difference

   between right and _____.

                                        NOUN

MAD LIBS® is fun to play with friends, but you can also play it by yourself! To begin with, DO NOT look at the story on the page below. Fill in the blanks on this page with the words called for. Then, using the words you have selected, fill in the blank spaces in the story.

Now you've created your own hilarious MAD LIBS® game!

GOD SAVE THE QUEEN

PERSON IN ROOM (MALE) _____

PERSON IN ROOM (FEMALE) _____

NUMBER _____

NOUN _____

VERB ENDING IN "ING" _____

ADJECTIVE _____

FIRST NAME (MALE) _____

ADJECTIVE _____

PERSON IN ROOM _____

A PLACE _____

A PLACE _____

PLURAL NOUN _____

ADJECTIVE _____

PLURAL NOUN _____

NOUN _____

PART OF THE BODY _____

MAD LIBS
GOD SAVE THE QUEEN

Elizabeth I of England was the daughter of King _____ VIII
_{PERSON IN ROOM (MALE)}

and his wife _____. At age _____, she was crowned
_{PERSON IN ROOM (FEMALE)}   _{NUMBER}

_____ of England in a royal _____ ceremony. During
_{NOUN}   _{VERB ENDING IN "ING"}

her reign, England was a very _____ place to live. Famous writer
_{ADJECTIVE}

_____ Shakespeare wrote many _____ plays, and explorer
_{FIRST NAME (MALE)}   _{ADJECTIVE}

_____ discovered (the) _____. In a war against
_{PERSON IN ROOM}   _{A PLACE}

(the) _____, Queen Elizabeth I led her army of _____ to
_{A PLACE}   _{PLURAL NOUN}

a/an _____ victory. Today, many _____ consider Queen
_{ADJECTIVE}   _{PLURAL NOUN}

Elizabeth the most famous _____ in English history. Some even say she
_{NOUN}

ruled England with an iron _____!
_{PART OF THE BODY}

MAD LIBS® is fun to play with friends, but you can also play it by yourself! To begin with, DO NOT look at the story on the page below. Fill in the blanks on this page with the words called for. Then, using the words you have selected, fill in the blank spaces in the story.

Now you've created your own hilarious MAD LIBS® game!

WHAT A
WONDERFUL WORLD

NOUN _____

ADJECTIVE _____

NOUN _____

ADJECTIVE _____

PERSON IN ROOM (FEMALE) _____

NOUN _____

CELEBRITY (FEMALE) _____

COLOR _____

CELEBRITY (MALE) _____

PERSON IN ROOM _____

PERSON IN ROOM _____

A PLACE _____

CELEBRITY (MALE) _____

A PLACE _____

NOUN _____

MAD LIBS
WHAT A
WONDERFUL WORLD

These are considered the Seven Wonders of the Ancient _____:

NOUN

1. **The Giza Necropolis** is a site in Egypt where you can see the Great Pyramids

   and the _____ Sphinx.

ADJECTIVE

2. **The Hanging Gardens** were in the ancient _____ of Babylon and

NOUN

   were built as a gift from Nebuchadnezzar II to his _____ wife,

ADJECTIVE

   _____.

PERSON IN ROOM (FEMALE)

3. **The Temple of Artemis at Ephesus** was a Greek _____ dedicated to

NOUN

   the goddess _____.

CELEBRITY (FEMALE)

4. **The Statue of Zeus at Olympia** was a giant forty-three-foot ivory and

   _____ statue of _____.

COLOR   CELEBRITY (MALE)

5. **The Mausoleum at Halicarnassus** was a tomb built by _____

PERSON IN ROOM

   and _____ of (the) _____.

PERSON IN ROOM   A PLACE

6. **The Colossus of Rhodes** was a statue of Greek god _____, built

CELEBRITY (MALE)

   to commemorate victory over (the) _____.

A PLACE

7. **The Lighthouse of Alexandria** was at one time the tallest _____ on

NOUN

   Earth.

From HISTORY OF THE WORLD MAD LIBS® • Copyright © 2015 by Penguin Random House LLC

MAD LIBS® is fun to play with friends, but you can also play it by yourself! To begin with, DO NOT look at the story on the page below. Fill in the blanks on this page with the words called for. Then, using the words you have selected, fill in the blank spaces in the story.

Now you've created your own hilarious MAD LIBS® game!

FAMOUS FIRSTS

PERSON IN ROOM _____

NOUN _____

PERSON IN ROOM _____

NOUN _____

NOUN _____

PERSON IN ROOM _____

PERSON IN ROOM _____

PLURAL NOUN _____

PERSON IN ROOM _____

PART OF THE BODY _____

A PLACE _____

PERSON IN ROOM _____

VERB _____

PERSON IN ROOM _____

ANIMAL _____

MAD LIBS
FAMOUS FIRSTS

- In 1901, _____ became the first person to go over Niagara
  <u>PERSON IN ROOM</u>

  Falls in a/an _____ and survive.
  <u>NOUN</u>

- In 1933, _____ became the first _____ to fly an
  <u>PERSON IN ROOM</u>   <u>NOUN</u>

  airplane around the _____.
  <u>NOUN</u>

- In 1953, _____ and _____ became the first
  <u>PERSON IN ROOM</u>   <u>PERSON IN ROOM</u>

  _____ to climb to the top of Mount Everest.
  <u>PLURAL NOUN</u>

- In 1963, _____ became the first person to receive a/an
  <u>PERSON IN ROOM</u>

  _____ transplant in (the) _____, South Africa.
  <u>PART OF THE BODY</u>   <u>A PLACE</u>

- In 1969, _____ became the first person to _____ on
  <u>PERSON IN ROOM</u>   <u>VERB</u>

  the moon.

- In 1996, in Scotland, _____ became the world's first clone
  <u>PERSON IN ROOM</u>

  of a/an _____.
  <u>ANIMAL</u>

MAD LIBS® is fun to play with friends, but you can also play it by yourself! To begin with, DO NOT look at the story on the page below. Fill in the blanks on this page with the words called for. Then, using the words you have selected, fill in the blank spaces in the story.

Now you've created your own hilarious MAD LIBS® game!

LAND, HO!

PLURAL NOUN _____

PLURAL NOUN _____

ADJECTIVE _____

NOUN _____

VERB (PAST TENSE) _____

ADJECTIVE _____

NOUN _____

NOUN _____

NOUN _____

NOUN _____

PLURAL NOUN _____

NOUN _____

PERSON IN ROOM (FEMALE) _____

PLURAL NOUN _____

PART OF THE BODY _____

PLURAL NOUN _____

MAD LIBS

LAND, HO!

Throughout history, _____ with a sense of adventure have traveled
PLURAL NOUN

the world in search of new lands and _____. Here are a few of the
PLURAL NOUN

most _____ explorers:
ADJECTIVE

Leif Ericson was a famous Viking _____ who _____ to
NOUN   VERB (PAST TENSE)

the Americas five hundred years before _____ Christopher Columbus.
ADJECTIVE

Ferdinand Magellan, a Portuguese _____, became the first _____
NOUN   NOUN

to cross the Pacific Ocean while he tried to discover a route to the _____
NOUN

Islands.

Marco Polo traveled in a/an _____ from Italy to China and helped many
NOUN

Western _____ learn about the Eastern _____.
PLURAL NOUN   NOUN

Lewis and Clark, led by _____, were the first _____
PERSON IN ROOM (FEMALE)   PLURAL NOUN

to travel by _____ across the continental United _____.
PART OF THE BODY   PLURAL NOUN

MAD LIBS® is fun to play with friends, but you can also play it by yourself! To begin with, DO NOT look at the story on the page below. Fill in the blanks on this page with the words called for. Then, using the words you have selected, fill in the blank spaces in the story.

Now you've created your own hilarious MAD LIBS® game!

WALK LIKE AN EGYPTIAN

ADJECTIVE _____

NOUN _____

ADJECTIVE _____

ADJECTIVE _____

PLURAL NOUN _____

ADJECTIVE _____

PLURAL NOUN _____

ADVERB _____

NOUN _____

NOUN _____

VERB (PAST TENSE) _____

ADJECTIVE _____

OCCUPATION _____

NOUN _____

CELEBRITY (FEMALE) _____

MAD LIBS®
WALK LIKE AN EGYPTIAN

Cleopatra was a/an _____ Egyptian pharaoh. Well-educated and clever
                         ADJECTIVE

as a/an _____ , Cleopatra spoke many _____ languages. She
            NOUN   ADJECTIVE

was also known for being particularly _____ . When she was eighteen,
                                              ADJECTIVE

Cleopatra took the throne, though she was chased out by a bunch of unruly

_____ . In response, Cleopatra put together an army of _____
PLURAL NOUN   ADJECTIVE

_____ , marched _____ back into Egypt, and took back the
PLURAL NOUN   ADVERB

_____ for herself. Cleopatra fell in love with the Roman _____
   NOUN   NOUN

Julius Caesar. After Caesar _____ , Cleopatra fell in love
                              VERB (PAST TENSE)

with another _____ Roman, Mark Antony. Cleopatra was the most
                ADJECTIVE

famous and powerful _____ to rule a/an _____ . She was even
                        OCCUPATION   NOUN

played by the legendary actress _____ in a movie!
                                  CELEBRITY (FEMALE)

MAD LIBS® is fun to play with friends, but you can also play it by yourself! To begin with, DO NOT look at the story on the page below. Fill in the blanks on this page with the words called for. Then, using the words you have selected, fill in the blank spaces in the story.

Now you've created your own hilarious MAD LIBS® game!

CROOKS DOWN UNDER

NOUN _____

ADJECTIVE _____

PLURAL NOUN _____

ADJECTIVE _____

PERSON IN ROOM _____

ADJECTIVE _____

NUMBER _____

PLURAL NOUN _____

ADJECTIVE _____

VERB _____

PLURAL NOUN _____

PERSON IN ROOM (FEMALE) _____

ANIMAL _____

NUMBER _____

PART OF THE BODY _____

MAD LIBS®
CROOKS DOWN UNDER

Australia—known as the _____ Down Under—has a/an
                                    NOUN

_____ criminal past. In the late 1700s, Britain's prisons were overrun
ADJECTIVE

with _____, so they began transporting their _____ prisoners
      PLURAL NOUN   ADJECTIVE

to Australia. Captain _____was in charge of setting up the first
                     PERSON IN ROOM

_____ colony for prisoners. Over _____ years, fifty-five thousand
ADJECTIVE   NUMBER

criminal _____ came from England to live there! With _____
        PLURAL NOUN   ADJECTIVE

behavior, these prisoners could _____ their way to freedom and gain
                              VERB

work as butchers, farmers, and professional _____. One resident in
                                       PLURAL NOUN

the colony was a thirteen-year-old named _____, who had
                               PERSON IN ROOM (FEMALE)

come to the colony for stealing a/an _____. She eventually became one
                           ANIMAL

of Australia's first businesswomen, and today, Australia's _____-dollar bill
                                            NUMBER

features her _____!
       PART OF THE BODY

MAD LIBS® is fun to play with friends, but you can also play it by yourself! To begin with, DO NOT look at the story on the page below. Fill in the blanks on this page with the words called for. Then, using the words you have selected, fill in the blank spaces in the story.

Now you've created your own hilarious MAD LIBS® game!

WHEREFORE ART THOU, SHAKESPEARE?

NOUN _____

PERSON IN ROOM (FEMALE) _____

NOUN _____

ADJECTIVE _____

ADJECTIVE _____

NOUN _____

ADJECTIVE _____

PLURAL NOUN _____

NOUN _____

NOUN _____

NOUN _____

PLURAL NOUN _____

PART OF THE BODY (PLURAL) _____

NOUN _____

William Shakespeare is the most famous writer in the history of the

_____. He wrote many plays, including *Romeo and* _____
　　NOUN　　　　　　　　　　　　　　　　　　　　　　PERSON IN ROOM (FEMALE)

and *A Midsummer Night's* _____. He also wrote many _____
　　　　　　　　　　　　　　　　　NOUN　　　　　　　　　　　　　ADJECTIVE

poems. Here is a selection from one of his most _____ sonnets:
　　　　　　　　　　　　　　　　　　　　　　　　　ADJECTIVE

Shall I compare thee to a summer's _____?
　　　　　　　　　　　　　　　　　　　NOUN

Thou art more lovely and more _____.
　　　　　　　　　　　　　　　　　ADJECTIVE

Rough winds do shake the darling _____ of May,
　　　　　　　　　　　　　　　　　　PLURAL NOUN

And summer's _____ hath all too short a/an _____ . . .
　　　　　　　　NOUN　　　　　　　　　　　　　　　　NOUN

But thy eternal _____ shall not fade . . .
　　　　　　　　　NOUN

So long as _____ can breathe,
　　　　　　　PLURAL NOUN

or _____ can see,
　　PART OF THE BODY (PLURAL)

So long lives this, and this gives _____ to thee.
　　　　　　　　　　　　　　　　　　NOUN

MAD LIBS® is fun to play with friends, but you can also play it by yourself! To begin with, DO NOT look at the story on the page below. Fill in the blanks on this page with the words called for. Then, using the words you have selected, fill in the blank spaces in the story.

Now you've created your own hilarious MAD LIBS® game!

WANTED:
FOUNTAIN OF YOUTH

ADJECTIVE _____

VERB ENDING IN "S" _____

ANIMAL _____

PART OF THE BODY _____

ADJECTIVE _____

PLURAL NOUN _____

A PLACE _____

ADJECTIVE _____

SILLY WORD _____

NOUN _____

PLURAL NOUN _____

NOUN _____

Spanish explorer Ponce de Leon seeks a/an _____ Fountain of
ADJECTIVE

Youth. Anyone who drinks or _____ in its waters will
VERB ENDING IN "S"

have eternal youth. It can also cure illnesses from _____ pox to the
ANIMAL

_____ flu. It has been rumored for many _____
PART OF THE BODY   ADJECTIVE

years that the Fountain of Youth exists. Some _____ believe
PLURAL NOUN

it is either in the New World or (the) _____. If you find this
A PLACE

_____ fountain, please contact Ponce de Leon at 555-_____ or
ADJECTIVE   SILLY WORD

poncedeleon@-_____-mail.com. You will be rewarded with gold and
NOUN

_____, as well as eternal _____.
PLURAL NOUN   NOUN

MAD LIBS® is fun to play with friends, but you can also play it by yourself! To begin with, DO NOT look at the story on the page below. Fill in the blanks on this page with the words called for. Then, using the words you have selected, fill in the blank spaces in the story.

Now you've created your own hilarious MAD LIBS® game!

O.M.O. (OH MY ODIN)

PLURAL NOUN _____

A PLACE _____

ADJECTIVE _____

A PLACE _____

PLURAL NOUN _____

VERB _____

ADJECTIVE _____

COLOR _____

SAME COLOR _____

ADJECTIVE _____

ADJECTIVE _____

PLURAL NOUN _____

PLURAL NOUN _____

PLURAL NOUN _____

PLURAL NOUN _____

NOUN _____

Vikings were seafaring _____ from Scandinavia, which includes
                        PLURAL NOUN

modern-day countries like Denmark, Norway, and (the) _____. Vikings
                                                       A PLACE

traveled in their _____ boats from Europe to Russia and then to (the)
                     ADJECTIVE

_____, raiding _____ and establishing villages to _____
   A PLACE   PLURAL NOUN   VERB

in. The Vikings were known to be _____ fighters. One famous Viking
                                    ADJECTIVE

warrior was Erik the _____, who was nicknamed this because of his
                        COLOR

flowing _____ beard. There were also _____ Viking female
         SAME COLOR   ADJECTIVE

warriors who wore _____ shields when fighting _____. The
                     ADJECTIVE   PLURAL NOUN

Vikings even had their own gods and goddesses, like Odin, who was thought

to be the ruler of all _____, and who also represented war, battle, and
                          PLURAL NOUN

_____. The Vikings were a serious bunch of _____—you
   PLURAL NOUN   PLURAL NOUN

sure didn't want to get on their bad _____!
                                        NOUN

MAD LIBS® is fun to play with friends, but you can also play it by yourself! To begin with, DO NOT look at the story on the page below. Fill in the blanks on this page with the words called for. Then, using the words you have selected, fill in the blank spaces in the story.

Now you've created your own hilarious MAD LIBS® game!

PEACE, LOVE, AND

_____
PLURAL NOUN

PLURAL NOUN _____

ADJECTIVE _____

PLURAL NOUN _____

NOUN _____

PLURAL NOUN _____

A PLACE _____

VERB ENDING IN "ING" _____

PLURAL NOUN _____

NOUN _____

NOUN _____

A PLACE _____

ADJECTIVE _____

A PLACE _____

PLURAL NOUN _____

PLURAL NOUN _____

MAD LIBS®
PEACE, LOVE, AND
_____
PLURAL NOUN

Since the beginning of time, _____ have fought with one another
                              PLURAL NOUN

for many _____ reasons. But these brave people devoted their lives to
         ADJECTIVE

helping their fellow _____:
                     PLURAL NOUN

Gandhi led India to freedom from the British _____, who had taken
                                                 NOUN

it over. He inspired people all over the world to be peaceful _____.
                                                             PLURAL NOUN

Martin Luther King Jr. led the Civil Rights Movement in (the) _____,
                                                                 A PLACE

helping gain equal rights for African Americans by _____
                                                   VERB ENDING IN "ING"

peacefully.

Nelson Mandela helped end racist _____ in South Africa. For his
                                     PLURAL NOUN

hard work, he won the Nobel Peace _____ and the US Presidential
                                  NOUN

_____ of Freedom.
NOUN

Mother Teresa was a nun from (the) _____ who devoted her life to helping
                                       A PLACE

sick and _____ people all over (the) _____.
         ADJECTIVE   A PLACE

Clara Barton was a nurse who helped found the American Red Cross, which

educates _____ and gives assistance to _____ in need.
         PLURAL NOUN   PLURAL NOUN

MAD LIBS® is fun to play with friends, but you can also play it by yourself! To begin with, DO NOT look at the story on the page below. Fill in the blanks on this page with the words called for. Then, using the words you have selected, fill in the blank spaces in the story.

Now you've created your own hilarious MAD LIBS® game!

DID I DO THAT?

PLURAL NOUN _____

PLURAL NOUN _____

PERSON IN ROOM _____

NOUN _____

PLURAL NOUN _____

VERB _____

NOUN _____

PERSON IN ROOM (MALE) _____

VERB _____

VERB _____

ADJECTIVE _____

A PLACE _____

ADJECTIVE _____

PERSON IN ROOM _____

NOUN _____

ADJECTIVE _____

MAD LIBS®
DID I DO THAT?

Oops! We should thank our lucky _____ for these _____
                                   PLURAL NOUN   PLURAL NOUN

that were invented by accident!

The microwave: In 1945, _____ was experimenting with
                              PERSON IN ROOM

a/an _____ when he discovered it could melt _____ and make
      NOUN   PLURAL NOUN

popcorn _____. He then built the first microwave _____.
         VERB   NOUN

The Slinky: In 1943, naval engineer _____ attempted to
                                        PERSON IN ROOM (MALE)

create a spring to help ships _____, when he got the idea for a toy spring
                              VERB

that could _____ down the stairs all by itself. It became the _____
            VERB   ADJECTIVE

Slinky!

Potato chips: At a restaurant in (the) _____ in 1853, a customer
                                           A PLACE

complained that his fried potatoes were too _____. The chef,
                                             ADJECTIVE

_____, cut the potatoes as thin as possible and fried them
PERSON IN ROOM

to a/an _____, accidentally inventing the _____ potato chip!
         NOUN   ADJECTIVE

MAD LIBS® is fun to play with friends, but you can also play it by yourself! To begin with, DO NOT look at the story on the page below. Fill in the blanks on this page with the words called for. Then, using the words you have selected, fill in the blank spaces in the story.

Now you've created your own hilarious MAD LIBS® game!

STATE OF WONDER

NOUN _____

PLURAL NOUN _____

ADJECTIVE _____

PLURAL NOUN _____

A PLACE _____

A PLACE _____

ADJECTIVE _____

PLURAL NOUN _____

PLURAL NOUN _____

ADJECTIVE _____

NOUN _____

ADJECTIVE _____

NOUN _____

ADJECTIVE _____

PERSON IN ROOM (MALE) _____

CELEBRITY _____

MAD LIBS®
STATE OF WONDER

The Seven Wonders of the Modern _____ were chosen by _____
NOUN   PLURAL NOUN

like me and you!

1. **The Great Wall of China** is a/an _____ wall made of stones, bricks,
ADJECTIVE

and _____ that stretches all the way from (the) _____ to
PLURAL NOUN   A PLACE

(the) _____.
A PLACE

2. **Petra** is a/an _____ city in Jordan, also known as the Rose City
ADJECTIVE

for its pink-colored _____.
PLURAL NOUN

3. **The Colosseum** is an ancient Roman amphitheater built by _____.
PLURAL NOUN

4. **Chichén Itzá** is a/an _____ city in Mexico built during the
ADJECTIVE

_____ Empire.
NOUN

5. **Machu Picchu** is a/an _____ citadel built into a huge _____
ADJECTIVE   NOUN

in Peru.

6. **Taj Mahal** is a/an _____ mausoleum in India, built by Emperor
ADJECTIVE

_____.
PERSON IN ROOM (MALE)

7. **Christ the Redeemer** in Brazil is a hundred-foot-tall statue of

_____.
CELEBRITY

MAD LIBS® is fun to play with friends, but you can also play it by yourself! To begin with, DO NOT look at the story on the page below. Fill in the blanks on this page with the words called for. Then, using the words you have selected, fill in the blank spaces in the story.

Now you've created your own hilarious MAD LIBS® game!

MONGOLIAN WARRIOR

ADJECTIVE _____

NUMBER _____

ADJECTIVE _____

PLURAL NOUN _____

ADJECTIVE _____

A PLACE _____

PLURAL NOUN _____

ADJECTIVE _____

PLURAL NOUN _____

PLURAL NOUN _____

ADJECTIVE _____

NOUN _____

ADJECTIVE _____

VERB (PAST TENSE) _____

ADJECTIVE _____

MAD LIBS®
MONGOLIAN WARRIOR

Genghis Khan was a/an _____ Mongolian leader. Starting at the
                              ADJECTIVE

young age of _____, Genghis Khan began to build a/an _____
              NUMBER   ADJECTIVE

army of _____. He wanted to destroy _____ tribes in (the)
        PLURAL NOUN   ADJECTIVE

Northeast _____ so he could rule over all the _____ in the
           A PLACE   PLURAL NOUN

land. He and his _____ armies marched into _____
                ADJECTIVE   PLURAL NOUN

all around Asia. They brutally fought and killed many _____ and
                                      PLURAL NOUN

eventually created the _____ Mongolian Empire, which was the largest
                      ADJECTIVE

_____ in the world. Today, Genghis Khan is considered one of the most
    NOUN

ruthless and _____ warriors that ever _____. You
             ADJECTIVE   VERB (PAST TENSE)

wouldn't have wanted to meet him alone in a/an _____ alley!
                                          ADJECTIVE

MAD LIBS® is fun to play with friends, but you can also play it by yourself! To begin with, DO NOT look at the story on the page below. Fill in the blanks on this page with the words called for. Then, using the words you have selected, fill in the blank spaces in the story.

Now you've created your own hilarious MAD LIBS® game!

NAPOLEON COMPLEX

OCCUPATION _____

PLURAL NOUN _____

PLURAL NOUN _____

ADJECTIVE _____

NOUN _____

NOUN _____

NOUN _____

ADJECTIVE _____

NOUN _____

PLURAL NOUN _____

PLURAL NOUN _____

ADJECTIVE _____

A PLACE _____

A PLACE _____

PLURAL NOUN _____

VERB (PAST TENSE) _____

ADJECTIVE _____

MAD LIBS
NAPOLEON COMPLEX

Napoleon Bonaparte was the first _____ of France. He made his way to
                                    OCCUPATION

the top during the French Revolution, where regular old _____ rose
                                                         PLURAL NOUN

up to fight against royal _____. But Napoleon was known for having
                          PLURAL NOUN

a/an _____ temper. He would fly off the _____ at the drop
     ADJECTIVE   NOUN

of a/an _____. Napoleon was also not a very tall _____. Some
        NOUN   NOUN

say his small size made him feel _____. In order to feel like more of
                                 ADJECTIVE

a/an _____, he would act out, invade _____, and fight wars
     NOUN   PLURAL NOUN

with _____! This made him feel _____ and powerful, despite
     PLURAL NOUN   ADJECTIVE

his small size. And, for a while, it worked, and Napoleon ruled over all of (the)

_____. But eventually, at the Battle of (the) _____, Napoleon was
   A PLACE   A PLACE

captured by British _____, and he _____.
                    PLURAL NOUN   VERB (PAST TENSE)

One thing's for sure: What Napoleon lacked in size, he made up for with his

_____ personality!
   ADJECTIVE

MAD LIBS® is fun to play with friends, but you can also play it by yourself! To begin with, DO NOT look at the story on the page below. Fill in the blanks on this page with the words called for. Then, using the words you have selected, fill in the blank spaces in the story.

Now you've created your own hilarious MAD LIBS® game!

WHEN IN ROME

ADJECTIVE _____

PLURAL NOUN _____

ADJECTIVE _____

ADJECTIVE _____

PLURAL NOUN _____

ADJECTIVE _____

PLURAL NOUN _____

VERB _____

ADJECTIVE _____

PART OF THE BODY (PLURAL) _____

PLURAL NOUN _____

NOUN _____

NOUN _____

NOUN _____

The Roman Empire is one of the most _____ empires in world history.
ADJECTIVE

Two thousand years ago, one in four _____ lived under Roman rule.
PLURAL NOUN

The Roman Empire was led by _____ emperors—a bunch of
ADJECTIVE

powerful men who wore _____ robes and decided the fate of Rome's
ADJECTIVE

many _____. The most famous Roman emperor was Caesar
PLURAL NOUN

Augustus, a/an _____ leader who helped Rome become one of the most
ADJECTIVE

powerful _____ the world had ever seen. The Roman people, rich and
PLURAL NOUN

poor, loved to mingle, gossip, and _____ at the _____ Roman
VERB   ADJECTIVE

baths, a place for bathing and exercising your _____.
PART OF THE BODY (PLURAL)

Romans also enjoyed watching gladiators fight wild _____ in coliseums
PLURAL NOUN

and racing chariots around a/an _____. For about five hundred years,
NOUN

Romans ruled the _____—which is why the Roman Empire is thought
NOUN

of by some people as the most powerful _____ to ever exist.
NOUN

MAD LIBS® is fun to play with friends, but you can also play it by yourself! To begin with, DO NOT look at the story on the page below. Fill in the blanks on this page with the words called for. Then, using the words you have selected, fill in the blank spaces in the story.

Now you've created your own hilarious MAD LIBS® game!

AN APPLE A DAY

ADJECTIVE _____

ADJECTIVE _____

ADJECTIVE _____

ADJECTIVE _____

PERSON IN ROOM (FEMALE) _____

SILLY WORD _____

A PLACE _____

VERB ENDING IN "ING" _____

NOUN _____

ADVERB _____

NOUN _____

ADJECTIVE _____

NOUN _____

ADJECTIVE _____

VERB _____

MAD LIBS®
AN APPLE A DAY

Here is the story of how a/an _____ scientist named Sir Isaac Newton
<u>ADJECTIVE</u>

came up with the _____ theory of gravity. One day, a/an _____
<u>ADJECTIVE</u> <u>ADJECTIVE</u>

Isaac went to visit his _____ mother, _____ ,
<u>ADJECTIVE</u> <u>PERSON IN ROOM (FEMALE)</u>

at _____ Manor, her country home in (the) _____ . While
<u>SILLY WORD</u> <u>A PLACE</u>

_____ in the garden, Isaac saw an apple fall from a/an
<u>VERB ENDING IN "ING"</u>

_____ . *Why does that apple fall* _____ *to the ground?* thought
<u>NOUN</u> <u>ADVERB</u>

Isaac. *Why doesn't the apple fall sideways, or go upward, toward the* _____
<u>NOUN</u>

in the sky? Before long, Isaac decided that the _____ apple must be
<u>ADJECTIVE</u>

drawn to the Earth's core, right in the middle of the _____ . And thus,
<u>NOUN</u>

Sir Isaac Newton came up with the _____ concept of gravity—that
<u>ADJECTIVE</u>

whatever goes up must _____ down.
<u>VERB</u>

MAD LIBS®

SPY MAD LIBS

MAD LIBS®

INSTRUCTIONS

MAD LIBS® is a game for people who don't like games!
It can be played by one, two, three, four, or forty.

• RIDICULOUSLY SIMPLE DIRECTIONS

In this tablet you will find stories containing blank spaces where words are left out.
One player, the READER, selects one of these stories. The READER does not tell anyone
what the story is about. Instead, he/she asks the other players, the WRITERS, to give
him/her words. These words are used to fill in the blank spaces in the story.

• TO PLAY

The READER asks each WRITER in turn to call out a word—an adjective or a noun or
whatever the space calls for—and uses them to fill in the blank spaces in the story. The
result is a MAD LIBS® game.

When the READER then reads the completed MAD LIBS® game to the other players,
they will discover that they have written a story that is fantastic, screamingly funny,
shocking, silly, crazy, or just plain dumb—depending upon which words each WRITER
called out.

• EXAMPLE (*Before* and *After*)

"_____!" he said _____
        EXCLAMATION   ADVERB

as he jumped into his convertible _____ and
                                                    NOUN

drove off with his _____ wife.
                          ADJECTIVE

"_____OUCH_____!" he said _____HAPPILY_____
        EXCLAMATION   ADVERB

as he jumped into his convertible _____CAT_____ and
                                                    NOUN

drove off with his _____BRAVE_____ wife.
                          ADJECTIVE

MAD LIBS®

QUICK REVIEW

In case you have forgotten what adjectives, adverbs, nouns, and verbs are, here is a quick review:

An ADJECTIVE describes something or somebody. *Lumpy, soft, ugly, messy,* and *short* are adjectives.

An ADVERB tells how something is done. It modifies a verb and usually ends in "ly." *Modestly, stupidly, greedily,* and *carefully* are adverbs.

A NOUN is the name of a person, place, or thing. *Sidewalk, umbrella, bridle, bathtub,* and *nose* are nouns.

A VERB is an action word. *Run, pitch, jump,* and *swim* are verbs. Put the verbs in past tense if the directions say PAST TENSE. *Ran, pitched, jumped,* and *swam* are verbs in the past tense.

When we ask for A PLACE, we mean any sort of place: a country or city *(Spain, Cleveland)* or a room *(bathroom, kitchen).*

An EXCLAMATION or SILLY WORD is any sort of funny sound, gasp, grunt, or outcry, like *Wow!, Ouch!, Whomp!, Ick!,* and *Gadzooks!*

When we ask for specific words, like a NUMBER, a COLOR, an ANIMAL, or a PART OF THE BODY, we mean a word that is one of those things, like *seven, blue, horse,* or *head.*

When we ask for a PLURAL, it means more than one. For example, *cat* pluralized is *cats.*

MAD LIBS® is fun to play with friends, but you can also play it by yourself! To begin with, DO NOT look at the story on the page below. Fill in the blanks on this page with the words called for. Then, using the words you have selected, fill in the blank spaces in the story.

Now you've created your own hilarious MAD LIBS® game!

THE ART OF ESPIONAGE

VERB ENDING IN "ING" _____

ADJECTIVE _____

ADJECTIVE _____

PLURAL NOUN _____

ADJECTIVE _____

PERSON IN ROOM _____

PLURAL NOUN _____

A PLACE _____

ADJECTIVE _____

CELEBRITY _____

NOUN _____

PLURAL NOUN _____

ADJECTIVE _____

PLURAL NOUN _____

PLURAL NOUN _____

NOUN _____

PLURAL NOUN _____

MAD LIBS®
THE ART OF ESPIONAGE

Espionage is the formal word for _____. In the shadowy

                  VERB ENDING IN "ING"

world of spies, a/an _____ organization like the US government uses

            ADJECTIVE

spies to infiltrate _____ groups for the purpose of obtaining top secret

           ADJECTIVE

_____. For example, spies might have to crack the code for accessing

   PLURAL NOUN

confidential, _____ files, or their mission could be far more

            ADJECTIVE

dangerous—like stealing the key ingredient for making _____'s

                                PERSON IN ROOM

award-winning Explosive Fudgy _____. Spies are found all over (the)

                       PLURAL NOUN

_____—but they are not allowed to reveal their _____ identities.

   A PLACE   ADJECTIVE

A teacher, _____, or even the little old _____ with the cane and

          CELEBRITY   NOUN

fifteen pet _____ who lives next door to you could be a spy. The world

       PLURAL NOUN

of spying might seem glamorous and _____—but it's filled with risks

                          ADJECTIVE

and _____! Sure, spies have a never-ending supply of supercool

       PLURAL NOUN

electronic _____, but they can't trust any _____—which is why

       PLURAL NOUN   NOUN

the number one rule of spies is to keep friends close—and _____ closer!

                                               PLURAL NOUN

MAD LIBS® is fun to play with friends, but you can also play it by yourself! To begin with, DO NOT look at the story on the page below. Fill in the blanks on this page with the words called for. Then, using the words you have selected, fill in the blank spaces in the story.

Now you've created your own hilarious MAD LIBS® game!

SPY HALL OF FAME

PLURAL NOUN _____

ADJECTIVE _____

PERSON IN ROOM (MALE) _____

NUMBER _____

ADJECTIVE _____

NOUN _____

PART OF THE BODY _____

ADJECTIVE _____

PART OF THE BODY _____

ADJECTIVE _____

PLURAL NOUN _____

NOUN _____

PART OF THE BODY _____

NOUN _____

NOUN _____

VERB _____

CELEBRITY _____

NOUN _____

MAD LIBS®
SPY HALL OF FAME

The Spy Hall of Fame honors the brave _____ of that
                                         PLURAL NOUN
_____ profession known as spying. Inductees include:
ADJECTIVE

- _____ **Bond**—Famously known as Agent Double
  PERSON IN ROOM (MALE)

  "O" _____, this spy was as handsome as he was _____. Not
        NUMBER   ADJECTIVE

  only did Bond nab the bad _____ every time, he always won the
                              NOUN

  _____ of the _____ woman, as well.
  PART OF THE BODY   ADJECTIVE

- **Chuck "Eagle _____" Spyglass**—Whether it was
                    PART OF THE BODY

  designing a/an _____ pair of night-vision _____ or hiding a
                  ADJECTIVE   PLURAL NOUN

  tiny camera inside a gold _____ that a spy could wear around
                              NOUN

  his _____, Chuck was the go-to _____ for his
       PART OF THE BODY   NOUN

  wizardry in surveillance.

- **Joe the Spy**—Joe was your typical _____ next door. His high-
                                         NOUN

  school yearbook denoted him as "Most Likely to _____." Who
                                                   VERB

  would have thought this Average Joe would be the _____ of the spy
                                                     CELEBRITY

  world when he single-handedly took down an international ring of

  _____ robbers?!
  NOUN

MAD LIBS® is fun to play with friends, but you can also play it by yourself! To begin with, DO NOT look at the story on the page below. Fill in the blanks on this page with the words called for. Then, using the words you have selected, fill in the blank spaces in the story.

Now you've created your own hilarious MAD LIBS® game!

HOW TO SPEAK LIKE A SPY

ADJECTIVE _____

NOUN _____

VERB _____

NOUN _____

VERB ENDING IN "ING" _____

PLURAL NOUN _____

ADJECTIVE _____

NOUN _____

ADJECTIVE _____

CELEBRITY _____

PERSON IN ROOM _____

NOUN _____

NOUN _____

PLURAL NOUN _____

ADJECTIVE _____

PLURAL NOUN _____

MAD LIBS
HOW TO SPEAK LIKE A SPY

Spies speak their own _____ language. Common terms include:
ADJECTIVE

- **Target**—a person or a/an _____ of interest whom a spy watches
  NOUN

  come and _____
  VERB

- **Surveillance**—to monitor or observe a/an _____ with visual,
  NOUN

  listening, or _____ equipment like cameras, satellites, or
  VERB ENDING IN "ING"

  long-distance _____
  PLURAL NOUN

- **Bug**—a/an _____ device that can be planted on an object such
  ADJECTIVE

  as a car, remote control, or _____ phone to listen in on a target's
  NOUN

  _____ conversations
  ADJECTIVE

- **Alias**—the name a spy uses, like _____ or _____, while
  CELEBRITY   PERSON IN ROOM

  undercover

- **Mole**—a/an _____ from one spy organization who gets a job
  NOUN

  within a rival _____ organization in order to obtain inside
  NOUN

  information or other secret _____
  PLURAL NOUN

- **Classified**—sensitive and _____ information that only certain
  ADJECTIVE

  levels of _____ have authorized clearance to access
  PLURAL NOUN

MAD LIBS® is fun to play with friends, but you can also play it by yourself! To begin with, DO NOT look at the story on the page below. Fill in the blanks on this page with the words called for. Then, using the words you have selected, fill in the blank spaces in the story.

Now you've created your own hilarious MAD LIBS® game!

A SPY BIRTHDAY PARTY

NUMBER _____

NOUN _____

ADJECTIVE _____

PLURAL NOUN _____

ADJECTIVE _____

PART OF THE BODY (PLURAL) _____

ADJECTIVE _____

VERB _____

ADJECTIVE _____

PLURAL NOUN _____

NOUN _____

NOUN _____

PLURAL NOUN _____

PART OF THE BODY (PLURAL) _____

PLURAL NOUN _____

ADJECTIVE _____

ADJECTIVE _____

NOUN _____

PLURAL NOUN _____

MAD LIBS®
A SPY BIRTHDAY PARTY

When I turned _____ years old, my mom and _____ threw a/an
                         NUMBER   NOUN

_____ spy-themed birthday party for me. I invited ten of my closest
 ADJECTIVE

_____, and we spent a/an _____ afternoon doing cool spy stuff.
PLURAL NOUN   ADJECTIVE

We slipped black sunglasses over our _____, grabbed
                                     PART OF THE BODY (PLURAL)

_____ toy cell phones, and practiced our surveillance techniques with a
 ADJECTIVE

game of hide-and-_____ around my backyard. We decoded _____
                    VERB   ADJECTIVE

messages that my parents had written on colorful _____. We pounded on
                                                  PLURAL NOUN

a/an _____-shaped piñata with a wooden _____, and we put spy
      NOUN   NOUN

tattoos like binoculars, computers, and micro-_____ all over our
                                               PLURAL NOUN

_____. Later my mom served cake and _____, and
PART OF THE BODY (PLURAL)   PLURAL NOUN

everyone sang "_____ Birthday" to me. I got a ton of _____ gifts,
                ADJECTIVE   ADJECTIVE

but my favorite was the motion-activated _____ that would alert me to
                                          NOUN

any _____ about to sneak into my room. Every good spy needs one of
     PLURAL NOUN

these!

MAD LIBS® is fun to play with friends, but you can also play it by yourself! To begin with, DO NOT look at the story on the page below. Fill in the blanks on this page with the words called for. Then, using the words you have selected, fill in the blank spaces in the story.

Now you've created your own hilarious MAD LIBS® game!

FROM THE SPY FILE

PERSON IN ROOM _____

ADJECTIVE _____

CELEBRITY _____

VERB ENDING IN "ING" _____

NOUN _____

ADJECTIVE _____

ADJECTIVE _____

NOUN _____

ADJECTIVE _____

ADJECTIVE _____

A PLACE _____

ADJECTIVE _____

NOUN _____

PART OF THE BODY _____

PLURAL NOUN _____

ADJECTIVE _____

PART OF THE BODY _____

ADJECTIVE _____

To Agent _____ : At this morning's _____ management
          PERSON IN ROOM   ADJECTIVE

meeting, it was decided by Agency Chief _____ that you are being
                                          CELEBRITY

assigned to the case known internally as Operation _____
                                                    VERB ENDING IN "ING"

_____ . This memo will provide the _____ details of the case, and
   NOUN   ADJECTIVE

you will be briefed further in the coming week. As you may know, this case

involves a band of _____ thieves who stole the blueprints to a top secret
                    ADJECTIVE

robot _____ that threatens the security of our _____ country. They
        NOUN   ADJECTIVE

have hidden the prints somewhere in a/an _____ location on the
                                          ADJECTIVE

outskirts of (the) _____ . Their leader's name is Uno Ojo, which translates
                    A PLACE

to _____ _____ . You will know him by the black eye patch he
   ADJECTIVE   NOUN

wears over his _____ . Be advised that he and his group of
                PART OF THE BODY

evil _____ are armed and _____ , so use extreme caution if you
     PLURAL NOUN   ADJECTIVE

come face-to-_____ with any of them. As any good spy
              PART OF THE BODY

knows, you're of no use to the agency if you're _____ .
                                                 ADJECTIVE

MAD LIBS® is fun to play with friends, but you can also play it by yourself! To begin with, DO NOT look at the story on the page below. Fill in the blanks on this page with the words called for. Then, using the words you have selected, fill in the blank spaces in the story.

Now you've created your own hilarious MAD LIBS® game!

WELCOME TO HEADQUARTERS

NOUN _____

VERB _____

ADJECTIVE _____

ADJECTIVE _____

NOUN _____

PERSON IN ROOM _____

ADJECTIVE _____

PLURAL NOUN _____

PART OF THE BODY _____

CELEBRITY _____

ADJECTIVE _____

PLURAL NOUN _____

VERB ENDING IN "ING" _____

PART OF THE BODY _____

The new spy headquarters that just opened on the corner of Fifth Avenue and

_____ Street really makes people stop and _____. The building
  NOUN   VERB

itself features _____, modern architecture on the outside and _____,
           ADJECTIVE   ADJECTIVE

state-of-the-art technology on the inside. To gain entrance, you must step

through an electronic _____ while a security guard named
                            NOUN

_____ pats you down with a/an _____ wand to make sure
PERSON IN ROOM   ADJECTIVE

you aren't carrying any dangerous _____. Then you have to wear a
                              PLURAL NOUN

name badge around your _____ that says, "Hi! My name is
                          PART OF THE BODY

_____." There's a/an _____ elevator to take you anywhere
CELEBRITY   ADJECTIVE

you need to go. There are closed-circuit _____ everywhere, so if anyone
                                    PLURAL NOUN

in the building starts _____ inappropriately, security will
                      VERB ENDING IN "ING"

instantly remove them. Certain areas are completely off-limits—unless, of

course, you place your _____ on the scanner and it gives
                      PART OF THE BODY

you authorized clearance.

MAD LIBS® is fun to play with friends, but you can also play it by yourself! To begin with, DO NOT look at the story on the page below. Fill in the blanks on this page with the words called for. Then, using the words you have selected, fill in the blank spaces in the story.

Now you've created your own hilarious MAD LIBS® game!

GEAR & GADGETS, PART 1

ADJECTIVE _____

ADJECTIVE _____

PART OF THE BODY _____

NOUN _____

PLURAL NOUN _____

PLURAL NOUN _____

ADJECTIVE _____

COLOR _____

VERB ENDING IN "ING" _____

TYPE OF LIQUID _____

ADJECTIVE _____

ADJECTIVE _____

CELEBRITY _____

PART OF THE BODY (PLURAL) _____

VERB ENDING IN "ING" _____

One of the most _____ parts about being a spy are the gadgets you get to

ADJECTIVE

use! Here are some examples:

- **Spy phones**—These do much more than make _____ calls. They

ADJECTIVE

  can scan _____-prints on a drinking _____

PART OF THE BODY   NOUN

  or shoot laser _____ if a spy is being chased.

PLURAL NOUN

- **X-ray vision** _____—These _____ glasses are so powerful

PLURAL NOUN   ADJECTIVE

  that they can help spies determine if an enemy is wearing _____

COLOR

  underwear.

- _____ **beans**—A must-have defense weapon for any

VERB ENDING IN "ING"

  spy, the beans are dropped in a glass of _____ to render

TYPE OF LIQUID

  an enemy _____.

ADJECTIVE

- **Mini flashlight**—This clever and _____ little tool projects a

ADJECTIVE

  holographic image of _____ to distract bad guys.

CELEBRITY

- **Eavesdropping ears**—Spies affix long-range earpieces to their

  _____ to detect where their targets are

PART OF THE BODY (PLURAL)

  _____.

VERB ENDING IN "ING"

MAD LIBS® is fun to play with friends, but you can also play it by yourself! To begin with, DO NOT look at the story on the page below. Fill in the blanks on this page with the words called for. Then, using the words you have selected, fill in the blank spaces in the story.

Now you've created your own hilarious MAD LIBS® game!

I, SPY

PERSON IN ROOM _____

NUMBER _____

ADJECTIVE _____

ADJECTIVE _____

A PLACE _____

NOUN _____

ADJECTIVE _____

PLURAL NOUN _____

SILLY WORD _____

PART OF THE BODY _____

ADJECTIVE _____

CELEBRITY _____

VERB ENDING IN "ING" _____

PLURAL NOUN _____

NOUN _____

PLURAL NOUN _____

ADJECTIVE _____

PLURAL NOUN _____

ADJECTIVE _____

PART OF THE BODY (PLURAL) _____

MAD LIBS®
I, SPY

My name is _____, and I became a spy when I was only
                    PERSON IN ROOM

_____ years old. It certainly was an exciting, _____ time in my life!
    NUMBER   ADJECTIVE

I was sent to _____ locations all over the world, including London, Paris,
                 ADJECTIVE

and (the) _____. Depending on the assignment, there could be
              A PLACE

_____ chases, _____ explosions, or _____ collapsing around
    NOUN   ADJECTIVE   PLURAL NOUN

me. _____, I'm lucky I didn't lose a/an _____
       SILLY WORD   PART OF THE BODY

during some of my _____ spy adventures! One time my partner
                        ADJECTIVE

_____ and I were _____ in an alley in pursuit of a target
   CELEBRITY   VERB ENDING IN "ING"

when a shower of flaming _____ shot out of the darkness. Another
                            PLURAL NOUN

time I was piloting a/an _____ when a flock of _____ flew right
                            NOUN   PLURAL NOUN

into the engines. Fortunately, I crash-landed in a/an _____ lake, so I
                                                         ADJECTIVE

managed to walk away with only a few scrapes and _____. Now that
                                                      PLURAL NOUN

I'm retired, my life isn't nearly as _____, but on the other hand, it's nice
                                        ADJECTIVE

just to be able to put my _____ up and relax.
                            PART OF THE BODY (PLURAL)

MAD LIBS® is fun to play with friends, but you can also play it by yourself! To begin with, DO NOT look at the story on the page below. Fill in the blanks on this page with the words called for. Then, using the words you have selected, fill in the blank spaces in the story.

Now you've created your own hilarious MAD LIBS® game!

DRESSING IN DISGUISE

ADJECTIVE _____

ARTICLE OF CLOTHING (PLURAL) _____

ADJECTIVE _____

CELEBRITY _____

PERSON IN ROOM (MALE) _____

ADJECTIVE _____

PART OF THE BODY _____

NOUN _____

PLURAL NOUN _____

VERB _____

PLURAL NOUN _____

ADJECTIVE _____

PLURAL NOUN _____

COLOR _____

ADJECTIVE _____

PART OF THE BODY (PLURAL) _____

MAD LIBS®
DRESSING IN DISGUISE

A superspy must excel in the _____ art of disguise. They need to be
                                    ADJECTIVE

able to use _____, makeup, and _____ acting
              ARTICLE OF CLOTHING (PLURAL)   ADJECTIVE

skills to morph into other characters, such as a superstar like _____
                                                                    CELEBRITY

or just a regular guy like _____. Disguises can range from
                            PERSON IN ROOM (MALE)

simple to outrageously _____. One of the easiest disguises is a pair of
                         ADJECTIVE

eyeglasses with a large _____ and mustache attached.
                          PART OF THE BODY

Other disguises are more complicated, like a full-body _____ costume.
                                                          NOUN

Sometimes spies even have to dress as _____—a particularly challenging
                                        PLURAL NOUN

disguise as it's difficult to _____ while wearing _____! Once a
                               VERB   PLURAL NOUN

person advances to the level of spy, they get a/an _____ Spy Disguise
                                                     ADJECTIVE

Kit containing everything they need to become anyone they want. The

kits contain helpful disguise tools like _____ to color your hair
                                           PLURAL NOUN

_____, _____ wigs, and—best of all—fake
    COLOR   ADJECTIVE

_____.
  PART OF THE BODY (PLURAL)

MAD LIBS® is fun to play with friends, but you can also play it by yourself! To begin with, DO NOT look at the story on the page below. Fill in the blanks on this page with the words called for. Then, using the words you have selected, fill in the blank spaces in the story.

Now you've created your own hilarious MAD LIBS® game!

ULTIMATE SPYMOBILE

NOUN _____

ADJECTIVE _____

PLURAL NOUN _____

NOUN _____

SILLY WORD _____

PLURAL NOUN _____

VERB _____

ADJECTIVE _____

NOUN _____

PART OF THE BODY _____

PLURAL NOUN _____

PLURAL NOUN _____

ADJECTIVE _____

NOUN _____

NOUN _____

ADJECTIVE _____

CELEBRITY _____

MAD LIBS
ULTIMATE SPYMOBILE

A top-notch spy deserves to drive a world-class _____ with all these
NOUN

_____ features:
ADJECTIVE

- Computers and TV monitors to communicate with _____ back
PLURAL NOUN

  at headquarters

- _____-activated doors that slide open when the password
NOUN

  "_____" is spoken
SILLY WORD

- Jet sprays that shoot _____ so that any enemy in pursuit will
PLURAL NOUN

  crash and _____
VERB

- A/An _____ punching _____ that will bonk an enemy on
ADJECTIVE   NOUN

  the _____ if he gets inside the vehicle
PART OF THE BODY

- Razor-sharp _____ along the outside edges of the car to slice the
PLURAL NOUN

  tires of other passing _____
PLURAL NOUN

- A/An _____ battering ram on the front end to bash into a/an
ADJECTIVE

  _____ barricade
NOUN

- _____-boosters that will propel the vehicle into the air
NOUN

- Best of all, a/an _____ sound system that fills the vehicle with
ADJECTIVE

  the sweet melodies of _____
CELEBRITY

MAD LIBS® is fun to play with friends, but you can also play it by yourself! To begin with, DO NOT look at the story on the page below. Fill in the blanks on this page with the words called for. Then, using the words you have selected, fill in the blank spaces in the story.

Now you've created your own hilarious MAD LIBS® game!

A TRIP TO THE SPY MUSEUM

A PLACE _____

ADJECTIVE _____

VERB ENDING IN "ING" _____

PLURAL NOUN _____

PLURAL NOUN _____

ADJECTIVE _____

NOUN _____

PLURAL NOUN _____

ADJECTIVE _____

VERB ENDING IN "ING" _____

PLURAL NOUN _____

NOUN _____

ADJECTIVE _____

VERB ENDING IN "ING" _____

NOUN _____

ADJECTIVE _____

NOUN _____

PLURAL NOUN _____

ADJECTIVE _____

MAD LIBS

A TRIP TO THE SPY MUSEUM

Located in (the) _____, the International Spy Museum is the only
___A PLACE___

_____ museum in the United States dedicated to the covert profession of
___ADJECTIVE___

_____. The museum features the largest collection of spy-
___VERB ENDING IN "ING"___

themed _____ ever placed on public display. These items bring to life the
___PLURAL NOUN___

work of famous _____ as well as history-making _____ espionage
___PLURAL NOUN___ ___ADJECTIVE___

missions. The stories of spies are told through films, an interactive _____,
___NOUN___

and state-of-the-art _____. The museum contains a/an _____
___PLURAL NOUN___ ___ADJECTIVE___

gift shop and a restaurant called _____ Spy Café. Young
___VERB ENDING IN "ING"___

_____ love to visit the spy museum for _____ parties, field
___PLURAL NOUN___ ___NOUN___

trips, and _____ scavenger hunts. The exhibits teach up-
___ADJECTIVE___

and-_____ spies about _____ surveillance, threat analysis,
___VERB ENDING IN "ING"___ ___NOUN___

and maintaining one's _____ cover. The goal of the International
___ADJECTIVE___

_____ Museum is to teach _____ about espionage in a fun,
___NOUN___ ___PLURAL NOUN___

_____ way. Who knows? It might even make them want to join
___ADJECTIVE___

the team someday!

MAD LIBS® is fun to play with friends, but you can also play it by yourself! To begin with, DO NOT look at the story on the page below. Fill in the blanks on this page with the words called for. Then, using the words you have selected, fill in the blank spaces in the story.

Now you've created your own hilarious MAD LIBS® game!

THE BEST SPY MOVIES

NOUN _____

ADVERB _____

PLURAL NOUN _____

NOUN _____

SILLY WORD _____

ADJECTIVE _____

CELEBRITY _____

NOUN _____

ADJECTIVE _____

PERSON IN ROOM (FEMALE) _____

NOUN _____

NOUN _____

NOUN _____

PART OF THE BODY _____

ADJECTIVE _____

COLOR _____

PART OF THE BODY _____

TYPE OF FOOD _____

MAD LIBS
THE BEST SPY MOVIES

Here are the best spy movies to curl up on the _____ and watch:

NOUN

- *Spy Story*: In this _____ epic tale, toy _____ come to life!

ADVERB   PLURAL NOUN

  The main character is a space-_____ named _____

NOUN   SILLY WORD

  Lightyear who thinks he is an intergalactic spy, and a/an _____

ADJECTIVE

  cowboy action figure named _____ must convince him he's just

CELEBRITY

  a/an _____.

NOUN

- *Beauty and the Spy*: A beautiful, _____ young girl named

ADJECTIVE

  _____ wanders into a castle in the middle of a/an

PERSON IN ROOM (FEMALE)

  _____ and meets a spy who's under the spell of a wicked old

NOUN

  _____. He has been turned into a hideous _____

NOUN   NOUN

  with hair all over his _____, and only she can break the

PART OF THE BODY

  enchantment.

- *Spy Wars*: A space tale in which spies from the _____ Rebel Forces

ADJECTIVE

  go up against a scary, robotic man in flowing _____ robes who

COLOR

  wears a large helmet on his _____ and calls himself Lord

PART OF THE BODY

  _____.

TYPE OF FOOD

MAD LIBS® is fun to play with friends, but you can also play it by yourself! To begin with, DO NOT look at the story on the page below. Fill in the blanks on this page with the words called for. Then, using the words you have selected, fill in the blank spaces in the story.

Now you've created your own hilarious MAD LIBS® game!

TALES FROM SPY CAMP

ADJECTIVE _____

NOUN _____

VERB _____

ADJECTIVE _____

CELEBRITY _____

PLURAL NOUN _____

PLURAL NOUN _____

ADJECTIVE _____

VERB _____

PLURAL NOUN _____

ADVERB _____

EXCLAMATION _____

NOUN _____

PART OF THE BODY _____

VERB _____

NOUN _____

PLURAL NOUN _____

PLURAL NOUN _____

PERSON IN ROOM _____

MAD LIBS®
TALES FROM SPY CAMP

Dear Mom and Dad,

Spy Camp is totally _____! Being a real _____-in-training is
_____ADJECTIVE_____NOUN

the coolest thing ever! We start each day with a/an _____ around
_____VERB

the campground for exercise. Next we do different _____ activities that
_____ADJECTIVE

Counselor _____ assigns. Sometimes we get buckets full of screws,
_____CELEBRITY

magnets, and other _____ to build surveillance gadgets. Or we use leaves,
_____PLURAL NOUN

twigs, and _____ to make camouflage disguises. My favorite is when we
_____PLURAL NOUN

play _____ games like Spy Paintball. We team up and _____
_____ADJECTIVE_____VERB

behind trees, boulders, and other large _____. We need to be _____
_____PLURAL NOUN_____ADVERB

stealthy to avoid detection; otherwise, we'll get nailed—and, _____, a
_____EXCLAMATION

paintball _____ to the _____ *really hurts*! Sometimes
_____NOUN_____PART OF THE BODY

we just _____ by a roaring _____ and roast _____—like
_____VERB_____NOUN_____PLURAL NOUN

regular campers do. See you in a few weeks!

Hugs and _____, _____
_____PLURAL NOUN_____PERSON IN ROOM

MAD LIBS® is fun to play with friends, but you can also play it by yourself! To begin with, DO NOT look at the story on the page below. Fill in the blanks on this page with the words called for. Then, using the words you have selected, fill in the blank spaces in the story.

Now you've created your own hilarious MAD LIBS® game!

WANTED: A FEW GOOD SPIES

ADJECTIVE _____

PART OF THE BODY (PLURAL) _____

NOUN _____

TYPE OF FOOD _____

ADJECTIVE _____

A PLACE _____

ADJECTIVE _____

ADJECTIVE _____

PART OF THE BODY (PLURAL) _____

ADJECTIVE _____

ADJECTIVE _____

ARTICLE OF CLOTHING (PLURAL) _____

NUMBER _____

PLURAL NOUN _____

NOUN _____

VERB _____

MAD LIBS®
WANTED: A FEW GOOD SPIES

Are you sneaky and _____? Do you keep your eyes and
    _____ADJECTIVE_____

_____ open at all times to things going on around you?
PART OF THE BODY (PLURAL)

Can you take items like a piece of string, a cell phone, a/an _____, and
                                                                NOUN

some day-old _____ and build a makeshift homing device to track
            TYPE OF FOOD

a/an _____ target? If so, then we want you to join our exclusive spy
    ADJECTIVE

agency. We are hired out by the military, private corporations, and occasionally

the mayor of (the) _____ to infiltrate a/an _____ enemy and
                  A PLACE   ADJECTIVE

steal plans, crack codes, or perform other _____ duties as assigned.
                                            ADJECTIVE

Although previous experience is not required, candidates who are fast on their

_____ when it comes to solving _____ problems
PART OF THE BODY (PLURAL)   ADJECTIVE

will be given top consideration. Spy gear—including a backpack of

_____ gadgets and black _____—is provided.
ADJECTIVE   ARTICLE OF CLOTHING (PLURAL)

Starting salary is _____ _____ a week. If you can move with the
                  NUMBER   PLURAL NOUN

stealth of a two-ton _____, then the job of a spy could be right for you.
                    NOUN

_____ today for an application!
VERB

MAD LIBS® is fun to play with friends, but you can also play it by yourself! To begin with, DO NOT look at the story on the page below. Fill in the blanks on this page with the words called for. Then, using the words you have selected, fill in the blank spaces in the story.

Now you've created your own hilarious MAD LIBS® game!

ODE TO SPIES

VERB ENDING IN "ING" _____

NOUN _____

ADJECTIVE _____

PLURAL NOUN _____

PLURAL NOUN _____

VERB _____

PART OF THE BODY (PLURAL) _____

ADJECTIVE _____

NOUN _____

NOUN _____

VERB _____

ADJECTIVE _____

PLURAL NOUN _____

PLURAL NOUN _____

PERSON IN ROOM _____

ADJECTIVE _____

NOUN _____

They're pros at _____ stealthily and the art of surprise.

VERB ENDING IN "ING"

Is that a/an _____ that I see—or a/an _____ spy in disguise?

NOUN   ADJECTIVE

They're sneaky as _____ so their covers don't get blown.

PLURAL NOUN

They hang with their best _____, but they *always* _____

PLURAL NOUN   VERB

alone.

Spies think with their _____, and they're fast on their feet.

PART OF THE BODY (PLURAL)

The high-tech gadgets they use are _____ and neat,

ADJECTIVE

Like _____-shaped bugs to plant on a moving car

NOUN

Or telescopic _____-glasses to help them _____ far.

NOUN   VERB

They crack _____ codes with _____ and speed.

ADJECTIVE   PLURAL NOUN

Steal _____? Learn secrets? They'll get what you need!

PLURAL NOUN

So don't you fear, _____! Don't make a/an _____ fuss!

PERSON IN ROOM   ADJECTIVE

Just pick up the _____ and dial 1-800-SPIES-R-US.

NOUN

MAD LIBS® is fun to play with friends, but you can also play it by yourself! To begin with, DO NOT look at the story on the page below. Fill in the blanks on this page with the words called for. Then, using the words you have selected, fill in the blank spaces in the story.

Now you've created your own hilarious MAD LIBS® game!

MOST WANTED LIST

PLURAL NOUN _____

ADJECTIVE _____

PLURAL NOUN _____

NOUN _____

ADVERB _____

NOUN _____

ADJECTIVE _____

PERSON IN ROOM _____

COLOR _____

NOUN _____

PART OF THE BODY (PLURAL) _____

PLURAL NOUN _____

NOUN _____

A PLACE _____

CELEBRITY _____

NOUN _____

ADJECTIVE _____

PLURAL NOUN _____

PART OF THE BODY (PLURAL) _____

PLURAL NOUN _____

MAD LIBS®
MOST WANTED LIST

The Global Spy Organization's list of most wanted _____ is a long
                                                        PLURAL NOUN

one. Here are _____ profiles of the most notorious criminals:
                   ADJECTIVE

- **Max Von** _____ **III** is wanted for the kidnapping of Sir
                 PLURAL NOUN

  Puffy-_____, the _____ overweight pet _____ of His
           NOUN   ADVERB   NOUN

  _____ Majesty, King _____.
   ADJECTIVE   PERSON IN ROOM

- **The** _____ **Shadow** is the head of an international ring of
              COLOR

  _____ thieves whose sticky _____ have lifted
     NOUN   PART OF THE BODY (PLURAL)

  valuable _____ from museums around the world, including the
             PLURAL NOUN

  famous Le _____ located in (the) _____.
               NOUN   A PLACE

- _____, a world-famous super-_____, is actually
     CELEBRITY   NOUN

  the mastermind behind a/an _____ group of computer
                                 ADJECTIVE

  geeks and techno-_____ whose ultra-intelligent
                        PLURAL NOUN

  _____ enable them to breach the highest levels of
   PART OF THE BODY (PLURAL)

  security and steal US military _____.
                                     PLURAL NOUN

MAD LIBS® is fun to play with friends, but you can also play it by yourself! To begin with, DO NOT look at the story on the page below. Fill in the blanks on this page with the words called for. Then, using the words you have selected, fill in the blank spaces in the story.

Now you've created your own hilarious MAD LIBS® game!

SPY VIDEO GAMES

PART OF THE BODY (PLURAL) _____

ADJECTIVE _____

COLOR _____

PLURAL NOUN _____

ADJECTIVE _____

A PLACE _____

PLURAL NOUN _____

NOUN _____

PERSON IN ROOM _____

ADJECTIVE _____

PLURAL NOUN _____

NOUN _____

PLURAL NOUN _____

PLURAL NOUN _____

VERB ENDING IN "ING" _____

ADJECTIVE _____

NOUN _____

NUMBER _____

PLURAL NOUN _____

PLURAL NOUN _____

NOUN _____

Grab your favorite controller, flex your _____, and get
PART OF THE BODY (PLURAL)

ready to play spy in these _____ video games:
ADJECTIVE

- *Operation* _____ _____: You are a spy in the hot,
  COLOR   PLURAL NOUN

  _____ jungles of (the) _____. Your mission?
  ADJECTIVE   A PLACE

  Vaporize poisonous _____ as you search for the missing
  PLURAL NOUN

  and priceless _____ Diamond, stolen by the rogue operative
  NOUN

  _____.
  PERSON IN ROOM

- *Spies in Space*: The _____, evil scientist, Dr. Smarty
  ADJECTIVE

  _____, has launched a/an _____ into space
  PLURAL NOUN   NOUN

  containing deadly _____ that, if sprinkled into the Earth's
  PLURAL NOUN

  atmosphere, will destroy all living _____.
  PLURAL NOUN

- *Speedway Spies*: It's spy-on-spy _____ action on the
  VERB ENDING IN "ING"

  racetrack! You and your _____ opponent burn up the race
  ADJECTIVE

  _____ at speeds topping _____ mph as you swerve to
  NOUN   NUMBER

  avoid toppling _____, slippery spills of _____, and,
  PLURAL NOUN   PLURAL NOUN

  occasionally, a/an _____ trying to cross the road.
  NOUN

MAD LIBS® is fun to play with friends, but you can also play it by yourself! To begin with, DO NOT look at the story on the page below. Fill in the blanks on this page with the words called for. Then, using the words you have selected, fill in the blank spaces in the story.

Now you've created your own hilarious MAD LIBS® game!

GEAR & GADGETS, PART 2

ADJECTIVE _____

PLURAL NOUN _____

PLURAL NOUN _____

PLURAL NOUN _____

ADJECTIVE _____

PART OF THE BODY (PLURAL) _____

VERB _____

TYPE OF LIQUID _____

ADJECTIVE _____

PLURAL NOUN _____

VERB _____

PART OF THE BODY (PLURAL) _____

NOUN _____

NOUN _____

PLURAL NOUN _____

PART OF THE BODY (PLURAL) _____

MAD LIBS®
GEAR & GADGETS, PART 2

Whether it's to locate a/an _____ target or protect themselves from
_____ADJECTIVE

enemy _____, spies are always armed with the coolest gear and
_____PLURAL NOUN

_____ imaginable.
PLURAL NOUN

- **Smoke** _____—When thrown at enemies, these explode
  _____PLURAL NOUN

  and send _____ smoke billowing into the bad guys'
  _____ADJECTIVE

  _____, making them unable to _____
  PART OF THE BODY (PLURAL)   VERB

  any longer.

- **Laser Pen**—This tool functions as a pen that writes with invisible

  _____, a telescope so spies can track _____
  TYPE OF LIQUID   ADJECTIVE

  enemies from a safe distance, and a flashlight that contains different

  color _____—yellow means "_____ with caution," blue
  _____PLURAL NOUN   VERB

  means "put up your _____ or else," and red means
  PART OF THE BODY (PLURAL)

  "abort the _____."
  NOUN

- **Laser Trip Wire** _____—This gadget has invisible beams
  _____NOUN

  that alert spies to intruding _____ whenever their
  PLURAL NOUN

  _____ hit the beam.
  PART OF THE BODY (PLURAL)

MAD LIBS® is fun to play with friends, but you can also play it by yourself! To begin with, DO NOT look at the story on the page below. Fill in the blanks on this page with the words called for. Then, using the words you have selected, fill in the blank spaces in the story.

Now you've created your own hilarious MAD LIBS® game!

SPY ROLES

ADJECTIVE _____

NOUN _____

NUMBER _____

PLURAL NOUN _____

PLURAL NOUN _____

NOUN _____

ADJECTIVE _____

NOUN _____

ADJECTIVE _____

PLURAL NOUN _____

ADJECTIVE _____

PLURAL NOUN _____

NOUN _____

PLURAL NOUN _____

ADJECTIVE _____

MAD LIBS®
SPY ROLES

There are lots of ways that spies can use their _____ training, including

ADJECTIVE

these:

- A *double agent* is a/an _____ who works for at least _____

NOUN   NUMBER

  intelligence agencies and whose job is to secure classified _____

PLURAL NOUN

  at one agency and deliver them to the _____ in charge at the

PLURAL NOUN

  other agency.

- A *sleeper agent* lives as a regular _____ in a foreign country and

NOUN

  is only called upon when a hostile or otherwise _____ situation

ADJECTIVE

  develops.

- A *cobbler* is a/an _____ who creates false passports, diplomas,

NOUN

  and other _____ documents to help create identities for

ADJECTIVE

  _____ going undercover.

PLURAL NOUN

- A *ghoul* is an agent who searches _____ death notices and

ADJECTIVE

  graveyards for names of dead _____ and gives them to cobblers

PLURAL NOUN

  for their documents.

- A *handler* is a/an _____ who handles _____ as they

NOUN   PLURAL NOUN

  undergo _____ missions.

ADJECTIVE

From SPY MAD LIBS® • Copyright © 2012 by Penguin Random House LLC

MAD LIBS® is fun to play with friends, but you can also play it by yourself! To begin with, DO NOT look at the story on the page below. Fill in the blanks on this page with the words called for. Then, using the words you have selected, fill in the blank spaces in the story.

Now you've created your own hilarious MAD LIBS® game!

SPY U

NOUN _____

ADJECTIVE _____

PLURAL NOUN _____

VERB ENDING IN "ING" _____

PLURAL NOUN _____

CELEBRITY _____

ADJECTIVE _____

ADJECTIVE _____

ADJECTIVE _____

PLURAL NOUN _____

VERB ENDING IN "ING" _____

PERSON IN ROOM _____

A PLACE _____

ADJECTIVE _____

PART OF THE BODY (PLURAL) _____

PLURAL NOUN _____

PART OF THE BODY _____

VERB _____

MAD LIBS®
SPY U

Grab a pen and a/an _____ and get ready to take notes! Spy University
        NOUN

offers _____ classes for aspiring _____ who wish to enter
        ADJECTIVE   PLURAL NOUN

the covert world of espionage:

- **Introduction to** _____: Do you have the patience,
                    VERB ENDING IN "ING"

  street smarts, and _____ to be a spy? Taught by world-renowned
                    PLURAL NOUN

  instructor _____, this class offers a/an _____ overview on
            CELEBRITY   ADJECTIVE

  what it takes to be a/an _____ spy.
                        ADJECTIVE

- **Stealth Mode:** A great spy has the _____ ability to sneak up on
                                    ADJECTIVE

  unsuspecting _____ without detection. This course provides
              PLURAL NOUN

  field experience in _____ within different environments,
                    VERB ENDING IN "ING"

  such as _____'s room or even (the) _____.
          PERSON IN ROOM   A PLACE

- **Wise Spies:** Spies have many gadgets and _____ tools they use to
                                            ADJECTIVE

  pull the wool over their opponents' _____. But it's
                                    PART OF THE BODY (PLURAL)

  their wits and clever _____ that give them an advantage. Learn
                        PLURAL NOUN

  how to use your _____ to get your opponent to
                PART OF THE BODY

  _____ exactly the way you want him to.
  VERB

MAD LIBS® is fun to play with friends, but you can also play it by yourself! To begin with, DO NOT look at the story on the page below. Fill in the blanks on this page with the words called for. Then, using the words you have selected, fill in the blank spaces in the story.

Now you've created your own hilarious MAD LIBS® game!

CRACK THE CODE

ADJECTIVE _____

A PLACE _____

ADJECTIVE _____

COLOR _____

VERB ENDING IN "ING" _____

NOUN _____

PART OF THE BODY _____

PLURAL NOUN _____

PLURAL NOUN _____

SAME PLURAL NOUN _____

NOUN _____

ADJECTIVE _____

ADJECTIVE _____

PERSON IN ROOM _____

PLURAL NOUN _____

NOUN _____

A PLACE _____

ADJECTIVE _____

CELEBRITY _____

Cracking _____ codes is a prized spy skill, like in this example:
ADJECTIVE

Coded message: The circus has come to (the) _____, and
A PLACE

there are _____ clowns with big _____ noses _____
ADJECTIVE   COLOR   VERB ENDING IN "ING"

in the streets. If you try to run away, they will stick out their _____ and trip
NOUN

you so you fall _____-first into a puddle of _____.
PART OF THE BODY   PLURAL NOUN

Beware those _____—I repeat, beware those _____!
PLURAL NOUN   SAME PLURAL NOUN

Decoded message: To the brave _____ who deciphers this _____
NOUN   ADJECTIVE

note—be forewarned! Our agency has experienced a breach of security involving

_____ double agents. Agency Chief _____ desperately
ADJECTIVE   PERSON IN ROOM

needs _____ who have not been corrupted to be trained as new agents.
PLURAL NOUN

Report promptly to _____ Headquarters located near (the) _____
NOUN   A PLACE

and await further instructions. Keep this _____ message confidential.
ADJECTIVE

Apply in person using the code phrase "I am president of the _____ Fan
CELEBRITY

Club."

MAD●LIBS®

INSTRUCTIONS

MAD LIBS® is a game for people who don't like games!
It can be played by one, two, three, four, or forty.

● RIDICULOUSLY SIMPLE DIRECTIONS

In this tablet you will find stories containing blank spaces where words are left out.
One player, the READER, selects one of these stories. The READER does not tell anyone
what the story is about. Instead, he/she asks the other players, the WRITERS, to give
him/her words. These words are used to fill in the blank spaces in the story.

● TO PLAY

The READER asks each WRITER in turn to call out a word—an adjective or a noun or
whatever the space calls for—and uses them to fill in the blank spaces in the story. The
result is a MAD LIBS® game.

When the READER then reads the completed MAD LIBS® game to the other players,
they will discover that they have written a story that is fantastic, screamingly funny,
shocking, silly, crazy, or just plain dumb—depending upon which words each WRITER
called out.

● EXAMPLE (*Before* and *After*)

"_____!" he said _____
        EXCLAMATION   ADVERB

as he jumped into his convertible _____ and
                                              NOUN

drove off with his _____ wife.
                          ADJECTIVE

"_____OUCH_____!" he said _____HAPPILY_____
        EXCLAMATION   ADVERB

as he jumped into his convertible _____CAT_____ and
                                              NOUN

drove off with his _____BRAVE_____ wife.
                          ADJECTIVE

MAD LIBS®

QUICK REVIEW

In case you have forgotten what adjectives, adverbs, nouns, and verbs are, here is a quick review:

An ADJECTIVE describes something or somebody. *Lumpy, soft, ugly, messy,* and *short* are adjectives.

An ADVERB tells how something is done. It modifies a verb and usually ends in "ly." *Modestly, stupidly, greedily,* and *carefully* are adverbs.

A NOUN is the name of a person, place, or thing. *Sidewalk, umbrella, bridle, bathtub,* and *nose* are nouns.

A VERB is an action word. *Run, pitch, jump,* and *swim* are verbs. Put the verbs in past tense if the directions say PAST TENSE. *Ran, pitched, jumped,* and *swam* are verbs in the past tense.

When we ask for A PLACE, we mean any sort of place: a country or city *(Spain, Cleveland)* or a room *(bathroom, kitchen).*

An EXCLAMATION or SILLY WORD is any sort of funny sound, gasp, grunt, or outcry, like *Wow!, Ouch!, Whomp!, Ick!,* and *Gadzooks!*

When we ask for specific words, like a NUMBER, a COLOR, an ANIMAL, or a PART OF THE BODY, we mean a word that is one of those things, like *seven, blue, horse,* or *head.*

When we ask for a PLURAL, it means more than one. For example, *cat* pluralized is *cats.*

MAD LIBS® is fun to play with friends, but you can also play it by yourself! To begin with, DO NOT look at the story on the page below. Fill in the blanks on this page with the words called for. Then, using the words you have selected, fill in the blank spaces in the story.

Now you've created your own hilarious MAD LIBS® game!

UNIDENTIFIED FLYING OBJECTS

ADJECTIVE _____

VEHICLE (PLURAL) _____

NOUN _____

NOUN _____

ADJECTIVE _____

NOUN _____

ANIMAL (PLURAL) _____

NOUN _____

ADJECTIVE _____

ADJECTIVE _____

PLURAL NOUN _____

OCCUPATION (PLURAL) _____

PLURAL NOUN _____

MAD LIBS®
UNIDENTIFIED FLYING OBJECTS

Did you know that UFOs aren't just _____-looking _____
                                    ADJECTIVE   VEHICLE (PLURAL)

flying around in the sky? The term is actually a nickname for any unidentified

flying _____! Currently, the _____ community is split
       NOUN   NOUN

between three schools of thought on this _____ subject. Scientists are
                                          ADJECTIVE

adamant that there is a rational _____ for every UFO sighting. Often,
                                  NOUN

UFOs are officially recognized as weather balloons, asteroids, or a flock of

_____ after they're initially spotted. However, _____ enthusiasts
ANIMAL (PLURAL)   NOUN

believe these _____ objects are actually spacecraft driven by
               ADJECTIVE

_____ extraterrestrials from faraway _____. Finally, there's a
ADJECTIVE   PLURAL NOUN

growing number of _____ who insist that UFOs are in fact
                   OCCUPATION (PLURAL)

experimental _____ the military is secretly testing. So what do you
              PLURAL NOUN

think?

MAD LIBS® is fun to play with friends, but you can also play it by yourself! To begin with, DO NOT look at the story on the page below. Fill in the blanks on this page with the words called for. Then, using the words you have selected, fill in the blank spaces in the story.

Now you've created your own hilarious MAD LIBS® game!

ABDUCTION JUNCTION

VERB _____

NOUN _____

PLURAL NOUN _____

PLURAL NOUN _____

VERB _____

ADJECTIVE _____

VEHICLE (PLURAL) _____

ADJECTIVE _____

PLURAL NOUN _____

ADJECTIVE _____

PLURAL NOUN _____

NOUN _____

ADJECTIVE _____

MAD LIBS®
ABDUCTION JUNCTION

Spacecraft sightings occur all over the world. Here are some places aliens are most

likely to _____:
                VERB

Roswell, New Mexico: The birthplace of _____ 51, a haven for top-secret
                                              NOUN

government _____ and a veritable breeding ground for alien
              PLURAL NOUN

_____. UFO fanatics can even _____ down the "Extraterrestrial
   PLURAL NOUN   VERB

Highway" that runs through this _____ town.
                                    ADJECTIVE

Nazca City, Peru: Thought to be a landing zone for alien _____, the
                                                            VEHICLE (PLURAL)

famous Nazca Lines in the ground reveal _____ designs of animals and
                                            ADJECTIVE

other _____ when viewed from high in the sky.
         PLURAL NOUN

The M-Triangle, Russia: Located in the mountains, this area is a hot spot of

UFO sightings, _____ symbols written in the sky, and encounters with
                   ADJECTIVE

translucent _____ and humanoid figures that glow in the
                PLURAL NOUN

_____. It's rumored that people who venture into this region
   NOUN

sometimes return having developed _____-powers and superhuman
                                       ADJECTIVE

abilities.

MAD LIBS® is fun to play with friends, but you can also play it by yourself! To begin with, DO NOT look at the story on the page below. Fill in the blanks on this page with the words called for. Then, using the words you have selected, fill in the blank spaces in the story.

Now you've created your own hilarious MAD LIBS® game!

CIA ITINERARY

VERB _____

ADJECTIVE _____

ADJECTIVE _____

PLURAL NOUN _____

ANIMAL _____

NOUN _____

TYPE OF FOOD _____

NOUN _____

PERSON IN ROOM (MALE) _____

PLURAL NOUN _____

NOUN _____

ADJECTIVE _____

A PLACE _____

MAD LIBS®
CIA ITINERARY

Here's a peek at a typical day in the life of a CIA agent working at Area 51:

9:00 a.m.: Check on the resident Martians to make sure they didn't _____
VERB
all the light bulbs for their _____ experiments again—the CIA can't
ADJECTIVE
afford to keep replacing these!

10:30 a.m.: Oversee _____ peace negotiations between the
ADJECTIVE
_____ of Earth and the _____-people of Planet Nebula.
PLURAL NOUN   ANIMAL

11:00 a.m.: Make sure the antigravity _____ in the kitchen is turned
NOUN
off. Last time we were scraping _____ off the ceiling for a week.
TYPE OF FOOD

1:30 p.m.: A well-deserved _____ break.
NOUN

2:00 p.m.: Drive out to Dundy County, Nebraska, and talk to Farmer
_____ about the crop _____ appearing in his
PERSON IN ROOM (MALE)   PLURAL NOUN
cornfields.

4:30 p.m.: Investigate reports of a/an _____ that crash-landed in a/an
NOUN
_____ field on the outskirts of (the) _____.
ADJECTIVE   A PLACE

MAD LIBS® is fun to play with friends, but you can also play it by yourself! To begin with, DO NOT look at the story on the page below. Fill in the blanks on this page with the words called for. Then, using the words you have selected, fill in the blank spaces in the story.

Now you've created your own hilarious MAD LIBS® game!

THE CONSPIRACY THEORIST'S SURVIVAL GUIDE

ADJECTIVE _____

ARTICLE OF CLOTHING _____

PART OF THE BODY _____

PLURAL NOUN _____

NOUN _____

PLURAL NOUN _____

ARTICLE OF CLOTHING _____

VERB ENDING IN "ING" _____

PLURAL NOUN _____

ANIMAL _____

PLURAL NOUN _____

PLURAL NOUN _____

VERB _____

SILLY WORD _____

MAD LIBS®
THE CONSPIRACY THEORIST'S
SURVIVAL GUIDE

Here's a list of _____ survival tips from our resident conspiracy theorist:
<u>ADJECTIVE</u>

• Protect your thoughts by making a stylish tinfoil _____ to wear
<u>ARTICLE OF CLOTHING</u>

on your _____.
<u>PART OF THE BODY</u>

• The FBI is recording all of your _____, so you might as well
<u>PLURAL NOUN</u>

throw your cell phone in the _____.
<u>NOUN</u>

• The government is spraying chemtrails to control the _____ of the
<u>PLURAL NOUN</u>

population, so wear a gas _____ to avoid breathing any mind-
<u>ARTICLE OF CLOTHING</u>

_____ chemicals.
<u>VERB ENDING IN "ING"</u>

• Trust no one! Most _____ in positions of authority belong to the
<u>PLURAL NOUN</u>

Illuminati and are actually _____-people in disguise.
<u>ANIMAL</u>

• Companies will try to get you to buy their _____ by exposing you to
<u>PLURAL NOUN</u>

subliminal _____ hidden in their advertising. To avoid commercials
<u>PLURAL NOUN</u>

altogether, just _____ your television.
<u>VERB</u>

• Scientists say aliens aren't real, but that's a load of _____! The truth
<u>SILLY WORD</u>

is out there . . .

MAD LIBS® is fun to play with friends, but you can also play it by yourself! To begin with, DO NOT look at the story on the page below. Fill in the blanks on this page with the words called for. Then, using the words you have selected, fill in the blank spaces in the story.

Now you've created your own hilarious MAD LIBS® game!

LITTLE RED PLANET

NOUN _____

ADJECTIVE _____

PLURAL NOUN _____

ADJECTIVE _____

ADJECTIVE _____

VERB _____

PLURAL NOUN _____

ADJECTIVE _____

NOUN _____

TYPE OF LIQUID _____

OCCUPATION (PLURAL) _____

NOUN _____

NOUN _____

ADJECTIVE _____

PLURAL NOUN _____

NOUN _____

MAD LIBS®
LITTLE RED PLANET

Mars is the fourth _____ from the Sun and close enough to Earth that
NOUN

you can see it in the sky on _____ nights. It gets its trademark reddish
ADJECTIVE

color from a high concentration of _____ on the planet's surface. Some
PLURAL NOUN

say that there are "little _____ men from Mars," but is there any merit
ADJECTIVE

to this claim? Since the planet's atmosphere is so thin and _____, there
ADJECTIVE

is no air to _____, making it uninhabitable. However, this doesn't mean
VERB

it can't support _____ in the future! _____ tests of Mars's
PLURAL NOUN   ADJECTIVE

soil reveal all the building blocks for life, including nitrogen, carbon, oxygen, and

_____. A key component for survival is _____.
NOUN   TYPE OF LIQUID

_____ recently discovered underground ice buried deep below the
OCCUPATION (PLURAL)

planet's _____. Explorers claim that space is the final _____.
NOUN   NOUN

With so many _____ advances, maybe our future _____
ADJECTIVE   PLURAL NOUN

will colonize this little red _____ after all!
NOUN

From UNIDENTIFIED FLYING MAD LIBS® • Copyright © 2018 by Penguin Random House LLC

MAD LIBS® is fun to play with friends, but you can also play it by yourself! To begin with, DO NOT look at the story on the page below. Fill in the blanks on this page with the words called for. Then, using the words you have selected, fill in the blank spaces in the story.

Now you've created your own hilarious MAD LIBS® game!

ROSWELL OR BUST

NOUN _____

ADJECTIVE _____

PLURAL NOUN _____

NOUN _____

ADJECTIVE _____

PERSON IN ROOM _____

ADJECTIVE _____

NOUN _____

NOUN _____

PLURAL NOUN _____

PLURAL NOUN _____

ADJECTIVE _____

PLURAL NOUN _____

VERB _____

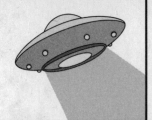

MAD LIBS®
ROSWELL OR BUST

Each summer, Mom and Dad pack up the _____ and we drive across
                                        NOUN

the country to the _____ town of Roswell, New Mexico, to see if we can
                      ADJECTIVE

encounter some _____. We pay a quick visit to the International
                   PLURAL NOUN

UFO _____ & Research Center and take a peek at the _____
         NOUN   ADJECTIVE

exhibits. Then I get my photo taken with a local mascot, _____, the
                                                          PERSON IN ROOM

_____ alien! I know it's just some _____ wearing a costume,
   ADJECTIVE   NOUN

but I heard the design was based on a real-life _____ from Mars. At
                                                    NOUN

night, we sit around a campfire and watch the _____ twinkle in the
                                                  PLURAL NOUN

sky. I save up my _____ all year so I can buy some souvenirs. Once
                     PLURAL NOUN

we met a/an _____ old man who claimed he'd been abducted over a
               ADJECTIVE

dozen times. He sold me a map of alien hot spots in the area for only fifty

_____! This year I know I'll finally _____ some aliens.
   PLURAL NOUN   VERB

MAD LIBS® is fun to play with friends, but you can also play it by yourself! To begin with, DO NOT look at the story on the page below. Fill in the blanks on this page with the words called for. Then, using the words you have selected, fill in the blank spaces in the story.

Now you've created your own hilarious MAD LIBS® game!

MILKY WAY GALAXY

ADJECTIVE _____

ADJECTIVE _____

ADJECTIVE _____

NOUN _____

ADJECTIVE _____

NOUN _____

COLOR _____

PLURAL NOUN _____

PLURAL NOUN _____

ANIMAL _____

NOUN _____

PLURAL NOUN _____

VERB ENDING IN "ING" _____

Home sweet home! Our _____ planet is merely a/an _____
                        ADJECTIVE   ADJECTIVE

speck in a sea of stars that make up the Milky Way Galaxy. It gets its name from

the strip of bright, _____ stars that resemble a milky _____
                      ADJECTIVE   NOUN

coursing through the sky. Like so many other _____ galaxies in the
                                              ADJECTIVE

universe, ours is in the shape of a/an _____. Billions of stars, like
                                        NOUN

_____ dwarfs and super-_____, litter our galaxy, and
 COLOR   PLURAL NOUN

there is enough gas and _____ to create billions more! Many of these
                         PLURAL NOUN

stars form constellations like Aries and Leo, which resembles a/an _____.
                                                                    ANIMAL

At the center of our galaxy sits a supermassive black _____, greedily
                                                       NOUN

feeding on nearby _____ and stardust. The Milky Way's closest
                   PLURAL NOUN

neighbor is nearby Andromeda. These two galaxies are actually _____
                                                               VERB ENDING IN "ING"

through space and are set to collide four billion years from now!

MAD LIBS® is fun to play with friends, but you can also play it by yourself! To begin with, DO NOT look at the story on the page below. Fill in the blanks on this page with the words called for. Then, using the words you have selected, fill in the blank spaces in the story.

Now you've created your own hilarious MAD LIBS® game!

WELCOME, EARTHLINGS!

ADJECTIVE _____

SILLY WORD _____

PART OF THE BODY _____

EXCLAMATION _____

PLURAL NOUN _____

TYPE OF FOOD _____

ANIMAL (PLURAL) _____

VERB _____

ADJECTIVE _____

NOUN _____

ARTICLE OF CLOTHING (PLURAL) _____

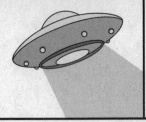

MAD LIBS®
WELCOME, EARTHLINGS!

Greetings, Earthlings! Here are some dos and don'ts for when you meet the

_____ inhabitants of Planet _____:
    ADJECTIVE   SILLY WORD

• Wiggle your _____ and shout "_____!" whenever you
             PART OF THE BODY   EXCLAMATION

meet someone new.

• As an act of peace, give gifts of golden _____ and fragrant
                        PLURAL NOUN

_____.
  TYPE OF FOOD

• _____ are highly respected, so don't make fun of them or you'll
    ANIMAL (PLURAL)

be asked to _____.
            VERB

• Don't be offended if you're called a/an _____ _____—
                         ADJECTIVE   NOUN

this is a common term of endearment.

• These aliens don't wear _____—feel free to leave
                   ARTICLE OF CLOTHING (PLURAL)

yours at home!

MAD LIBS® is fun to play with friends, but you can also play it by yourself! To begin with, DO NOT look at the story on the page below. Fill in the blanks on this page with the words called for. Then, using the words you have selected, fill in the blank spaces in the story.

Now you've created your own hilarious MAD LIBS® game!

THE WAR OF THE WORLDS, A BOOK REPORT

NOUN _____

CELEBRITY _____

NOUN _____

PLURAL NOUN _____

ADJECTIVE _____

LETTER OF THE ALPHABET _____

PLURAL NOUN _____

VERB ENDING IN "ING" _____

PLURAL NOUN _____

ADJECTIVE _____

ADJECTIVE _____

ADVERB _____

PLURAL NOUN _____

VERB (PAST TENSE) _____

ADJECTIVE _____

ADJECTIVE _____

MAD LIBS®
THE WAR OF THE WORLDS,
A BOOK REPORT

The War of the Worlds is a/an _____ novel published in 1898 by
<u>NOUN</u>

_____ and is told as a factual account of a/an _____ invasion on
CELEBRITY   NOUN

Earth. The narrator describes cylindrical _____ that crash to Earth and
PLURAL NOUN

release aliens with _____ skin, _____-shaped mouths,
ADJECTIVE   LETTER OF THE ALPHABET

and spindly _____ for arms. They begin _____
PLURAL NOUN   VERB ENDING IN "ING"

humans with their heat-rays and other advanced _____. The narrator
PLURAL NOUN

flees and after some _____ experiences is finally reunited with his
ADJECTIVE

_____ wife. _____, the aliens are defeated by the smallest
ADJECTIVE   ADVERB

line of defense on our planet: _____. In 1938, Orson Welles
PLURAL NOUN

infamously _____ a radio drama based on the _____
VERB (PAST TENSE)   ADJECTIVE

novel, causing _____ panic among listeners who were convinced the
ADJECTIVE

report was real!

MAD LIBS® is fun to play with friends, but you can also play it by yourself! To begin with, DO NOT look at the story on the page below. Fill in the blanks on this page with the words called for. Then, using the words you have selected, fill in the blank spaces in the story.

Now you've created your own hilarious MAD LIBS® game!

THE TRUTH BEHIND
THE MOON LANDING

NOUN _____

CELEBRITY _____

ADJECTIVE _____

A COUNTRY _____

PART OF THE BODY (PLURAL) _____

ADJECTIVE _____

PLURAL NOUN _____

NOUN _____

ADJECTIVE _____

ADJECTIVE _____

PLURAL NOUN _____

ADJECTIVE _____

TYPE OF FOOD _____

MAD LIBS®
THE TRUTH BEHIND
THE MOON LANDING

Any _____ textbook will tell you all about _____ landing
_{NOUN} _{CELEBRITY}

on the moon, but what it won't mention is the _____ scandal that was
_{ADJECTIVE}

covered up. The government claims it was a space race with _____, but
_{A COUNTRY}

they were actually trying to get their _____ on the
_{PART OF THE BODY (PLURAL)}

_____ treasure hidden deep in the moon's _____. The
_{ADJECTIVE} _{PLURAL NOUN}

footage from the first _____ landing was intentionally _____
_{NOUN} _{ADJECTIVE}

so people couldn't make out any _____ details of the surface. After the
_{ADJECTIVE}

astronauts returned home, they were paid large sums of _____ to keep
_{PLURAL NOUN}

quiet. The _____ secret the government was trying to keep? The moon
_{ADJECTIVE}

is actually made of _____!
_{TYPE OF FOOD}

MAD LIBS® is fun to play with friends, but you can also play it by yourself! To begin with, DO NOT look at the story on the page below. Fill in the blanks on this page with the words called for. Then, using the words you have selected, fill in the blank spaces in the story.

Now you've created your own hilarious MAD LIBS® game!

EXTRATERRESTRIALS

ADJECTIVE _____

ANIMAL _____

PART OF THE BODY (PLURAL) _____

OCCUPATION _____

ADJECTIVE _____

PLURAL NOUN _____

ADJECTIVE _____

NOUN _____

COLOR _____

VERB _____

PLURAL NOUN _____

SILLY WORD (PLURAL) _____

VERB (PAST TENSE) _____

PLURAL NOUN _____

ADJECTIVE _____

MAD LIBS
EXTRATERRESTRIALS

There are many types of aliens living in the universe. Here are a few of the most recognizable species:

The Reptilians: Hailing from the Alpha Draconis system, this species resembles a/an _____, scaly _____ with webbed _____.
<u>ADJECTIVE</u>   <u>ANIMAL</u>   <u>PART OF THE BODY (PLURAL)</u>
They are a/an _____ race and have _____ tempers.
<u>OCCUPATION</u>   <u>ADJECTIVE</u>

The Greys: These are the most common type of _____ seen by humans.
<u>PLURAL NOUN</u>
They have distinctive features such as their _____ heads, large
<u>ADJECTIVE</u>
_____-shaped eyes, and their namesake _____ skin. These guys can't
<u>NOUN</u>   <u>COLOR</u>
_____ with their feet and instead get around by floating inside
<u>VERB</u>
_____.
<u>PLURAL NOUN</u>

The _____**:** This group _____ ancient human
<u>SILLY WORD (PLURAL)</u>   <u>VERB (PAST TENSE)</u>
civilizations and were viewed as divine _____. They're said to have a/an
<u>PLURAL NOUN</u>
_____ influence on our culture.
<u>ADJECTIVE</u>

MAD LIBS® is fun to play with friends, but you can also play it by yourself! To begin with, DO NOT look at the story on the page below. Fill in the blanks on this page with the words called for. Then, using the words you have selected, fill in the blank spaces in the story.

Now you've created your own hilarious MAD LIBS® game!

MY BEST FRIEND IS AN ALIEN

NOUN _____

PERSON IN ROOM (MALE) _____

NOUN _____

ADJECTIVE _____

ARTICLE OF CLOTHING _____

NOUN _____

ADJECTIVE _____

NOUN _____

VEHICLE _____

PLURAL NOUN _____

NOUN _____

PLURAL NOUN _____

PART OF THE BODY _____

PERSON IN ROOM (MALE) _____

ADJECTIVE _____

MAD LIBS®
MY BEST FRIEND IS AN ALIEN

My best friend is the new foreign exchange _____ and he's a little out of
                                           NOUN

this world. _____ comes from a faraway _____. He's
            PERSON IN ROOM (MALE)   NOUN

just like everyone else, except his skin is a/an _____ shade of green and
                                                 ADJECTIVE

he has two antennas he keeps hidden under a/an _____. He
                                               ARTICLE OF CLOTHING

comes to school in a giant metal _____ that beats the pants off of my
                                 NOUN

mom's _____ minivan. Last month, he helped me win the _____
      ADJECTIVE   NOUN

fair by building a fully functional model _____. Did I mention he can
                                          VEHICLE

walk through _____ and teleport from one _____ to the
             PLURAL NOUN   NOUN

other in the blink of an eye? We're so close that we can finish each other's

_____—sometimes I swear I can even hear his voice inside my
PLURAL NOUN

_____! _____ says one day he'll take me
PART OF THE BODY   PERSON IN ROOM (MALE)

to visit his _____ home. Boy, I sure hope Mom lets me go!
             ADJECTIVE

MAD LIBS® is fun to play with friends, but you can also play it by yourself! To begin with, DO NOT look at the story on the page below. Fill in the blanks on this page with the words called for. Then, using the words you have selected, fill in the blank spaces in the story.

Now you've created your own hilarious MAD LIBS® game!

SPACE INVADERS

ADJECTIVE _____

NOUN _____

PLURAL NOUN _____

PLURAL NOUN _____

ADJECTIVE _____

VERB (PAST TENSE) _____

NOUN _____

ANIMAL _____

VERB _____

TYPE OF FOOD _____

ADJECTIVE _____

ADJECTIVE _____

SILLY WORD _____

SILLY WORD _____

NOUN _____

ADJECTIVE _____

VERB _____

MAD LIBS®
SPACE INVADERS

I live next to the most _____ neighbors ever and I'm almost at the end

ADJECTIVE

of my _____. Boy, these _____ are annoying. I've been woken

NOUN ... PLURAL NOUN

up by blinding white _____ and _____ noises every night this

PLURAL NOUN ... ADJECTIVE

week and I haven't _____ a wink. My neighbors have three children

VERB (PAST TENSE)

who shot a toy rocket through my front _____ and I'm still waiting for

NOUN

them to pay the damages. Their pet is a fifty-foot space _____ that likes

ANIMAL

to _____ holes in the garden and eat all my _____ plants. I've

VERB ... TYPE OF FOOD

tried talking to them about these _____ problems, but they don't seem

ADJECTIVE

to understand. I think they speak a different language because they're always using

_____ words I've never heard before, like _____ and

ADJECTIVE ... SILLY WORD

_____. I know they're not from this _____ and being so far

SILLY WORD ... NOUN

from home can be _____, but they could at least try to _____

ADJECTIVE ... VERB

a little more normal!

MAD LIBS® is fun to play with friends, but you can also play it by yourself! To begin with, DO NOT look at the story on the page below. Fill in the blanks on this page with the words called for. Then, using the words you have selected, fill in the blank spaces in the story.

Now you've created your own hilarious MAD LIBS® game!

ANCIENT CIVILIZATIONS

ADJECTIVE _____

VERB _____

ADJECTIVE _____

NOUN _____

NOUN _____

ADJECTIVE _____

ADJECTIVE _____

PART OF THE BODY (PLURAL) _____

PLURAL NOUN _____

ADJECTIVE _____

ADJECTIVE _____

PLURAL NOUN _____

VEHICLE (PLURAL) _____

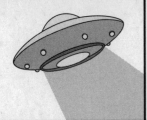

MAD LIBS®
ANCIENT CIVILIZATIONS

Man has created many wonders, but here's a list of famous sites where aliens may have lent a helping hand:

The Egyptian Pyramids: Some theorize the ancient Egyptians' technology wasn't

_____ enough to build the Pyramids and that aliens helped to

ADJECTIVE

_____ these structures.

VERB

Stonehenge: These _____ stone monuments are laid out in a/an

ADJECTIVE

_____ shape and are thought to act as a landing _____ for

NOUN ... NOUN

intergalactic spacecraft. It doesn't hurt that the area is known for sightings of

_____ lights in the sky.

ADJECTIVE

Easter Island *moai*: This coast is littered with hundreds of _____ statues

ADJECTIVE

carved with human-like _____. It's believed their design was

PART OF THE BODY (PLURAL)

based on extraterrestrial _____ that visited _____

PLURAL NOUN ... ADJECTIVE

civilizations.

The Bermuda Triangle: This place is famous for countless _____

ADJECTIVE

disappearances. Some suspect this popular spot is where aliens abduct

unsuspecting _____—and their _____!

PLURAL NOUN ... VEHICLE (PLURAL)

MAD LIBS® is fun to play with friends, but you can also play it by yourself! To begin with, DO NOT look at the story on the page below. Fill in the blanks on this page with the words called for. Then, using the words you have selected, fill in the blank spaces in the story.

Now you've created your own hilarious MAD LIBS® game!

SPACE CAMP 101

NOUN _____

OCCUPATION _____

NOUN _____

ADJECTIVE _____

VERB _____

NUMBER _____

TYPE OF FOOD _____

TYPE OF LIQUID _____

PLURAL NOUN _____

PLURAL NOUN _____

NOUN _____

NOUN _____

ADJECTIVE _____

ADJECTIVE _____

VEHICLE _____

NOUN _____

VERB _____

It's almost here! Tomorrow I leave for space _____ to learn what it's like

NOUN

to be a/an _____ in outer space! First we'll board a replica _____

OCCUPATION .... NOUN

and take a/an _____ ride in the centrifuge, which can _____

ADJECTIVE .... VERB

us around in circles at _____ times the normal force of gravity. Just make

NUMBER

sure not to eat any _____ or drink _____ beforehand,

TYPE OF FOOD .... TYPE OF LIQUID

otherwise you might lose your _____! Speaking of, later we can

PLURAL NOUN

sample some astronaut chow, like freeze-dried _____ and powdered

PLURAL NOUN

_____. Then we'll visit the zero-gravity _____. Think

NOUN .... NOUN

of all the _____ tricks I can do when my body becomes as _____

ADJECTIVE .... ADJECTIVE

as air. We even get to build our own _____ and fly it to the

VEHICLE

_____. I can't wait to _____ at camp!

NOUN .... VERB

MAD LIBS® is fun to play with friends, but you can also play it by yourself! To begin with, DO NOT look at the story on the page below. Fill in the blanks on this page with the words called for. Then, using the words you have selected, fill in the blank spaces in the story.

Now you've created your own hilarious MAD LIBS® game!

DIARY OF A CIA AGENT

ADJECTIVE _____

PERSON IN ROOM _____

NOUN _____

ADJECTIVE _____

NOUN _____

NOUN _____

ADJECTIVE _____

ADJECTIVE _____

PLURAL NOUN _____

NOUN _____

ADJECTIVE _____

SILLY WORD _____

VERB _____

OCCUPATION _____

NOUN _____

ADJECTIVE _____

MAD LIBS®
DIARY OF A CIA AGENT

Dear Diary,

Today was an absolutely _____ day at Area 51! Agent _____
ADJECTIVE   PERSON IN ROOM

accidentally let Specimen X escape from its containment _____ and we
NOUN

spent all morning searching the _____ areas of the lab for it. Then, we had
ADJECTIVE

a toxic _____ spill in sector C. I had to clean the entire _____
NOUN   NOUN

because the janitor was out sick with a/an _____ cold. I had an incredibly
ADJECTIVE

_____ meeting with some new _____ from Alpha Draconis,
ADJECTIVE   PLURAL NOUN

but I was running late due to a/an _____ jam in the main hallway. These
NOUN

aliens can't stand to wait, and boy, they were _____ with me for the rest
ADJECTIVE

of the day! Later, I met with Commissioner _____ and I was convinced
SILLY WORD

he was going to _____ me. Instead, he said he was promoting me to
VERB

executive _____ of the _____ division. What a great surprise!
OCCUPATION   NOUN

I guess today wasn't so _____ after all!
ADJECTIVE

MAD LIBS® is fun to play with friends, but you can also play it by yourself! To begin with, DO NOT look at the story on the page below. Fill in the blanks on this page with the words called for. Then, using the words you have selected, fill in the blank spaces in the story.

Now you've created your own hilarious MAD LIBS® game!

IT CAME FROM OUTER SPACE

PERSON IN ROOM (FEMALE) _____

PLURAL NOUN _____

ADJECTIVE _____

NOUN _____

ANIMAL _____

VEHICLE _____

ADJECTIVE _____

NOUN _____

ADJECTIVE _____

PLURAL NOUN _____

ADJECTIVE _____

PART OF THE BODY (PLURAL) _____

ANIMAL (PLURAL) _____

ADJECTIVE _____

OCCUPATION _____

PLURAL NOUN _____

ADJECTIVE _____

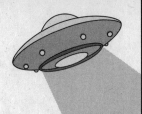

MAD LIBS
IT CAME FROM OUTER SPACE

At 3:00 a.m. this morning, a local woman, _____ , awoke to

PERSON IN ROOM (FEMALE)

thunderous _____ and a/an _____ flash of light. Armed

PLURAL NOUN · ADJECTIVE

with a heavy _____ and her pet _____ for protection, she

NOUN · ANIMAL

ventured outside to find that the smoldering remains of a/an _____

VEHICLE

had left a/an _____ hole the size of a/an _____ in her backyard.

ADJECTIVE · NOUN

To her horror, something _____ slithered out of the hole and left a trail of

ADJECTIVE

_____ as it escaped to the nearby woods. Authorities advise citizens to

PLURAL NOUN

remain _____ at all times, keep their _____ peeled for

ADJECTIVE · PART OF THE BODY (PLURAL)

any purple _____ , and to report any _____ occurrences

ANIMAL (PLURAL) · ADJECTIVE

to their local _____ . A reward of five thousand _____ is

OCCUPATION · PLURAL NOUN

being offered to anyone with a lead on the location of this _____ invader.

ADJECTIVE

MAD LIBS® is fun to play with friends, but you can also play it by yourself! To begin with, DO NOT look at the story on the page below. Fill in the blanks on this page with the words called for. Then, using the words you have selected, fill in the blank spaces in the story.

Now you've created your own hilarious MAD LIBS® game!

SPACESHIP SUPERSALE EMPORIUM

VERB ENDING IN "ING" _____

VEHICLE (PLURAL) _____

ADJECTIVE _____

PLURAL NOUN _____

COLOR _____

ADJECTIVE _____

NOUN _____

NUMBER _____

ADJECTIVE _____

NOUN _____

VERB ENDING IN "ING" _____

NOUN _____

NOUN _____

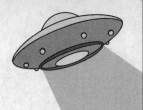

MAD LIBS®
SPACESHIP SUPERSALE
EMPORIUM

Tired of the same old _____ saucers? Then come on down to the

VERB ENDING IN "ING"

Spaceship Supersale Emporium and browse our wide selection of

_____, where you're sure to find a/an _____ solution

VEHICLE (PLURAL) · ADJECTIVE

to all your intergalactic travel needs! Our SUV shuttles are equipped with ample

room to store your abducted _____. All our vehicles come in a variety of

PLURAL NOUN

colors, including cobalt and avocado _____. If you're feeling

COLOR

_____, splurge for our turbo-drive model and kick your _____

ADJECTIVE · NOUN

up to _____ times the speed of light! Happy with your current vehicle?

NUMBER

Then come get it upgraded with the latest _____ gizmo, like the

ADJECTIVE

_____ Ray 5000, capable of _____ an entire _____

NOUN · VERB ENDING IN "ING" · · · · · · · · · · · · · NOUN

with a single blast! You'd have to be out of your _____ to pass on these

NOUN

deals!

MAD LIBS® is fun to play with friends, but you can also play it by yourself! To begin with, DO NOT look at the story on the page below. Fill in the blanks on this page with the words called for. Then, using the words you have selected, fill in the blank spaces in the story.

Now you've created your own hilarious MAD LIBS® game!

THE BENEFITS OF
BLACK HOLES

PLURAL NOUN _____

PART OF THE BODY _____

NOUN _____

ADJECTIVE _____

A PLACE (PLURAL) _____

ADJECTIVE _____

VERB _____

ADJECTIVE _____

PLURAL NOUN _____

NOUN _____

A PLACE _____

ARTICLE OF CLOTHING _____

Black holes are crushing, gravitational _____ of nature. Although
(PLURAL NOUN)

they can't be seen by the naked _____, we know when one exists by
(PART OF THE BODY)

the way it manipulates the _____ nearby. No one knows what resides
(NOUN)

inside these _____ holes, but some believe they are used as portals to
(ADJECTIVE)

other _____. Like a doorway to the universe, aliens utilizing these
(A PLACE (PLURAL))

_____ wormholes can easily _____ from one galaxy to the
(ADJECTIVE)   (VERB)

next in a matter of seconds. This explains why people often claim UFOs disappear

into _____ air. If we can speak to these _____ and receive help
(ADJECTIVE)   (PLURAL NOUN)

with interdimensional travel, it could totally change _____ as we know
(NOUN)

it! Imagine waking up and deciding you wanted to visit (the) _____.
(A PLACE)

You could just pull on your space-_____ and teleport over.
(ARTICLE OF CLOTHING)

Incredible!

MAD LIBS® is fun to play with friends, but you can also play it by yourself! To begin with, DO NOT look at the story on the page below. Fill in the blanks on this page with the words called for. Then, using the words you have selected, fill in the blank spaces in the story.

Now you've created your own hilarious MAD LIBS® game!

FIRST CONTACT

VERB ENDING IN "ING" _____

SILLY WORD _____

PLURAL NOUN _____

NOUN _____

ADJECTIVE _____

NOUN _____

VERB _____

PLURAL NOUN _____

ADJECTIVE _____

EXCLAMATION _____

NOUN _____

PLURAL NOUN _____

TYPE OF FOOD _____

ADJECTIVE _____

TYPE OF LIQUID _____

MAD LIBS®
FIRST CONTACT

Scientists and aliens have finally established a means of long-distance communication. Here is their first recorded conversation:

Alien: Hello? Is this planet Earth?

Scientist: Yes! With whom am I _____?
_____VERB ENDING IN "ING"

Alien: I am _____. My family and I hail from the planet of
_____SILLY WORD

_____.
PLURAL NOUN

Scientist: Are you here to take over our _____?
_____NOUN

Alien: No, we are _____ beings and mean you no _____. We come
_____ADJECTIVE _____NOUN

in peace.

Scientist: Shall I _____ you to our leader?
_____VERB

Alien: No. We've traveled many light-years and risked our _____ to
_____PLURAL NOUN

come here for a very _____ request.
_____ADJECTIVE

Scientist: _____! Well, what do you want?
_____EXCLAMATION

Alien: We would like one large _____ with pepperoni and green
_____NOUN

_____. Three orders of _____, fried extra _____.
PLURAL NOUN TYPE OF FOOD ADJECTIVE

And a diet _____.
_____TYPE OF LIQUID

Scientist: I think you have the wrong number . . .

MAD LIBS® is fun to play with friends, but you can also play it by yourself! To begin with, DO NOT look at the story on the page below. Fill in the blanks on this page with the words called for. Then, using the words you have selected, fill in the blank spaces in the story.

Now you've created your own hilarious MAD LIBS® game!

CLOSE ENCOUNTERS

PLURAL NOUN _____

NOUN _____

VERB (PAST TENSE) _____

NOUN _____

ADJECTIVE _____

ANIMAL _____

TYPE OF FOOD _____

ADJECTIVE _____

PART OF THE BODY (PLURAL) _____

PART OF THE BODY _____

PLURAL NOUN _____

NOUN _____

PLURAL NOUN _____

ADJECTIVE _____

MAD LIBS
CLOSE ENCOUNTERS

Let me tell you about the time I got abducted by _____. I was outside

PLURAL NOUN

one night, minding my own business, when suddenly a bright _____ lit

NOUN

up the sky and I was _____ up into a flying _____. Inside,

VERB (PAST TENSE)   NOUN

I came face-to-face with some _____ critters that looked like a cross

ADJECTIVE

between a/an _____ and a/an oversized _____. The creatures

ANIMAL   TYPE OF FOOD

could only make _____ noises that sounded even worse than someone

ADJECTIVE

scraping their _____ on a chalkboard. Yikes! Thankfully, the

PART OF THE BODY (PLURAL)

creatures could transmit their words straight into my _____ and we

PART OF THE BODY

could communicate using our _____. They asked to borrow my

PLURAL NOUN

_____ so they could call their mother ship. Turns out these strange

NOUN

_____ were lost and just needed _____ directions to return

PLURAL NOUN   ADJECTIVE

home!

MAD LIBS®

MUCH ADO ABOUT
MAD LIBS

by DW McCann

INSTRUCTIONS

MAD LIBS® is a game for people who don't like games!
It can be played by one, two, three, four, or forty.

• RIDICULOUSLY SIMPLE DIRECTIONS

In this tablet you will find stories containing blank spaces where words are left out. One player, the READER, selects one of these stories. The READER does not tell anyone what the story is about. Instead, he/she asks the other players, the WRITERS, to give him/her words. These words are used to fill in the blank spaces in the story.

• TO PLAY

The READER asks each WRITER in turn to call out a word—an adjective or a noun or whatever the space calls for—and uses them to fill in the blank spaces in the story. The result is a MAD LIBS® game.

When the READER then reads the completed MAD LIBS® game to the other players, they will discover that they have written a story that is fantastic, screamingly funny, shocking, silly, crazy, or just plain dumb—depending upon which words each WRITER called out.

• EXAMPLE (*Before* and *After*)

"_____!" he said _____
    EXCLAMATION   ADVERB

as he jumped into his convertible _____ and
                   NOUN

drove off with his _____ wife.
         ADJECTIVE

"____OUCH____!" he said ____HAPPILY____
    EXCLAMATION   ADVERB

as he jumped into his convertible ____CAT____ and
                   NOUN

drove off with his ____BRAVE____ wife.
         ADJECTIVE

MAD LIBS®

QUICK REVIEW

In case you have forgotten what adjectives, adverbs, nouns, and verbs are, here is a quick review:

An ADJECTIVE describes something or somebody. *Lumpy, soft, ugly, messy,* and *short* are adjectives.

An ADVERB tells how something is done. It modifies a verb and usually ends in "ly." *Modestly, stupidly, greedily,* and *carefully* are adverbs.

A NOUN is the name of a person, place, or thing. *Sidewalk, umbrella, bridle, bathtub,* and *nose* are nouns.

A VERB is an action word. *Run, pitch, jump,* and *swim* are verbs. Put the verbs in past tense if the directions say PAST TENSE. *Ran, pitched, jumped,* and *swam* are verbs in the past tense.

When we ask for A PLACE, we mean any sort of place: a country or city *(Spain, Cleveland)* or a room *(bathroom, kitchen).*

An EXCLAMATION or SILLY WORD is any sort of funny sound, gasp, grunt, or outcry, like *Wow!, Ouch!, Whomp!, Ick!,* and *Gadzooks!*

When we ask for specific words, like a NUMBER, a COLOR, an ANIMAL, or a PART OF THE BODY, we mean a word that is one of those things, like *seven, blue, horse,* or *head.*

When we ask for a PLURAL, it means more than one. For example, *cat* pluralized is *cats.*

MAD LIBS® is fun to play with friends, but you can also play it by yourself! To begin with, DO NOT look at the story on the page below. Fill in the blanks on this page with the words called for. Then, using the words you have selected, fill in the blank spaces in the story.

Now you've created your own hilarious MAD LIBS® game!

AS YOU LIKE IT
(ACT 2, SCENE 7—PART 1)

NOUN _____

OCCUPATION (PLURAL) _____

VERB ENDING IN "S" _____

NUMBER _____

VERB ENDING IN "ING" _____

VERB ENDING IN "ING" _____

ADJECTIVE _____

ANIMAL _____

NOUN _____

ADJECTIVE _____

PART OF THE BODY _____

ADJECTIVE _____

ADJECTIVE _____

NOUN _____

Jaques: All the world's a/an _____,
NOUN

And all the men and women merely _____.
OCCUPATION (PLURAL)

They have their exits and their entrances,

And one man in his time _____ many parts,
VERB ENDING IN "S"

His acts being _____ ages. At first the infant,
NUMBER

_____ and puking in the nurse's arms.
VERB ENDING IN "ING"

Then the _____ schoolboy with his satchel
VERB ENDING IN "ING"

And _____ morning face, creeping like _____
ADJECTIVE   ANIMAL

Unwillingly to school. And then the lover,

Sighing like _____, with a/an _____ ballad
NOUN   ADJECTIVE

Made to his mistress' _____. Then a soldier,
PART OF THE BODY

Full of _____ oaths and bearded like the pard,
ADJECTIVE

Jealous in honor, sudden and _____ in quarrel,
ADJECTIVE

Seeking the bubble reputation

Even in the _____'s mouth.
NOUN

MAD LIBS® is fun to play with friends, but you can also play it by yourself! To begin with, DO NOT look at the story on the page below. Fill in the blanks on this page with the words called for. Then, using the words you have selected, fill in the blank spaces in the story.

Now you've created your own hilarious MAD LIBS® game!

AS YOU LIKE IT
(ACT 2, SCENE 7–PART 2)

TYPE OF FOOD _____

ADJECTIVE _____

ADJECTIVE _____

PLURAL NOUN _____

ADJECTIVE _____

PART OF THE BODY _____

NOUN _____

ADJECTIVE _____

NOUN _____

ADJECTIVE _____

NOUN _____

Jaques: And then the justice,

In fair round belly with good _____ lined,
<u>TYPE OF FOOD</u>

With eyes _____ and beard of _____ cut,
<u>ADJECTIVE</u>   <u>ADJECTIVE</u>

Full of wise _____ and modern instances;
<u>PLURAL NOUN</u>

And so he plays his part. The sixth age shifts

Into the _____ and slippered pantaloon
<u>ADJECTIVE</u>

With spectacles on _____ and pouch on side,
<u>PART OF THE BODY</u>

His youthful hose, well saved, a/an _____ too wide
<u>NOUN</u>

For his shrunk shank, and his _____ manly voice,
<u>ADJECTIVE</u>

Turning again toward childish treble, pipes

And whistles in his _____. Last scene of all,
<u>NOUN</u>

That ends this _____ eventful history,
<u>ADJECTIVE</u>

Is second childishness and mere oblivion,

Sans teeth, sans eyes, sans _____, sans everything.
<u>NOUN</u>

MAD LIBS® is fun to play with friends, but you can also play it by yourself! To begin with, DO NOT look at the story on the page below. Fill in the blanks on this page with the words called for. Then, using the words you have selected, fill in the blank spaces in the story.

Now you've created your own hilarious MAD LIBS® game!

SONNET #5

PLURAL NOUN _____

ADJECTIVE _____

PART OF THE BODY _____

PLURAL NOUN _____

ADJECTIVE _____

VERB ENDING IN "S" _____

ADJECTIVE _____

NOUN _____

ADJECTIVE _____

NOUN _____

NOUN _____

PLURAL NOUN _____

VERB _____

NOUN _____

MAD LIBS
SONNET #5

Those _____ that with gentle work did frame
PLURAL NOUN

The _____ gaze where every _____ doth dwell
ADJECTIVE   PART OF THE BODY

Will play the _____ to the very same
PLURAL NOUN

And that unfair which fairly doth excel;

For never-resting time leads summer on

To _____ winter and _____ him there,
ADJECTIVE   VERB ENDING IN "S"

Sap checked with frost and _____ leaves quite gone,
ADJECTIVE

Beauty o'er-snowed and bareness everywhere.

Then, were not summer's _____ left
NOUN

A/An _____ prisoner pent in walls of _____,
ADJECTIVE   NOUN

Beauty's _____ with beauty were bereft,
NOUN

Nor it nor no remembrance what it was.

But _____ distilled, though they with winter meet,
PLURAL NOUN

_____ but their show; their _____ still lives sweet.
VERB   NOUN

MAD LIBS® is fun to play with friends, but you can also play it by yourself! To begin with, DO NOT look at the story on the page below. Fill in the blanks on this page with the words called for. Then, using the words you have selected, fill in the blank spaces in the story.

Now you've created your own hilarious MAD LIBS® game!

HAMLET
(ACT 5, SCENE 1)

PART OF THE BODY _____

FIRST NAME (MALE) _____

ADJECTIVE _____

PART OF THE BODY _____

PART OF THE BODY (PLURAL) _____

VERB (PAST TENSE) _____

PLURAL NOUN _____

PLURAL NOUN _____

NOUN _____

VERB _____

A PLACE _____

VERB _____

PLURAL NOUN _____

(*Hamlet takes the* _____)
                             PART OF THE BODY

Alas, poor _____! I knew him, Horatio—a fellow of infinite jest,
          FIRST NAME (MALE)

of most _____ fancy. He hath bore me on his _____ a thousand
     ADJECTIVE   PART OF THE BODY

times, and now how abhorred in my imagination it is! My gorge rises at it. Here

hung those _____ that I have _____
      PART OF THE BODY (PLURAL)   VERB (PAST TENSE)

I know not how oft. Where be your _____ now? your gambols? your
                         PLURAL NOUN

songs? your _____ of merriment that were wont to set the _____
        PLURAL NOUN   NOUN

on a roar? Not one now to _____ your own grinning? Quite chapfallen?
                     VERB

Now get you to my lady's _____, and tell her, let her _____ an
                A PLACE   VERB

inch thick, to this favor she must come. Make her laugh at _____.
                                             PLURAL NOUN

MAD LIBS® is fun to play with friends, but you can also play it by yourself! To begin with, DO NOT look at the story on the page below. Fill in the blanks on this page with the words called for. Then, using the words you have selected, fill in the blank spaces in the story.

Now you've created your own hilarious MAD LIBS® game!

SONNET #18

NOUN _____

ADJECTIVE _____

PLURAL NOUN _____

ADJECTIVE _____

PLURAL NOUN _____

NOUN _____

PART OF THE BODY _____

NOUN _____

NOUN _____

SAME NOUN _____

NOUN _____

VERB _____

CELEBRITY _____

NOUN _____

VERB _____

PART OF THE BODY (PLURAL) _____

SILLY WORD _____

MAD LIBS
SONNET #18

Shall I compare thee to a/an _____'s day?
<u>NOUN</u>

Thou art more _____ and more temperate.
<u>ADJECTIVE</u>

Rough _____ do shake the _____ _____ of May,
<u>PLURAL NOUN</u>   <u>ADJECTIVE</u>   <u>PLURAL NOUN</u>

And summer's _____ hath all too short a date.
<u>NOUN</u>

Sometime too hot the _____ of heaven shines,
<u>PART OF THE BODY</u>

And often is his gold _____ dimmed;
<u>NOUN</u>

And every _____ from _____ sometime declines,
<u>NOUN</u>   <u>SAME NOUN</u>

By chance or nature's changing _____ untrimmed.
<u>NOUN</u>

But thy eternal summer shall not _____
<u>VERB</u>

Nor lose possession of that fair thou ow'st,

Nor shall _____ brag thou wand'rest in his shade,
<u>CELEBRITY</u>

When in eternal lines to _____ thou grow'st.
<u>NOUN</u>

So long as men can _____ or _____ can see,
<u>VERB</u>   <u>PART OF THE BODY (PLURAL)</u>

So long lives this, and this gives _____ to thee.
<u>SILLY WORD</u>

MAD LIBS® is fun to play with friends, but you can also play it by yourself! To begin with, DO NOT look at the story on the page below. Fill in the blanks on this page with the words called for. Then, using the words you have selected, fill in the blank spaces in the story.

Now you've created your own hilarious MAD LIBS® game!

MACBETH
(ACT 4, SCENE 1)

PLURAL NOUN _____

ADJECTIVE _____

NUMBER _____

NOUN _____

ADJECTIVE _____

VERB _____

PART OF THE BODY _____

ANIMAL _____

NOUN _____

NOUN _____

ADJECTIVE _____

NOUN _____

VERB _____

ADJECTIVE _____

MAD LIBS®
MACBETH
(ACT 4, SCENE 1)

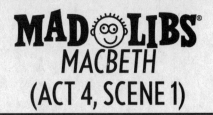

First Witch: Round about the cauldron go;

In the poisoned _____ throw.

PLURAL NOUN

Toad, that under _____ stone

ADJECTIVE

Days and nights has _____-one. . . .

NUMBER

All Three Witches: Double, double toil and trouble;

Fire burn, and _____ bubble.

NOUN

Second Witch: Fillet of a/an _____ snake

ADJECTIVE

In the cauldron _____ and bake.

VERB

_____ of newt and toe of frog,

PART OF THE BODY

Wool of _____ and tongue of dog. . . .

ANIMAL

Third Witch: Scale of dragon, _____ of wolf,

NOUN

Witches' mummy, _____ and gulf

NOUN

Of the _____ salt-sea shark,

ADJECTIVE

_____ of hemlock digged i' th' dark. . . .

NOUN

Second Witch: _____ it with a baboon's blood.

VERB

Then the charm is _____ and good.

ADJECTIVE

MAD LIBS® is fun to play with friends, but you can also play it by yourself! To begin with, DO NOT look at the story on the page below. Fill in the blanks on this page with the words called for. Then, using the words you have selected, fill in the blank spaces in the story.

Now you've created your own hilarious MAD LIBS® game!

SONNET #23

ADJECTIVE _____

NOUN _____

NOUN _____

ADJECTIVE _____

NOUN _____

ADJECTIVE _____

NOUN _____

NOUN _____

PLURAL NOUN _____

PLURAL NOUN _____

VERB ENDING IN "ING" _____

VERB _____

ADJECTIVE _____

VERB _____

MAD LIBS®
SONNET #23

As a/an _____ actor on the stage
ADJECTIVE

Who with his _____ is put beside his _____,
NOUN   NOUN

Or some _____ thing replete with too much rage,
ADJECTIVE

Whose strength's abundance weakens his own heart;

So I for fear of _____ forget to say
NOUN

The _____ _____ of love's rite,
ADJECTIVE   NOUN

And in mine own love's _____ seem to decay,
NOUN

O'ercharged with burden of mine own love's might.

O, let my _____ be then the eloquence
PLURAL NOUN

And dumb _____ of my _____ breast,
PLURAL NOUN   VERB ENDING IN "ING"

Who _____ for love and look for recompense
VERB

More than that tongue that more hath more expressed.

O, learn to read what _____ love hath writ.
ADJECTIVE

To _____ with eyes belongs to love's fine wit.
VERB

MAD LIBS® is fun to play with friends, but you can also play it by yourself! To begin with, DO NOT look at the story on the page below. Fill in the blanks on this page with the words called for. Then, using the words you have selected, fill in the blank spaces in the story.

Now you've created your own hilarious MAD LIBS® game!

JULIUS CAESAR
(ACT 3, SCENE 2)

PLURAL NOUN _____

PART OF THE BODY (PLURAL) _____

VERB _____

PLURAL NOUN _____

PERSON IN ROOM _____

ADJECTIVE _____

ADVERB _____

PERSON IN ROOM _____

SAME PERSON IN ROOM _____

NOUN _____

NOUN _____

PERSON IN ROOM _____

PLURAL NOUN _____

ADJECTIVE _____

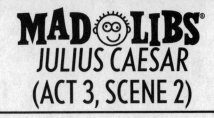

Antony: Friends, Romans, _____,
PLURAL NOUN
lend me your

_____.
PART OF THE BODY (PLURAL)

I come to bury Caesar, not to _____ him.
VERB

The evil that men do lives after them;

The good is oft interrèd with their _____.
PLURAL NOUN

So let it be with Caesar. The noble _____
PERSON IN ROOM

Hath told you Caesar was ambitious.

If it were so, it was a/an _____ fault,
ADJECTIVE

And _____ hath Caesar answered it.
ADVERB

Here, under leave of _____ and the rest
PERSON IN ROOM

(For _____ is an honorable _____....)
SAME PERSON IN ROOM   NOUN

Come I to speak in Caesar's funeral.

He was my _____, faithful and just to me,
NOUN

But _____ says he was ambitious. . . .
PERSON IN ROOM

He hath brought many _____ home to Rome,
PLURAL NOUN

Whose ransoms did the _____ coffers fill.
ADJECTIVE

Did this in Caesar seem ambitious?

MAD LIBS® is fun to play with friends, but you can also play it by yourself! To begin with, DO NOT look at the story on the page below. Fill in the blanks on this page with the words called for. Then, using the words you have selected, fill in the blank spaces in the story.

Now you've created your own hilarious MAD LIBS® game!

HENRY V
(ACT 4, SCENE 3)

NOUN _____

VERB _____

NOUN _____

PLURAL NOUN _____

NOUN _____

PART OF THE BODY _____

PERSON IN ROOM _____

PERSON IN ROOM _____

CELEBRITY _____

ADJECTIVE _____

NOUN _____

NOUN _____

PLURAL NOUN _____

ADJECTIVE _____

PLURAL NOUN _____

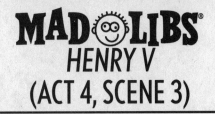
Henry: This day is called the feast of Crispian.

He that outlives this _____ and comes safe home
<u>NOUN</u>

Will _____ o' tiptoe when this day is nam'd. . . .
<u>VERB</u>

He that shall see this day, and live old _____,
<u>NOUN</u>

Will yearly on the vigil feast his _____
<u>PLURAL NOUN</u>

And say "Tomorrow is Saint Crispian."

Then will he strip his _____ and show his scars . . .
<u>NOUN</u>

Then shall our names,

Familiar in his _____ as household words,
<u>PART OF THE BODY</u>

_____ the King, Bedford and Exeter,
<u>PERSON IN ROOM</u>

Warwick and _____, Salisbury and _____,
<u>PERSON IN ROOM</u>   <u>CELEBRITY</u>

Be in their _____ cups freshly remembered.
<u>ADJECTIVE</u>

This story shall the good _____ teach his son,
<u>NOUN</u>

And Crispin Crispian shall ne'er go by,

From this day to the ending of the _____,
<u>NOUN</u>

But _____ in it shall be rememberèd—
<u>PLURAL NOUN</u>

We few, we _____ few, we band of _____. . . .
<u>ADJECTIVE</u>   <u>PLURAL NOUN</u>

MAD LIBS® is fun to play with friends, but you can also play it by yourself! To begin with, DO NOT look at the story on the page below. Fill in the blanks on this page with the words called for. Then, using the words you have selected, fill in the blank spaces in the story.

Now you've created your own hilarious MAD LIBS® game!

SONNET #29

PLURAL NOUN _____

ADJECTIVE _____

NOUN _____

VERB _____

PLURAL NOUN _____

NOUN _____

NOUN _____

PLURAL NOUN _____

VERB _____

ANIMAL _____

ADJECTIVE _____

NOUN _____

NOUN _____

MAD LIBS
SONNET #29

When in disgrace with _____ and men's eyes,
                           PLURAL NOUN

I all alone beweep my _____ state,
                           ADJECTIVE

And trouble deaf heaven with my _____-less cries,
                                   NOUN

And _____ upon myself and curse my fate,
        VERB

Wishing me like to one more rich in hope,

Featured like him, like him with _____ possessed,
                                   PLURAL NOUN

Desiring this man's _____ and that man's _____,
                       NOUN   NOUN

With what I most enjoy contented least;

Yet in these _____ myself almost despising,
                 PLURAL NOUN

Haply I _____ on thee, and then my state,
            VERB

Like to the _____ at break of day arising
                ANIMAL

From _____ earth, sings hymns at heaven's gate;
        ADJECTIVE

For thy sweet love remembered such _____ brings
                                       NOUN

That then I scorn to change my _____ with kings.
                                   NOUN

MAD LIBS® is fun to play with friends, but you can also play it by yourself! To begin with, DO NOT look at the story on the page below. Fill in the blanks on this page with the words called for. Then, using the words you have selected, fill in the blank spaces in the story.

Now you've created your own hilarious MAD LIBS® game!

ROMEO AND JULIET (ACT 1, SCENE 5)

VERB _____

ADJECTIVE _____

ADJECTIVE _____

NOUN _____

ADJECTIVE _____

PLURAL NOUN _____

PART OF THE BODY _____

SAME PART OF THE BODY _____

PART OF THE BODY (PLURAL) _____

SAME PART OF THE BODY (PLURAL) _____

ADJECTIVE _____

NOUN _____

VERB _____

SAME VERB _____

NOUN _____

ADVERB _____

Romeo: If I _____ with my unworthiest hand

VERB

This holy shrine, the _____ fine is this:

ADJECTIVE

My lips, two _____ pilgrims, ready stand

ADJECTIVE

To smooth that rough _____ with a tender kiss.

NOUN

Juliet: _____ pilgrim, you do wrong your hand too much,

ADJECTIVE

Which mannerly devotion shows in this;

For saints have _____ that pilgrims' hands do touch,

PLURAL NOUN

And _____ to _____ is holy palmers' kiss.

PART OF THE BODY — SAME PART OF THE BODY

Romeo: Have not saints _____, and holy palmers too?

PART OF THE BODY (PLURAL)

Juliet: Ay, _____ that they must use in prayer.

SAME PART OF THE BODY (PLURAL)

Romeo: O then, _____ saint, let lips do what hands do.

ADJECTIVE

They pray: grant thou, lest _____ turn to despair.

NOUN

Juliet: Saints do not _____, though grant for prayers' sake.

VERB

Romeo: Then _____ not while my prayer's _____ I take.

SAME VERB — NOUN

(*He kisses her.*) Thus from my lips, by thine, my sin is purged.

Juliet: Then have my lips the sin that they have took.

Romeo: Sin from thy lips? O trespass _____ urged!

ADVERB

MAD LIBS® is fun to play with friends, but you can also play it by yourself! To begin with, DO NOT look at the story on the page below. Fill in the blanks on this page with the words called for. Then, using the words you have selected, fill in the blank spaces in the story.

Now you've created your own hilarious MAD LIBS® game!

SONNET #30

ADJECTIVE _____

NOUN _____

PLURAL NOUN _____

VERB _____

PERSON IN ROOM _____

PERSON IN ROOM _____

NOUN _____

NOUN _____

SAME NOUN _____

ADJECTIVE _____

VERB _____

PLURAL NOUN _____

MAD LIBS®
SONNET #30

When to the sessions of sweet _____ thought
                    ADJECTIVE

I summon up remembrance of things past,

I sigh the lack of many a/an _____ I sought,
                         NOUN

And with old _____ new wail my dear time's waste;
             PLURAL NOUN

Then can I _____ an eye, unused to flow,
             VERB

For precious friends hid in _____'s dateless night,
                PERSON IN ROOM

And weep afresh _____'s long since canceled woe,
            PERSON IN ROOM

And moan th' _____ of many a vanished sight.
           NOUN

Then can I grieve at grievances foregone,

And heavily from _____ to _____ tell o'er
            NOUN   SAME NOUN

The _____ account of fore-bemoanèd moan,
      ADJECTIVE

Which I new pay as if not paid before.

But if the while I _____ on thee, dear friend,
             VERB

All _____ are restored and sorrows end.
   PLURAL NOUN

MAD LIBS® is fun to play with friends, but you can also play it by yourself! To begin with, DO NOT look at the story on the page below. Fill in the blanks on this page with the words called for. Then, using the words you have selected, fill in the blank spaces in the story.

Now you've created your own hilarious MAD LIBS® game!

MACBETH
(ACT 2, SCENE 1)

NOUN _____

VERB _____

ADJECTIVE _____

ADJECTIVE _____

NOUN _____

PART OF THE BODY _____

ADJECTIVE _____

VERB _____

VERB _____

NOUN _____

PART OF THE BODY (PLURAL) _____

PLURAL NOUN _____

TYPE OF LIQUID _____

ADJECTIVE _____

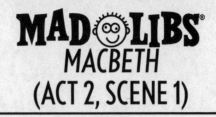

MACBETH
(ACT 2, SCENE 1)

Macbeth: Is this a/an _____ which I see before me,
NOUN

The handle toward my hand? Come, let me _____ thee.
VERB

I have thee not, and yet I see thee still.

Art thou not, _____ vision, sensible
ADJECTIVE

To feeling as to sight? Or art thou but

A dagger of the mind, a/an _____ _____
ADJECTIVE   NOUN

Proceeding from the heat-oppressèd _____?
PART OF THE BODY

I see thee yet, in form as _____
ADJECTIVE

As this which now I _____. (*He draws his dagger.*)
VERB

Thou _____'st me the way that I was going,
VERB

And such a/an _____ I was to use.
NOUN

Mine _____ are made the fools o' th' other senses
PART OF THE BODY (PLURAL)

Or else worth all the _____. I see thee still,
PLURAL NOUN

And, on thy blade and dudgeon, gouts of _____,
TYPE OF LIQUID

Which was not so before. There's no such thing.

It is the _____ business which informs
ADJECTIVE

Thus to mine eyes.

MAD LIBS® is fun to play with friends, but you can also play it by yourself! To begin with, DO NOT look at the story on the page below. Fill in the blanks on this page with the words called for. Then, using the words you have selected, fill in the blank spaces in the story.

Now you've created your own hilarious MAD LIBS® game!

SONNET #116

ADJECTIVE _____

PLURAL NOUN _____

VERB ENDING IN "S" _____

VERB (PAST TENSE) _____

PLURAL NOUN _____

NOUN _____

NOUN _____

PERSON IN ROOM (MALE) _____

ADJECTIVE _____

VERB ENDING IN "S" _____

NOUN _____

VERB _____

NOUN _____

MAD LIBS®
SONNET #116

Let me not to the marriage of _____ minds
  ADJECTIVE

Admit _____. Love is not love
  PLURAL NOUN

Which alters when it alteration finds

Or _____ with the remover to remove.
  VERB ENDING IN "S"

O, no, it is an ever-_____ mark
  VERB (PAST TENSE)

That looks on _____ and is never shaken;
  PLURAL NOUN

It is the _____ to every wand'ring bark,
  NOUN

Whose worth's unknown, although his _____ be taken.
  NOUN

Love's not _____'s fool, though _____
  PERSON IN ROOM (MALE)   ADJECTIVE

lips and cheeks

Within his bending sickle's compass come;

Love _____ not with his brief hours and weeks,
  VERB ENDING IN "S"

But bears it out even to the edge of doom.

If this be _____, and upon me proved,
  NOUN

I never _____, nor no _____ ever loved.
  VERB   NOUN

MAD LIBS® is fun to play with friends, but you can also play it by yourself! To begin with, DO NOT look at the story on the page below. Fill in the blanks on this page with the words called for. Then, using the words you have selected, fill in the blank spaces in the story.

Now you've created your own hilarious MAD LIBS® game!

RICHARD III
(ACT 1, SCENE 1)

NOUN _____

ADJECTIVE _____

PLURAL NOUN _____

ADJECTIVE _____

PART OF THE BODY (PLURAL) _____

ADJECTIVE _____

PLURAL NOUN _____

ADJECTIVE _____

PLURAL NOUN _____

NOUN _____

ADJECTIVE _____

VERB _____

ADVERB _____

ADJECTIVE _____

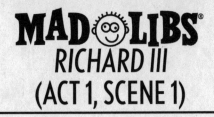
Richard: Now is the _____ of our discontent
NOUN

Made _____ summer by this son of York,
ADJECTIVE

And all the _____ that loured upon our house
PLURAL NOUN

In the _____ bosom of the ocean buried.
ADJECTIVE

Now are our _____ bound with _____ wreaths,
PART OF THE BODY (PLURAL)   ADJECTIVE

Our bruisèd arms hung up for _____,
PLURAL NOUN

Our _____ alarums changed to merry meetings,
ADJECTIVE

Our dreadful marches to delightful _____.
PLURAL NOUN

Grim-visaged war hath smoothed his wrinkled _____;
NOUN

And now, instead of mounting _____ steeds
ADJECTIVE

To _____ the souls of fearful adversaries,
VERB

He capers _____ in a lady's chamber
ADVERB

To the _____ pleasing of a lute.
ADJECTIVE

MAD LIBS® is fun to play with friends, but you can also play it by yourself! To begin with, DO NOT look at the story on the page below. Fill in the blanks on this page with the words called for. Then, using the words you have selected, fill in the blank spaces in the story.

Now you've created your own hilarious MAD LIBS® game!

HAMLET
(ACT 1, SCENE 3)

PART OF THE BODY _____

NOUN _____

NOUN _____

NOUN _____

NOUN _____

ADJECTIVE _____

NOUN _____

A PLACE _____

ADJECTIVE _____

OCCUPATION _____

VERB ENDING IN "S" _____

VERB ENDING IN "ING" _____

NOUN _____

ADJECTIVE _____

Polonius: Give thy thoughts no _____,
PART OF THE BODY

Nor any unproportioned thought his _____.
NOUN

Be thou familiar, but by no means vulgar. . . .

Give every _____ thy ear, but few thy voice.
NOUN

Take each man's _____, but reserve thy judgment.
NOUN

Costly thy _____ as thy purse can buy,
NOUN

But not expressed in fancy (_____, not gaudy),
ADJECTIVE

For the _____ oft proclaims the man,
NOUN

And they in (the) _____ of the best rank and station
A PLACE

Are of a most _____ and generous chief in that.
ADJECTIVE

Neither a borrower nor a/an _____ be,
OCCUPATION

For loan oft _____ both itself and friend,
VERB ENDING IN "S"

And _____ dulls the edge of husbandry.
VERB ENDING IN "ING"

This above all: to thine own _____ be true,
NOUN

And it must follow, as the night the day,

Thou canst not then be _____ to any man.
ADJECTIVE

MAD LIBS® is fun to play with friends, but you can also play it by yourself! To begin with, DO NOT look at the story on the page below. Fill in the blanks on this page with the words called for. Then, using the words you have selected, fill in the blank spaces in the story.

Now you've created your own hilarious MAD LIBS® game!

SONNET #126

NOUN _____

CELEBRITY (MALE) _____

VERB ENDING IN "ING" _____

ADJECTIVE _____

NOUN _____

VERB _____

VERB ENDING IN "S" _____

NOUN _____

NOUN _____

VERB _____

NOUN _____

VERB _____

MAD LIBS®
SONNET #126

O thou, my lovely _____, who in thy power
 <small>NOUN</small>

Dost hold _____'s fickle glass, his sickle hour;
 <small>CELEBRITY (MALE)</small>

Who hast by waning grown, and therein show'st

Thy lover's _____ as thy _____ self grow'st.
 <small>VERB ENDING IN "ING"</small> <small>ADJECTIVE</small>

If Nature, sovereign mistress over _____,
 <small>NOUN</small>

As thou goest onwards still will _____ thee back,
 <small>VERB</small>

She _____ thee to this purpose, that her skill
 <small>VERB ENDING IN "S"</small>

May _____ disgrace, and wretched minutes kill.
 <small>NOUN</small>

Yet fear her, O thou _____ of her pleasure!
 <small>NOUN</small>

She may _____, but not still keep, her treasure.
 <small>VERB</small>

Her _____, though delayed, answered must be,
 <small>NOUN</small>

And her quietus is to _____ thee.
 <small>VERB</small>

MAD LIBS® is fun to play with friends, but you can also play it by yourself! To begin with, DO NOT look at the story on the page below. Fill in the blanks on this page with the words called for. Then, using the words you have selected, fill in the blank spaces in the story.

Now you've created your own hilarious MAD LIBS® game!

TWELFTH NIGHT
(ACT 1, SCENE 1)

NOUN _____

VERB _____

NOUN _____

PART OF THE BODY _____

PLURAL NOUN _____

NOUN _____

ADJECTIVE _____

ADJECTIVE _____

VERB _____

NOUN _____

ADJECTIVE _____

PLURAL NOUN _____

ADJECTIVE _____

Orsino: If music be the food of love, play on.

Give me _____ of it, that, surfeiting,
_{NOUN}

The appetite may sicken and so _____.
_{VERB}

That _____ again! It had a dying fall.
_{NOUN}

O, it came o'er my _____ like the sweet sound
_{PART OF THE BODY}

That breathes upon a bank of _____,
_{PLURAL NOUN}

Stealing and giving _____. Enough; no more.
_{NOUN}

'Tis not so _____ now as it was before.
_{ADJECTIVE}

O spirit of love, how _____ and fresh art thou,
_{ADJECTIVE}

That, notwithstanding thy capacity

_____-eth as the sea, naught enters there,
_{VERB}

Of what _____ and pitch soe'er,
_{NOUN}

But falls into abatement and _____ price
_{ADJECTIVE}

Even in a minute. So full of _____ is fancy
_{PLURAL NOUN}

That it alone is _____ fantastical.
_{ADJECTIVE}

MAD LIBS® is fun to play with friends, but you can also play it by yourself! To begin with, DO NOT look at the story on the page below. Fill in the blanks on this page with the words called for. Then, using the words you have selected, fill in the blank spaces in the story.

Now you've created your own hilarious MAD LIBS® game!

SONNET #130

PERSON IN ROOM (FEMALE) _____

PART OF THE BODY (PLURAL) _____

PLURAL NOUN _____

COLOR _____

ADJECTIVE _____

ADJECTIVE _____

NOUN _____

ADJECTIVE _____

SILLY WORD _____

VERB ENDING IN "S" _____

A PLACE _____

NOUN _____

VERB (PAST TENSE) _____

MAD LIBS
SONNET #130

My _____'s eyes are nothing like the sun;
    PERSON IN ROOM (FEMALE)

Coral is far more red than her _____' red;
        PART OF THE BODY (PLURAL)

If snow be white, why then her _____ are dun;
        PLURAL NOUN

If hairs be wires, _____ wires grow on her head.
    COLOR

I have seen roses damasked, _____ and white,
     ADJECTIVE

But no such roses see I in her cheeks;

And in _____ perfumes is there more delight
   ADJECTIVE

Than in the breath that from my _____ reeks.
     NOUN

I love to hear her speak, yet well I know

That music hath a far more _____ sound.
    ADJECTIVE

I grant I never saw a goddess go;

My _____, when she walks, _____ on the ground.
SILLY WORD   VERB ENDING IN "S"

And yet, by (the) _____, I think my _____ as rare
     A PLACE   NOUN

As any she _____ with false compare.
    VERB (PAST TENSE)

MAD LIBS® is fun to play with friends, but you can also play it by yourself! To begin with, DO NOT look at the story on the page below. Fill in the blanks on this page with the words called for. Then, using the words you have selected, fill in the blank spaces in the story.

Now you've created your own hilarious MAD LIBS® game!

MACBETH
(ACT 5, SCENE 1)

ADJECTIVE _____

A PLACE _____

OCCUPATION _____

NOUN _____

ADJECTIVE _____

TYPE OF LIQUID _____

NOUN _____

PART OF THE BODY (PLURAL) _____

PLURAL NOUN _____

PART OF THE BODY _____

NOUN _____

CELEBRITY (MALE) _____

NOUN _____

Lady Macbeth: Yet here's a spot. . . . Out, _____ spot, out, I say! One.
ADJECTIVE

Two. Why then, 'tis time to do 't. (The) _____ is murky. Fie, my lord,
A PLACE

fie, a/an _____ and afeard? What need we fear who knows it,
OCCUPATION

when none can call our _____ to account? Yet who would have thought
NOUN

the _____ man to have had so much _____ in him? . . .
ADJECTIVE   TYPE OF LIQUID

The _____ of Fife had a wife. Where is she now? What, will these
NOUN

_____ ne'er be clean? No more o' that, my lord, no more
PART OF THE BODY (PLURAL)

o' that. You mar all with this starting. . . . Here's the smell of the blood still. All

the _____ of Arabia will not sweeten this little _____.
PLURAL NOUN   PART OF THE BODY

O, O, O! . . . Wash your hands. Put on your _____. Look not so pale.
NOUN

I tell you yet again, _____'s buried; he cannot come out on 's
CELEBRITY (MALE)

_____.
NOUN

MAD LIBS® is fun to play with friends, but you can also play it by yourself! To begin with, DO NOT look at the story on the page below. Fill in the blanks on this page with the words called for. Then, using the words you have selected, fill in the blank spaces in the story.

Now you've created your own hilarious MAD LIBS® game!

A MIDSUMMER NIGHT'S DREAM (ACT 5, SCENE 1)

PLURAL NOUN _____

VERB _____

VERB (PAST TENSE) _____

PLURAL NOUN _____

ADJECTIVE _____

PLURAL NOUN _____

VERB _____

ADJECTIVE _____

ANIMAL _____

SILLY WORD _____

EXCLAMATION _____

PLURAL NOUN _____

PERSON IN ROOM _____

PLURAL NOUN _____

Puck: If we _____ have offended,
<u>PLURAL NOUN</u>

_____ but this and all is mended:
<u>VERB</u>

That you have but _____ here
<u>VERB (PAST TENSE)</u>

While these _____ did appear.
<u>PLURAL NOUN</u>

And this _____ and idle theme,
<u>ADJECTIVE</u>

No more yielding but a dream,

_____, do not reprehend.
<u>PLURAL NOUN</u>

If you _____, we will mend.
<u>VERB</u>

And, as I am a/an _____ Puck,
<u>ADJECTIVE</u>

If we have unearnèd luck

Now to 'scape the _____'s tongue,
<u>ANIMAL</u>

We will make amends ere long.

Else the Puck a/an _____ call.
<u>SILLY WORD</u>

So _____ unto you all.
<u>EXCLAMATION</u>

Give me your _____, if we be friends,
<u>PLURAL NOUN</u>

And _____ shall restore _____.
<u>PERSON IN ROOM</u>　　　　　　<u>PLURAL NOUN</u>

MAD LIBS®

UNICORNS, MERMAIDS, AND MAD LIBS

by Billy Merrell

MAD LIBS®

INSTRUCTIONS

MAD LIBS® is a game for people who don't like games!
It can be played by one, two, three, four, or forty.

• RIDICULOUSLY SIMPLE DIRECTIONS

In this tablet you will find stories containing blank spaces where words are left out. One player, the READER, selects one of these stories. The READER does not tell anyone what the story is about. Instead, he/she asks the other players, the WRITERS, to give him/her words. These words are used to fill in the blank spaces in the story.

• TO PLAY

The READER asks each WRITER in turn to call out a word—an adjective or a noun or whatever the space calls for—and uses them to fill in the blank spaces in the story. The result is a MAD LIBS® game.

When the READER then reads the completed MAD LIBS® game to the other players, they will discover that they have written a story that is fantastic, screamingly funny, shocking, silly, crazy, or just plain dumb—depending upon which words each WRITER called out.

• EXAMPLE (*Before* and *After*)

"_____!" he said _____
    EXCLAMATION   ADVERB

as he jumped into his convertible _____ and
                                  NOUN

drove off with his _____ wife.
                ADJECTIVE

"_____OUCH_____!" he said _____HAPPILY_____
    EXCLAMATION   ADVERB

as he jumped into his convertible _____CAT_____ and
                                    NOUN

drove off with his _____BRAVE_____ wife.
                ADJECTIVE

MAD LIBS®
QUICK REVIEW

In case you have forgotten what adjectives, adverbs, nouns, and verbs are, here is a quick review:

An ADJECTIVE describes something or somebody. *Lumpy, soft, ugly, messy,* and *short* are adjectives.

An ADVERB tells how something is done. It modifies a verb and usually ends in "ly." *Modestly, stupidly, greedily,* and *carefully* are adverbs.

A NOUN is the name of a person, place, or thing. *Sidewalk, umbrella, bridle, bathtub,* and *nose* are nouns.

A VERB is an action word. *Run, pitch, jump,* and *swim* are verbs. Put the verbs in past tense if the directions say PAST TENSE. *Ran, pitched, jumped,* and *swam* are verbs in the past tense.

When we ask for A PLACE, we mean any sort of place: a country or city *(Spain, Cleveland)* or a room *(bathroom, kitchen)*.

An EXCLAMATION or SILLY WORD is any sort of funny sound, gasp, grunt, or outcry, like *Wow!, Ouch!, Whomp!, Ick!,* and *Gadzooks!*

When we ask for specific words, like a NUMBER, a COLOR, an ANIMAL, or a PART OF THE BODY, we mean a word that is one of those things, like *seven, blue, horse,* or *head*.

When we ask for a PLURAL, it means more than one. For example, *cat* pluralized is *cats*.

MAD LIBS® is fun to play with friends, but you can also play it by yourself! To begin with, DO NOT look at the story on the page below. Fill in the blanks on this page with the words called for. Then, using the words you have selected, fill in the blank spaces in the story.

Now you've created your own hilarious MAD LIBS® game!

HOW TO HATCH A DRAGON EGG

ADJECTIVE _____

PLURAL NOUN _____

PLURAL NOUN _____

COLOR _____

NUMBER _____

VERB _____

TYPE OF LIQUID _____

ADJECTIVE _____

PLURAL NOUN _____

NUMBER _____

ADJECTIVE _____

NOUN _____

SILLY WORD _____

A PLACE _____

ADJECTIVE _____

NOUN _____

VERB ENDING IN "ING" _____

PART OF THE BODY (PLURAL) _____

MAD LIBS
HOW TO HATCH
A DRAGON EGG

While most eggs need _____ love and care for the _____
ADJECTIVE   PLURAL NOUN

inside to survive, dragon eggs thrive on danger! In fact, the _____
PLURAL NOUN

of _____ dragons *require* a/an _____-foot drop in order to
COLOR   NUMBER

_____ open. Eggs of _____ dragons depend on
VERB   TYPE OF LIQUID

_____ lava from underwater _____ to heat the shells to
ADJECTIVE   PLURAL NOUN

temperatures of _____ degrees or more. Only then can the _____
NUMBER   ADJECTIVE

dragonets inside finally hatch. But the _____ of the skies,
NOUN

the _____ dragon of (the) _____, is the most _____
SILLY WORD   A PLACE   ADJECTIVE

_____-layer of them all! They have been spotted
NOUN

_____ into the _____ of hungry predators,
VERB ENDING IN "ING"   PART OF THE BODY (PLURAL)

hoping to be swallowed. Once they hatch, they cause quite a bellyache!

MAD LIBS® is fun to play with friends, but you can also play it by yourself! To begin with, DO NOT look at the story on the page below. Fill in the blanks on this page with the words called for. Then, using the words you have selected, fill in the blank spaces in the story.

Now you've created your own hilarious MAD LIBS® game!

WHAT UNICORNS EAT

PLURAL NOUN _____

ADJECTIVE _____

NOUN _____

TYPE OF FOOD _____

ARTICLE OF CLOTHING (PLURAL) _____

VERB ENDING IN "ING" _____

PLURAL NOUN _____

PLURAL NOUN _____

NUMBER _____

CELEBRITY (FEMALE) _____

COLOR _____

VERB ENDING IN "ING" _____

TYPE OF FOOD (PLURAL) _____

PLURAL NOUN _____

ADJECTIVE _____

ADJECTIVE _____

MAD LIBS®
WHAT UNICORNS EAT

Would it surprise you to learn that the most majestic _____ in the
PLURAL NOUN

world eat garbage? Well, they do! Everything from _____
ADJECTIVE

soda cans to _____-stained _____ boxes to used
NOUN   _TYPE OF FOOD_

_____—and more! Some have been spotted
ARTICLE OF CLOTHING (PLURAL)

_____ dumpsters and then using their long _____
VERB ENDING IN "ING"   _PLURAL NOUN_

to spear as many bags of _____ as they can before being caught.
PLURAL NOUN

According to an interview with _____ _Minutes,_ _____
NUMBER   _CELEBRITY (FEMALE)_

once came home to find a/an _____ unicorn _____
COLOR   _VERB ENDING IN "ING"_

up in her recycling bin. The poor thing had mistaken her husband's leftover

_____ for dried-up _____. "It was a/an _____
TYPE OF FOOD (PLURAL)   _PLURAL NOUN_   _ADJECTIVE_

mistake," she said. "My husband is a/an _____ cook!"
ADJECTIVE

MAD LIBS® is fun to play with friends, but you can also play it by yourself! To begin with, DO NOT look at the story on the page below. Fill in the blanks on this page with the words called for. Then, using the words you have selected, fill in the blank spaces in the story.

Now you've created your own hilarious MAD LIBS® game!

BAD HOUSEKEEPING

NOUN _____

ADJECTIVE _____

NOUN _____

PLURAL NOUN _____

VERB ENDING IN "ING" _____

PLURAL NOUN _____

NOUN _____

PLURAL NOUN _____

TYPE OF FOOD _____

NOUN _____

SILLY WORD _____

A PLACE _____

NUMBER _____

NOUN _____

SAME NOUN _____

MAD LIBS®
BAD HOUSEKEEPING

The troll that lives under the _____ shares tips for keeping his home
NOUN

_____ clean.
ADJECTIVE

- **Decorate sparingly.** Don't clutter up your _____
  NOUN

  with sentimental garbage, like pictures of _____ or
  PLURAL NOUN

  _____ trophies. Having too many _____
  VERB ENDING IN "ING" PLURAL NOUN

  visible ruins the element of surprise!

- **Clean up immediately.** It's easy to let _____-work get
  NOUN

  away from you. Wash the _____ right after meals, so that
  PLURAL NOUN

  _____ doesn't sit too long in the sink. For a troll, scraps of
  TYPE OF FOOD

  _____ could be considered evidence!
  NOUN

- **Make the most of it.** Even if it doesn't win the _____ award
  SILLY WORD

  for best home in (the) _____, it's still yours! Spend at least
  A PLACE

  _____ minutes a day simply sitting back and appreciating your
  NUMBER

  "_____, sweet _____."
  NOUN SAME NOUN

MAD LIBS® is fun to play with friends, but you can also play it by yourself! To begin with, DO NOT look at the story on the page below. Fill in the blanks on this page with the words called for. Then, using the words you have selected, fill in the blank spaces in the story.

Now you've created your own hilarious MAD LIBS® game!

ENCOUNTER WITH BIGFOOT

NOUN _____

A PLACE _____

PART OF THE BODY _____

NOUN _____

ADJECTIVE _____

ADJECTIVE _____

PART OF THE BODY (PLURAL) _____

ADJECTIVE _____

ADJECTIVE _____

TYPE OF FOOD _____

VERB ENDING IN "ING" _____

ANIMAL _____

PART OF THE BODY (PLURAL) _____

VERB ENDING IN "ING" _____

CELEBRITY _____

NOUN _____

TYPE OF LIQUID _____

TYPE OF FOOD _____

Before they vanished, a well-trained _____ of explorers sent an SOS
                                          NOUN

from the snowy peaks of (the) _____, claiming to have spotted Big-
                                  A PLACE

_____. This is what their _____ said:
PART OF THE BODY   NOUN

OMG, he's real. I'm looking at _____-foot right now. And he's
                                     ADJECTIVE

_____! I've never seen such human _____on a
         ADJECTIVE   PART OF THE BODY (PLURAL)

creature so _____! At first he looked as _____as we all were.
                 ADJECTIVE   ADJECTIVE

But as we approached, he became cool as a/an _____, silently
                                                     TYPE OF FOOD

_____ us. "What's the matter?" I said. "_____
      VERB ENDING IN "ING"   ANIMAL

got your tongue?" But we couldn't believe our _____—he
                                                   PART OF THE BODY (PLURAL)

actually spoke! Now the creature won't stop _____ on and on
                                                 VERB ENDING IN "ING"

about _____ and _____-flavored _____.
           CELEBRITY   NOUN   TYPE OF LIQUID

Help! Someone make this beast shut his _____-hole!
                                           TYPE OF FOOD

MAD LIBS® is fun to play with friends, but you can also play it by yourself! To begin with, DO NOT look at the story on the page below. Fill in the blanks on this page with the words called for. Then, using the words you have selected, fill in the blank spaces in the story.

Now you've created your own hilarious MAD LIBS® game!

A-MAZE-ING MINOTAUR

ANIMAL _____

NOUN _____

PLURAL NOUN _____

ADJECTIVE _____

VERB _____

ADJECTIVE _____

PLURAL NOUN _____

VERB _____

ADJECTIVE _____

PART OF THE BODY (PLURAL) _____

PLURAL NOUN _____

NOUN _____

PLURAL NOUN _____

ADJECTIVE _____

NOUN _____

ANIMAL _____

Interviewer: So, what's it like having a/an _____ head, but a human
ANIMAL

_____?
NOUN

Mini: It's just about what you'd expect. _____ don't take me
PLURAL NOUN

seriously. My therapist misses every _____ appointment. I could
ADJECTIVE

_____!
VERB

Interviewer: How unfortunate! Do you think they are _____ against
ADJECTIVE

all non-_____, or what?
PLURAL NOUN

Mini: I do hunt and _____ people I find wandering lost inside the maze.
VERB

That could be the reason for the _____ look in their
ADJECTIVE

_____.
PART OF THE BODY (PLURAL)

Interviewer: That seems likely. After all, _____ speak louder than
PLURAL NOUN

words. With that in _____, do you have anything to say to the families
NOUN

of your _____?
PLURAL NOUN

Mini: Only that it's never _____ to judge a book by its _____.
ADJECTIVE   NOUN

Despite my looks, on the inside I have the heart of a/an _____.
ANIMAL

MAD LIBS® is fun to play with friends, but you can also play it by yourself! To begin with, DO NOT look at the story on the page below. Fill in the blanks on this page with the words called for. Then, using the words you have selected, fill in the blank spaces in the story.

Now you've created your own hilarious MAD LIBS® game!

A GENIE'S CONTRACT

ADJECTIVE _____

VERB ENDING IN "ING" _____

NUMBER _____

NOUN _____

NUMBER _____

NOUN _____

NOUN _____

ADJECTIVE _____

A PLACE _____

NUMBER _____

ADJECTIVE _____

VERB _____

VERB _____

NOUN _____

NOUN _____

PLURAL NOUN _____

ADVERB _____

MAD LIBS
A GENIE'S CONTRACT

Be sure to read the _____ print:
                        ADJECTIVE

The individual responsible for _____ the lamp is entitled to
                                VERB ENDING IN "ING"

_____ wishes, to be granted by the _____ inside. Limit
   NUMBER   NOUN

_____ wishes per master, or one (1) _____ per day. At the genie's
   NUMBER   NOUN

discretion, a/an _____ may be substituted for a lamp at any time.
                     NOUN

Offer only _____ at participating locations, excluding (the)
              ADJECTIVE

_____. Official wishes must be limited to _____ characters, in
  A PLACE   NUMBER

order to minimize _____ consequences that may _____ due
                    ADJECTIVE   VERB

to unnecessary verbosity. May not be used to make a person _____ in love
                                                              VERB

or combined with any other _____ or offer. The lamp (or substituted
                              NOUN

_____) must be surrendered after the final wish. Wishing for more
    NOUN

_____ is _____ prohibited.
 PLURAL NOUN   ADVERB

MAD LIBS® is fun to play with friends, but you can also play it by yourself! To begin with, DO NOT look at the story on the page below. Fill in the blanks on this page with the words called for. Then, using the words you have selected, fill in the blank spaces in the story.

Now you've created your own hilarious MAD LIBS® game!

WHY GIANTS DON'T SLEEP

VERB _____

NUMBER _____

ADJECTIVE _____

ADJECTIVE _____

EXCLAMATION _____

PART OF THE BODY _____

PART OF THE BODY _____

ADJECTIVE _____

PLURAL NOUN _____

VERB _____

COLOR _____

TYPE OF LIQUID _____

PLURAL NOUN _____

ADVERB _____

VERB ENDING IN "ING" _____

ANIMAL _____

ARTICLE OF CLOTHING (PLURAL) _____

MAD LIBS
WHY GIANTS DON'T SLEEP

Finding a place to sit and _____ when you're more than _____
                          VERB   NUMBER

feet tall is no _____ task. And lying down is next to _____!
                 ADJECTIVE   ADJECTIVE

_____! It would take an area the size of two _____-ball fields
 EXCLAMATION   PART OF THE BODY

for a giant to stretch out from head to _____. That's why, for a giant,
                                          PART OF THE BODY

waking up on the _____ side of the bed is all but inevitable. The
                   ADJECTIVE

closest that most _____ get to a comfortable place to _____
                   PLURAL NOUN   VERB

are bogs, where _____ mud, _____, and dead
                 COLOR   TYPE OF LIQUID

_____ form a kind of mattress. And even there, they must take care
 PLURAL NOUN

not to sleep too _____, or else they risk _____
                  ADVERB   VERB ENDING IN "ING"

in the mud and drowning. Besides, most giants would rather chug Red

_____ all night than get mud on their _____.
 ANIMAL   ARTICLE OF CLOTHING (PLURAL)

MAD LIBS® is fun to play with friends, but you can also play it by yourself! To begin with, DO NOT look at the story on the page below. Fill in the blanks on this page with the words called for. Then, using the words you have selected, fill in the blank spaces in the story.

Now you've created your own hilarious MAD LIBS® game!

CERBERUS TRAINING

PERSON IN ROOM (MALE) _____

NUMBER _____

ANIMAL _____

PLURAL NOUN _____

SILLY WORD _____

NOUN _____

VERB _____

VERB _____

TYPE OF FOOD _____

PART OF THE BODY (PLURAL) _____

VERB _____

PART OF THE BODY _____

ADJECTIVE _____

ADVERB _____

PLURAL NOUN _____

ADJECTIVE _____

VERB _____

NOUN _____

VERB ENDING IN "ING" _____

MAD LIBS®
CERBERUS TRAINING

Here are some tips for training _____, your _____-headed
PERSON IN ROOM (MALE)   NUMBER

guard _____.
ANIMAL

1. **Be consistent.** The same _____ and commands should always
PLURAL NOUN

   apply.

2. **Be concise.** Don't say _____ several times in a/an _____,
SILLY WORD   NOUN

   or else he'll _____ the word out entirely.
VERB

3. **Be generous.** _____ him for being right by giving him treats,
VERB

   like _____—yes, one for each of his _____.
TYPE OF FOOD   PART OF THE BODY (PLURAL)

   But don't over-_____ him! Verbal praise and _____
VERB   PART OF THE BODY

   massages can serve as _____ reinforcement, too.
ADJECTIVE

4. **Be patient.** Understand that training him _____ takes time.
ADVERB

   Don't expect immediate _____. Take a/an _____ tone
PLURAL NOUN   ADJECTIVE

   and _____ at him so he knows you're on his _____.
VERB   NOUN

5. **Lastly, enjoy!** Make sure you both have a good time, and he'll be

   _____ out of your hand in no time.
VERB ENDING IN "ING"

MAD LIBS® is fun to play with friends, but you can also play it by yourself! To begin with, DO NOT look at the story on the page below. Fill in the blanks on this page with the words called for. Then, using the words you have selected, fill in the blank spaces in the story.

Now you've created your own hilarious MAD LIBS® game!

PEGASUS BREAKS GROUND

ANIMAL _____

OCCUPATION _____

VERB ENDING IN "ING" _____

A PLACE _____

PERSON IN ROOM _____

PART OF THE BODY (PLURAL) _____

TYPE OF LIQUID _____

NOUN _____

NUMBER _____

A PLACE _____

CELEBRITY _____

NUMBER _____

CELEBRITY _____

NOUN _____

SILLY WORD _____

VERB ENDING IN "ING" _____

ADJECTIVE _____

Breaking news! A flying _____ escaped from his _____ today
                        ANIMAL   OCCUPATION

while _____ for the Muses in (the) _____.
         VERB ENDING IN "ING"   A PLACE

According to the witness, _____, when the creature dug his
                                PERSON IN ROOM

_____ into the soil, a spring of _____ bubbled
PART OF THE BODY (PLURAL)   TYPE OF LIQUID

up from the ground, forming a/an _____-clear fountain. For the past
                                     NOUN

_____ hours, Muses from as far away as (the) _____ have
   NUMBER   A PLACE

come to see the miracle for themselves. _____ offered to buy the
                                             CELEBRITY

creature for _____ dollars, but _____, backed by a
                 NUMBER   CELEBRITY

crowd of _____-rights activists, insisted the animal isn't for sale. In
            NOUN

related news, the _____ Corporation has already bought
                      SILLY WORD

_____ rights for the fountain and has plans to create a new
VERB ENDING IN "ING"

_____ drink with Pegasus as their mascot.
   ADJECTIVE

MAD LIBS® is fun to play with friends, but you can also play it by yourself! To begin with, DO NOT look at the story on the page below. Fill in the blanks on this page with the words called for. Then, using the words you have selected, fill in the blank spaces in the story.

Now you've created your own hilarious MAD LIBS® game!

COOKING WITH MERMAIDS

PERSON IN ROOM (FEMALE) _____

NUMBER _____

ADJECTIVE _____

NOUN _____

ANIMAL _____

TYPE OF LIQUID _____

NUMBER _____

VERB _____

ADVERB _____

COLOR _____

NUMBER _____

NOUN _____

ADJECTIVE _____

ADJECTIVE _____

PLURAL NOUN _____

VERB ENDING IN "ING" _____

ADJECTIVE _____

A PLACE _____

MAD LIBS®
COOKING WITH MERMAIDS

Here is a recipe for Kraken eggs, from _____'s Underwater
<u>PERSON IN ROOM (FEMALE)</u>

Kitchen. (Serves _____)
<u>NUMBER</u>

Ingredients:

1 _____ egg, stolen from a giant Kraken
<u>ADJECTIVE</u>

4 _____-spoons _____ milk (fresh if possible)
<u>NOUN</u> <u>ANIMAL</u>

3 _____-spoons squid ink
<u>TYPE OF LIQUID</u>

_____ sea urchins (for garnish)
<u>NUMBER</u>

Directions:

_____ the first three ingredients. Beat _____ until the
<u>VERB</u> <u>ADVERB</u>

mixture turns _____ and frothy, about _____ minutes. Using a
<u>COLOR</u> <u>NUMBER</u>

pastry _____, pipe _____ portions of egg batter into a/an
<u>NOUN</u> <u>ADJECTIVE</u>

_____ tide pool. Allow the _____ to cook for four minutes,
<u>ADJECTIVE</u> <u>PLURAL NOUN</u>

_____ them in a net as you go. Serve alongside the
<u>VERB ENDING IN "ING"</u>

_____ urchins. Season with _____ water, to taste.
<u>ADJECTIVE</u> <u>A PLACE</u>

MAD LIBS® is fun to play with friends, but you can also play it by yourself! To begin with, DO NOT look at the story on the page below. Fill in the blanks on this page with the words called for. Then, using the words you have selected, fill in the blank spaces in the story.

Now you've created your own hilarious MAD LIBS® game!

MYTHICAL MONSTERS IN HISTORY

NOUN _____

PART OF THE BODY _____

ANIMAL (PLURAL) _____

NOUN _____

PART OF THE BODY (PLURAL) _____

NOUN _____

ADJECTIVE _____

ADJECTIVE _____

VERB ENDING IN "ING" _____

NOUN _____

PERSON IN ROOM (FEMALE) _____

ANIMAL _____

NOUN _____

TYPE OF LIQUID _____

ADVERB _____

PLURAL NOUN _____

NUMBER _____

MAD●LIBS®
MYTHICAL MONSTERS
IN HISTORY

- **Medusa** was a/an _____ with a hideous _____ and
  NOUN PART OF THE BODY

  venomous _____ for hair. According to _____
  ANIMAL (PLURAL) NOUN

  mythology, looking into Medusa's _____ could turn
  PART OF THE BODY (PLURAL)

  you to _____.
  NOUN

- **Arachne** was born a/an _____ human woman with
  ADJECTIVE

  nothing extra-_____ about her—aside from her talent for
  ADJECTIVE

  _____. After winning a/an _____ against
  VERB ENDING IN "ING" NOUN

  the goddess _____, Arachne was turned into a/an
  PERSON IN ROOM (FEMALE)

  _____.
  ANIMAL

- **The Loch Ness** _____ is a famous "_____ beast"
  NOUN TYPE OF LIQUID

  living in a Scottish lake. "Nessie," as the creature has been _____
  ADVERB

  nicknamed, supposedly appeared on satellite _____ as
  PLURAL NOUN

  recently as _____ years ago.
  NUMBER

MAD LIBS® is fun to play with friends, but you can also play it by yourself! To begin with, DO NOT look at the story on the page below. Fill in the blanks on this page with the words called for. Then, using the words you have selected, fill in the blank spaces in the story.

Now you've created your own hilarious MAD LIBS® game!

LAKE MONSTERS OF NORTH AMERICA

VERB _____

A PLACE _____

NOUN _____

PLURAL NOUN _____

NUMBER _____

TYPE OF LIQUID _____

PLURAL NOUN _____

ANIMAL _____

ADJECTIVE _____

PART OF THE BODY (PLURAL) _____

ANIMAL _____

PART OF THE BODY _____

NOUN _____

ANIMAL _____

FIRST NAME _____

NUMBER _____

Why _____ all the way to (the) _____ when there are
_{VERB} _{A PLACE}

_____ monsters right here at home? Between the United
_{NOUN}

_____ and Canada, North America is home to more than
_{PLURAL NOUN}

_____ lake and river monsters, like giant _____ serpents,
_{NUMBER} _{TYPE OF LIQUID}

crocodilian _____, and _____-like fish with _____
_{PLURAL NOUN} _{ANIMAL} _{ADJECTIVE}

necks and webbed _____. Ontario was once home to
_{PART OF THE BODY (PLURAL)}

Mishipeshu, an "underwater _____" with a catlike _____ and
_{ANIMAL} _{PART OF THE BODY}

claws. And British Columbia is still home to Ogopogo, a/an _____-
_{NOUN}

backed creature with a bearded _____ head. But Canada's favorite
_{ANIMAL}

just might be "_____," which has been described as looking
_{FIRST NAME}

somewhat like a/an _____-eyed Loch Ness Monster.
_{NUMBER}

MAD LIBS® is fun to play with friends, but you can also play it by yourself! To begin with, DO NOT look at the story on the page below. Fill in the blanks on this page with the words called for. Then, using the words you have selected, fill in the blank spaces in the story.

Now you've created your own hilarious MAD LIBS® game!

MOST FAMOUS MERMAIDS

ADJECTIVE _____

ADJECTIVE _____

VERB _____

PLURAL NOUN _____

NOUN _____

FIRST NAME _____

SILLY WORD _____

VERB ENDING IN "ING" _____

A PLACE _____

ADVERB _____

OCCUPATION (PLURAL) _____

NUMBER _____

ADJECTIVE _____

PERSON IN ROOM (FEMALE) _____

ADJECTIVE _____

NOUN _____

LAST NAME _____

NOUN _____

NOUN _____

MAD LIBS®
MOST FAMOUS MERMAIDS

Here is a list of some of the most _____ mermaids in history.

ADJECTIVE

- The Sirens of Greek mythology were _____ but

ADJECTIVE

  dangerous creatures who would _____ sailors with their

VERB

  _____, causing _____-wrecks. They appear in

PLURAL NOUN   NOUN

  both _____'s *Odyssey* and Ovid's _____.

FIRST NAME   SILLY WORD

- The _____ mermaids of Weeki Wachee Springs in (the)

VERB ENDING IN "ING"

  _____ are _____ famous. In the 1960s, these female

A PLACE   ADVERB

  _____ drew nearly _____ tourists per year!

OCCUPATION (PLURAL)   NUMBER

- The most _____ mermaid in the world is probably

ADJECTIVE

  _____, the main character of the animated film

PERSON IN ROOM (FEMALE)

  The _____ *Mermaid.* Based on the _____ tale by

ADJECTIVE   NOUN

  Hans Christian _____, the film tells the story of a teenage

LAST NAME

  _____ who is willing to do whatever it takes to become human.

NOUN

  Even if it means losing her _____!

NOUN

MAD LIBS® is fun to play with friends, but you can also play it by yourself! To begin with, DO NOT look at the story on the page below. Fill in the blanks on this page with the words called for. Then, using the words you have selected, fill in the blank spaces in the story.

Now you've created your own hilarious MAD LIBS® game!

FAERY SIGHTINGS ON THE RISE

NOUN _____

VERB _____

NOUN _____

PLURAL NOUN _____

NOUN _____

LAST NAME _____

OCCUPATION _____

PLURAL NOUN _____

NUMBER _____

ADVERB _____

ADJECTIVE _____

VERB _____

ADJECTIVE _____

PART OF THE BODY _____

PLURAL NOUN _____

NOUN _____

NUMBER _____

Since at least 1927, the Faery Investigation _____ has met to
NOUN

_____ and gather evidence of _____ life in all its reported
VERB   NOUN

forms. In the Society's heyday, it boasted several famous _____,
PLURAL NOUN

including decorated _____ hero Lord _____ and iconic
NOUN   LAST NAME

_____ Walt Disney. Though many of their _____ were
OCCUPATION   PLURAL NOUN

destroyed during World War _____, the Society grew _____
NUMBER   ADVERB

over the decades, until _____ ridicule in the '90s drove the Society to
ADJECTIVE

_____ underground. Today, however, they appear to be as
VERB

_____ as ever, with an active _____-book page and hundreds
ADJECTIVE   PART OF THE BODY

of devoted _____. A recent census conducted by the Society shows
PLURAL NOUN

_____ sightings are on the rise, with _____ occurring in the past
NOUN   NUMBER

year alone.

MAD LIBS® is fun to play with friends, but you can also play it by yourself! To begin with, DO NOT look at the story on the page below. Fill in the blanks on this page with the words called for. Then, using the words you have selected, fill in the blank spaces in the story.

Now you've created your own hilarious MAD LIBS® game!

SATYR PLAY

NOUN _____

ADJECTIVE _____

PERSON IN ROOM (MALE) _____

VERB _____

PLURAL NOUN _____

TYPE OF FOOD _____

NOUN _____

VERB ENDING IN "ING" _____

VERB _____

VERB ENDING IN "ING" _____

ANIMAL _____

SILLY WORD _____

VERB _____

VERB _____

EXCLAMATION _____

VERB ENDING IN "ING" _____

ADJECTIVE _____

MAD LIBS®
SATYR PLAY

First Satyr: OMG, I'm so bored.

Second Satyr: Me too. Let's play a/an _____ on someone!

NOUN

First Satyr: That's a/an _____ idea! But who?

ADJECTIVE

Second Satyr: How about _____? He's dumb enough to

PERSON IN ROOM (MALE)

_____ for anything.

VERB

(The two _____ hide under a/an _____ tree, waiting for

PLURAL NOUN .... TYPE OF FOOD

their _____ to pass by.)

NOUN

First Satyr: Why is he _____ so slow?

VERB ENDING IN "ING"

Second Satyr: I'm so bored I could _____ .

VERB

First Satyr: Wait! He's _____ back around.

VERB ENDING IN "ING"

(Second Satyr makes _____ sounds.)

ANIMAL

First Satyr: What are you doing, _____? He'll _____ you!

SILLY WORD .... VERB

Second Satyr: I know! Maybe he'll _____ this way.

VERB

First Satyr: _____! You totally scared him. Look, he's

EXCLAMATION

_____ away.

VERB ENDING IN "ING"

Second Satyr: Now we're going to be even *more* _____ .

ADJECTIVE

MAD LIBS® is fun to play with friends, but you can also play it by yourself! To begin with, DO NOT look at the story on the page below. Fill in the blanks on this page with the words called for. Then, using the words you have selected, fill in the blank spaces in the story.

Now you've created your own hilarious MAD LIBS® game!

WITNESS INTERVIEW

ANIMAL _____

VERB _____

A PLACE _____

NUMBER _____

PLURAL NOUN _____

PLURAL NOUN _____

NOUN _____

ANIMAL _____

VERB ENDING IN "ING" _____

ARTICLE OF CLOTHING _____

ADJECTIVE _____

ADVERB _____

EXCLAMATION _____

ADJECTIVE _____

PART OF THE BODY (PLURAL) _____

COLOR _____

VERB _____

MAD LIBS
WITNESS INTERVIEW

Kid: I'm telling you, my sister is a were-_____!

ANIMAL

Officer: Slow down! _____ at the beginning.

VERB

Kid: I got home from (the) _____ _____ hours after my curfew.

A PLACE   NUMBER

I tiptoed upstairs without my _____ noticing. That's when I heard

PLURAL NOUN

_____ coming from my sister's _____-room!

PLURAL NOUN   NOUN

Officer: What did you think was happening?

Kid: At first I thought there was a/an _____ in the room with her. Then

ANIMAL

I heard _____ sounds, like someone or something was ripping

VERB ENDING IN "ING"

her _____ apart. I asked her if she was _____, and

ARTICLE OF CLOTHING   ADJECTIVE

when she didn't answer, I knocked as _____ as I could.

ADVERB

Officer: According to your dad, you screamed, "_____!" Why

EXCLAMATION

didn't you call for help?

Kid: The door opened, and that's when I saw her! She had _____ claws,

ADJECTIVE

and whiskers had grown out of her _____. She looked at me

PART OF THE BODY (PLURAL)

with _____ eyes, and growled, "_____ your own business, twerp!"

COLOR   VERB

MAD LIBS® is fun to play with friends, but you can also play it by yourself! To begin with, DO NOT look at the story on the page below. Fill in the blanks on this page with the words called for. Then, using the words you have selected, fill in the blank spaces in the story.

Now you've created your own hilarious MAD LIBS® game!

RIDDLE OF THE SPHINX

A PLACE _____

NOUN _____

ANIMAL _____

VERB (PAST TENSE) _____

VERB ENDING IN "S" _____

PART OF THE BODY (PLURAL) _____

NUMBER _____

NOUN _____

FIRST NAME (MALE) _____

NOUN _____

VERB _____

VERB ENDING IN "S" _____

ADJECTIVE _____

NOUN _____

ADJECTIVE _____

NOUN _____

OCCUPATION _____

MAD LIBS®
RIDDLE OF THE SPHINX

According to legends of (the) _____, the Sphinx had the
                                    A PLACE

_____ of a human and the body of a/an _____. She killed
    NOUN   ANIMAL

and _____ any travelers who couldn't answer
            VERB (PAST TENSE)

the following question: "What creature _____ on four
                                            VERB ENDING IN "S"

_____ in the morning, _____ legs at noon, and three
PART OF THE BODY (PLURAL)   NUMBER

in the _____?" Only the hero _____ gave the correct
            NOUN   FIRST NAME (MALE)

answer, leading to the Sphinx's _____. "Man," he said. "Because a
                                        NOUN

baby has to _____ before he can walk. Then he _____
                 VERB   VERB ENDING IN "S"

on two legs until he's _____. At which point, he uses a/an
                            ADJECTIVE

_____ to keep his balance." The Sphinx was so _____ that
    NOUN   ADJECTIVE

her riddle had been solved that she threw herself off a high _____ and
                                                                  NOUN

died. Talk about a drama _____!
                              OCCUPATION

MAD LIBS® is fun to play with friends, but you can also play it by yourself! To begin with, DO NOT look at the story on the page below. Fill in the blanks on this page with the words called for. Then, using the words you have selected, fill in the blank spaces in the story.

Now you've created your own hilarious MAD LIBS® game!

HOW TO RIDE A UNICORN

NOUN _____

ADVERB _____

VERB _____

ADJECTIVE _____

TYPE OF FOOD _____

ADJECTIVE _____

PART OF THE BODY (PLURAL) _____

NOUN _____

SILLY WORD _____

VERB ENDING IN "ING" _____

PART OF THE BODY _____

SAME PART OF THE BODY _____

ADJECTIVE _____

VERB _____

TYPE OF LIQUID _____

VERB _____

Dos:

- Unicorns don't have _____-belts, so it's important to hold on
  NOUN

  _____ at all times.
  ADVERB

- Because they can _____ your mind, it's crucial to think only
  VERB

  _____ thoughts while riding a uni-_____.
  ADJECTIVE   TYPE OF FOOD

- If touching a unicorn's _____ horn becomes necessary, be
  ADJECTIVE

  sure to warm up your _____ first. (They are quite
  PART OF THE BODY (PLURAL)

  sensitive to changes in _____.)
  NOUN

Don'ts:

- Don't say "yeehaw" or "_____." The unicorn will think you're
  SILLY WORD

  _____ fun of it.
  VERB ENDING IN "ING"

- Never stand _____ to _____ with a unicorn for
  PART OF THE BODY   SAME PART OF THE BODY

  too long (for _____ reasons).
  ADJECTIVE

- Whatever you do, never, ever _____ unicorn
  VERB

  _____! It is deadly to the touch and will _____
  TYPE OF LIQUID   VERB

  you for sure. Happy riding!

MAD LIBS® is fun to play with friends, but you can also play it by yourself! To begin with, DO NOT look at the story on the page below. Fill in the blanks on this page with the words called for. Then, using the words you have selected, fill in the blank spaces in the story.

Now you've created your own hilarious MAD LIBS® game!

CENTAUR WRESTLING

ADJECTIVE _____

COLOR _____

SILLY WORD _____

ANIMAL _____

VERB _____

NOUN _____

CELEBRITY _____

COLOR _____

VERB ENDING IN "ING" _____

NOUN _____

PLURAL NOUN _____

OCCUPATION (PLURAL) _____

PART OF THE BODY _____

NUMBER _____

PLURAL NOUN _____

VERB ENDING IN "ING" _____

NOUN _____

MAD LIBS®
CENTAUR WRESTLING

The crowd goes _____ as the _____ Whiz and _____
           ADJECTIVE   COLOR   SILLY WORD

Joe enter the ring. Each of these twin centaurs is half Appaloosa _____
          ANIMAL

and half man. They are favored to _____ tonight at the match in
           VERB

_____ City. Entering the ring behind them is _____'s
  NOUN   CELEBRITY

dream duo, the _____ Stallions. The crowd makes _____
        COLOR   VERB ENDING IN "ING"

sounds at the hated visiting team. Following the sound of a/an

_____-shot, all four heavyweight _____ gallop against
  NOUN   PLURAL NOUN

one another. The Stallions have arms like human _____, which
                            OCCUPATION (PLURAL)

they use to put both their opponents in instant _____-locks. The
                      PART OF THE BODY

referee counts all the way to _____ before the Whiz and Joe break free.
           NUMBER

Against all _____, the hometown heroes manage to dominate the
    PLURAL NOUN

Stallions, _____ them to the mat for the full count. The referee
  VERB ENDING IN "ING"

calls it. The Stallions have lost. The _____ goes wild!
                        NOUN

MAD LIBS® is fun to play with friends, but you can also play it by yourself! To begin with, DO NOT look at the story on the page below. Fill in the blanks on this page with the words called for. Then, using the words you have selected, fill in the blank spaces in the story.

Now you've created your own hilarious MAD LIBS® game!

INTERVIEW WITH A BANSHEE

SILLY WORD _____

A PLACE _____

VERB _____

PART OF THE BODY (PLURAL) _____

NOUN _____

NOUN _____

VERB _____

ANIMAL (PLURAL) _____

ADJECTIVE _____

VERB ENDING IN "ING" _____

NUMBER _____

ADJECTIVE _____

PLURAL NOUN _____

NOUN _____

NOUN _____

News Anchor: I'm here with _____, a real-life banshee who
<u>SILLY WORD</u>

has agreed to talk to us about what it's like living as a monster in (the)

_____.
<u>A PLACE</u>

Banshee: Everyone expects me to _____ all the time, at the top of my
<u>VERB</u>

_____, but I'm actually a fairly quiet person.
<u>PART OF THE BODY (PLURAL)</u>

News Anchor: So you're a/an _____ that doesn't scream?
<u>NOUN</u>

Banshee: I scream as loudly as the next _____. But only when
<u>NOUN</u>

someone is about to _____. A kind of death call. And my neighbors
<u>VERB</u>

aren't exactly dropping like _____.
<u>ANIMAL (PLURAL)</u>

News Anchor: So you don't pose a/an _____ threat to the community
<u>ADJECTIVE</u>

here?

Banshee: Of course not! If anything, I'd be an asset to the

Neighborhood Watch because I can sense danger _____ from
<u>VERB ENDING IN "ING"</u>

_____ miles away.
<u>NUMBER</u>

News Anchor: I feel more _____ already! You heard it here first,
<u>ADJECTIVE</u>

_____ and gentlemen. Banshees mean no _____, so give
<u>PLURAL NOUN</u>   <u>NOUN</u>

them all a/an _____, why don't you?
<u>NOUN</u>

MAD LIBS® is fun to play with friends, but you can also play it by yourself! To begin with, DO NOT look at the story on the page below. Fill in the blanks on this page with the words called for. Then, using the words you have selected, fill in the blank spaces in the story.

Now you've created your own hilarious MAD LIBS® game!

MONSTER BONES

LAST NAME _____

OCCUPATION _____

NOUN _____

A PLACE _____

NUMBER _____

PLURAL NOUN _____

PLURAL NOUN _____

NUMBER _____

ADJECTIVE _____

VERB (PAST TENSE) _____

ANIMAL _____

ADJECTIVE _____

ADJECTIVE _____

NOUN _____

PART OF THE BODY _____

NOUN _____

ADJECTIVE _____

PLURAL NOUN _____

MAD LIBS®
MONSTER BONES

Dr. _____, the world's leading crypto-_____,
　　　LAST NAME　　　　　　　　　　　　　　　　　　　　OCCUPATION

asserts that there isn't a/an _____ of proof that the fabled Cyclops ever
　　　　　　　　　　　　　　　NOUN

existed in (the) _____. "For more than _____ years," she said,
　　　　　　　　A PLACE　　　　　　　　　　　　NUMBER

"_____ have brought me what they were certain were
　　PLURAL NOUN

_____ belonging to the _____-eyed beasts. But they were all
　　PLURAL NOUN　　　　　　　　　　NUMBER

_____. What they had _____ were in fact ordinary
　ADJECTIVE　　　　　　　　　　VERB (PAST TENSE)

_____ skulls! It was a/an _____ enough mistake considering
　ANIMAL　　　　　　　　　　　　ADJECTIVE

that each had a/an _____ hole at the center where the living animal's
　　　　　　　　　ADJECTIVE

_____ would be, the same size and position as a Cyclops's
　NOUN

_____ socket." The scholar wants nothing more than to put the
PART OF THE BODY

_____ to rest, once and for all. "I have _____ work to do!"
　NOUN　　　　　　　　　　　　　　　　　　　　　ADJECTIVE

she says. "I can't spend all day teaching elephant anatomy to _____."
　　　　　　　　　　　　　　　　　　　　　　　　　　　　　　PLURAL NOUN

MAD LIBS®

DOG ATE MY MAD LIBS

by Leigh Olsen

INSTRUCTIONS

MAD LIBS® is a game for people who don't like games!
It can be played by one, two, three, four, or forty.

• RIDICULOUSLY SIMPLE DIRECTIONS

In this tablet you will find stories containing blank spaces where words are left out. One player, the READER, selects one of these stories. The READER does not tell anyone what the story is about. Instead, he/she asks the other players, the WRITERS, to give him/her words. These words are used to fill in the blank spaces in the story.

• TO PLAY

The READER asks each WRITER in turn to call out a word—an adjective or a noun or whatever the space calls for—and uses them to fill in the blank spaces in the story. The result is a MAD LIBS® game.

When the READER then reads the completed MAD LIBS® game to the other players, they will discover that they have written a story that is fantastic, screamingly funny, shocking, silly, crazy, or just plain dumb—depending upon which words each WRITER called out.

• EXAMPLE (*Before* and *After*)

"_____!" he said _____
    EXCLAMATION   ADVERB

as he jumped into his convertible _____ and
                                               NOUN

drove off with his _____ wife.
                          ADJECTIVE

"_____OUCH_____!" he said _____HAPPILY_____
    EXCLAMATION   ADVERB

as he jumped into his convertible _____CAT_____ and
                                               NOUN

drove off with his _____BRAVE_____ wife.
                          ADJECTIVE

MAD LIBS®

QUICK REVIEW

In case you have forgotten what adjectives, adverbs, nouns, and verbs are, here is a quick review:

An ADJECTIVE describes something or somebody. *Lumpy, soft, ugly, messy,* and *short* are adjectives.

An ADVERB tells how something is done. It modifies a verb and usually ends in "ly." *Modestly, stupidly, greedily,* and *carefully* are adverbs.

A NOUN is the name of a person, place, or thing. *Sidewalk, umbrella, bridle, bathtub,* and *nose* are nouns.

A VERB is an action word. *Run, pitch, jump,* and *swim* are verbs. Put the verbs in past tense if the directions say PAST TENSE. *Ran, pitched, jumped,* and *swam* are verbs in the past tense.

When we ask for A PLACE, we mean any sort of place: a country or city *(Spain, Cleveland)* or a room *(bathroom, kitchen).*

An EXCLAMATION or SILLY WORD is any sort of funny sound, gasp, grunt, or outcry, like *Wow!, Ouch!, Whomp!, Ick!,* and *Gadzooks!*

When we ask for specific words, like a NUMBER, a COLOR, an ANIMAL, or a PART OF THE BODY, we mean a word that is one of those things, like *seven, blue, horse,* or *head.*

When we ask for a PLURAL, it means more than one. For example, *cat* pluralized is *cats.*

MAD LIBS® is fun to play with friends, but you can also play it by yourself! To begin with, DO NOT look at the story on the page below. Fill in the blanks on this page with the words called for. Then, using the words you have selected, fill in the blank spaces in the story.

Now you've created your own hilarious MAD LIBS® game!

DOG DAYS

VERB ENDING IN "ING" _____

PART OF THE BODY _____

PLURAL NOUN _____

VERB _____

NOUN _____

A PLACE _____

ADVERB _____

NOUN _____

PLURAL NOUN _____

PART OF THE BODY _____

PART OF THE BODY _____

PLURAL NOUN _____

PLURAL NOUN _____

NOUN _____

MAD LIBS®
DOG DAYS

Have you always wondered what it's like to be a dog?

7:00 a.m.: I wake up and my tummy is _____.
                                          VERB ENDING IN "ING"
I bug my human by licking her _____ until I get a bowl of _____.
                               PART OF THE BODY   PLURAL NOUN

7:30 a.m.: Potty time! My human takes me outside to _____ on a/an
                                                      VERB
_____.
    NOUN

8:00 a.m.: My human leaves to go to (the) _____. I am sad and pout
                                            A PLACE
_____.
   ADVERB

9:00 a.m.: Nap time. I cuddle on my favorite _____ and dream about
                                               NOUN
chasing _____.
         PLURAL NOUN

6:00 p.m.: MY HUMAN IS HOME! FINALLY! I wag my _____
                                                 PART OF THE BODY
back and forth, and give my human kisses on the _____.
                                                 PART OF THE BODY

6:30 p.m.: My human takes me for a walk, and I sniff lots of _____.
                                                              PLURAL NOUN

7:00 p.m.: Dinnertime! Eating _____ is my favorite!
                               PLURAL NOUN

9:00 p.m.: I snuggle up next to my human and fall asleep, happy as
a/an _____.
        NOUN

MAD LIBS® is fun to play with friends, but you can also play it by yourself! To begin with, DO NOT look at the story on the page below. Fill in the blanks on this page with the words called for. Then, using the words you have selected, fill in the blank spaces in the story.

Now you've created your own hilarious MAD LIBS® game!

WHO'S THAT DOG?, PART 1

A PLACE _____

NOUN _____

PLURAL NOUN _____

VERB _____

VERB ENDING IN "ING" _____

ADJECTIVE _____

ADJECTIVE _____

ADJECTIVE _____

NOUN _____

ADJECTIVE _____

ADJECTIVE _____

VERB _____

A PLACE _____

NOUN _____

With hundreds of breeds of dogs in (the) _____, there's one for every
<u>A PLACE</u>

kind of _____. Here are a few popular breeds:
<u>NOUN</u>

Golden retriever: The golden retriever is one of the most popular family

_____. Intelligent and eager to _____, the golden retriever
<u>PLURAL NOUN</u>   <u>VERB</u>

makes an excellent _____ companion, and is also a/an
<u>VERB ENDING IN "ING"</u>

_____ guide dog.
<u>ADJECTIVE</u>

Pug: The pug is a lot of dog in a very _____ package. It is known
<u>ADJECTIVE</u>

for being loving, outgoing, and _____. And it snores like a freight
<u>ADJECTIVE</u>

_____!
<u>NOUN</u>

Siberian husky: The husky was bred to pull _____ sleds, and it is
<u>ADJECTIVE</u>

known for its _____ endurance and willingness to _____.
<u>ADJECTIVE</u>   <u>VERB</u>

German shepherd: The German shepherd is not only the most popular police,

guard, and military dog in (the) _____, it is also a loving family
<u>A PLACE</u>

_____.
<u>NOUN</u>

MAD LIBS® is fun to play with friends, but you can also play it by yourself! To begin with, DO NOT look at the story on the page below. Fill in the blanks on this page with the words called for. Then, using the words you have selected, fill in the blank spaces in the story.

Now you've created your own hilarious MAD LIBS® game!

FAMOUS FIDOS: RIN TIN TIN

NOUN _____

PERSON IN ROOM _____

A PLACE _____

VERB _____

CELEBRITY _____

PERSON IN ROOM _____

ADJECTIVE _____

A PLACE _____

NOUN _____

NOUN _____

ADJECTIVE _____

PLURAL NOUN _____

NOUN _____

MAD LIBS
FAMOUS FIDOS: RIN TIN TIN

Rin Tin Tin was the biggest movie-star pooch to ever grace the silver

_____. During World War I, Rin Tin Tin's owner and future
　　　NOUN

trainer, _____, discovered the German shepherd puppy on a war-
　　　PERSON IN ROOM

torn battlefield in (the) _____. He brought Rin Tin Tin back
　　　　　　　　A PLACE

to the United States, trained him to _____, and brought him to
　　　　　　　　　　　　VERB

Hollywood, home to celebrities like _____ and _____.
　　　　　　　　　　　　　CELEBRITY　　　　　PERSON IN ROOM

Soon, Rin Tin Tin began to receive _____ roles in silent films!
　　　　　　　　　　　　　ADJECTIVE

He quickly became one of the most famous stars in (the) _____.
　　　　　　　　　　　　　　　　　　　A PLACE

In 1929, Rin Tin Tin even received the most votes for the Academy Award

for Best _____—but the Academy decided to give the award to
　　　NOUN

a/an _____ instead. All in all, this _____ dog starred in
　　　NOUN　　　　　　　　　　　　　ADJECTIVE

twenty-seven major motion _____. He even has his own star on the
　　　　　　　　　　PLURAL NOUN

Hollywood Walk of _____!
　　　　　　NOUN

MAD LIBS® is fun to play with friends, but you can also play it by yourself! To begin with, DO NOT look at the story on the page below. Fill in the blanks on this page with the words called for. Then, using the words you have selected, fill in the blank spaces in the story.

Now you've created your own hilarious MAD LIBS® game!

ODE TO THE MUTT

ADJECTIVE _____

PART OF THE BODY _____

PLURAL NOUN _____

PLURAL NOUN _____

PLURAL NOUN _____

NOUN _____

PART OF THE BODY _____

NOUN _____

NOUN _____

A PLACE _____

ANIMAL _____

ADJECTIVE _____

MAD LIBS®
ODE TO THE MUTT

A little bit of this and a little bit of that, the mutt is a/an _____
 ADJECTIVE

mixed-breed pup that will warm your _____ and chase your
 PART OF THE BODY

_____ away. First of all, mutts are just like snowflakes—no two
 PLURAL NOUN

_____ are alike! Mutts come in all shapes and _____.
 PLURAL NOUN   PLURAL NOUN

Big ones, small ones, fluffy ones, and scruffy ones—there's a mutt for every

_____. Mutts have a special way of worming their way into your
 NOUN

_____. There are millions in shelters that need your love and
 PART OF THE BODY

_____. They need your love more than the average _____,
 NOUN   NOUN

and they'll love you to (the) _____ and back! So next time you are
 A PLACE

thinking about bringing home a new _____, consider adopting a/an
 ANIMAL

_____ mutt!
 ADJECTIVE

MAD LIBS® is fun to play with friends, but you can also play it by yourself! To begin with, DO NOT look at the story on the page below. Fill in the blanks on this page with the words called for. Then, using the words you have selected, fill in the blank spaces in the story.

Now you've created your own hilarious MAD LIBS® game!

BEGGING 101

NOUN _____

ADJECTIVE _____

PLURAL NOUN _____

NOUN _____

NOUN _____

PART OF THE BODY (PLURAL) _____

ADJECTIVE _____

PART OF THE BODY (PLURAL) _____

ADVERB _____

ADJECTIVE _____

NOUN _____

TYPE OF FOOD _____

PERSON IN ROOM _____

Are your humans cooking a delicious-smelling _____? Learn to

NOUN

beg like a pro with these _____ tips, and you'll be eating tasty

ADJECTIVE

_____ in no time!

PLURAL NOUN

- Identify the weakest _____ at the dinner table. Who is the most likely

NOUN

 to sneak you a/an _____? Sit as close to that person as possible.

NOUN

- Stare up at your target with your biggest, saddest puppy-dog

 _____. If possible, think of something that makes you

PART OF THE BODY (PLURAL)

 feel _____ so you can work up some tears.

ADJECTIVE

- Squint your _____ so you look extra weak and hungry.

PART OF THE BODY (PLURAL)

 Lie down on the ground and pout _____. Basically, make yourself

ADVERB

 look as pathetic and _____ as possible.

ADJECTIVE

- Still not getting any food? Try crying like a/an _____.

NOUN

- If all else fails, grab that delicious _____ with your teeth and

TYPE OF FOOD

 make a run for it—quick! Before _____ catches you!

PERSON IN ROOM

MAD LIBS® is fun to play with friends, but you can also play it by yourself! To begin with, DO NOT look at the story on the page below. Fill in the blanks on this page with the words called for. Then, using the words you have selected, fill in the blank spaces in the story.

Now you've created your own hilarious MAD LIBS® game!

DOGGY DREAMS

ADJECTIVE _____

PART OF THE BODY (PLURAL) _____

ADVERB _____

ADJECTIVE _____

EXCLAMATION _____

VERB ENDING IN "ING" _____

NOUN _____

PART OF THE BODY (PLURAL) _____

EXCLAMATION _____

NOUN _____

SAME NOUN _____

PLURAL NOUN _____

VERB _____

PART OF THE BODY (PLURAL) _____

PLURAL NOUN _____

PERSON IN ROOM _____

PART OF THE BODY _____

ADJECTIVE _____

MAD LIBS®
DOGGY DREAMS

You know what it looks like when your sleeping dog is having a/an _____
                                                                    ADJECTIVE

dream: Their tail swishes, their _____ twitch, and they
                                 PART OF THE BODY (PLURAL)

bark _____. But what do dogs dream about? Here's one dog's
     ADVERB

_____ dream:
ADJECTIVE

_____! What's that little flash of white fur _____
EXCLAMATION   VERB ENDING IN "ING"

in my backyard? It's a bunny _____! I have to chase it! I run, run,
                             NOUN

run, as fast as my _____ will carry me. Oh, _____!
                   PART OF THE BODY (PLURAL)   EXCLAMATION

The bunny has hidden in a/an _____! I sniff the _____,
                            NOUN   SAME NOUN

and sure enough, it's in there with a den of baby _____! I want
                                                  PLURAL NOUN

to play with them so bad, I could _____! I bark at the top of my
                                  VERB

_____. Come out and play, you fluffy little _____!
PART OF THE BODY (PLURAL)   PLURAL NOUN

But before I can, _____ scratches my _____ and wakes
                  PERSON IN ROOM   PART OF THE BODY

me up. It was all just a/an _____ dream!
                            ADJECTIVE

MAD LIBS® is fun to play with friends, but you can also play it by yourself! To begin with, DO NOT look at the story on the page below. Fill in the blanks on this page with the words called for. Then, using the words you have selected, fill in the blank spaces in the story.

Now you've created your own hilarious MAD LIBS® game!

WHO'S THAT DOG?, PART 2

ADJECTIVE _____

VERB _____

ADJECTIVE _____

ADJECTIVE _____

PART OF THE BODY (PLURAL) _____

ADJECTIVE _____

ADJECTIVE _____

PLURAL NOUN _____

ADJECTIVE _____

PLURAL NOUN _____

NOUN _____

NOUN _____

More _____ dog breeds for you to love and _____!

ADJECTIVE · VERB

Poodle: The curly-haired poodle, best known for its _____ haircut,

ADJECTIVE

is exceptionally smart and _____.

ADJECTIVE

Dachshund: Known for its long body and short _____,

PART OF THE BODY (PLURAL)

the dachshund has a friendly personality and a/an _____ sense of

ADJECTIVE

smell.

Beagle: This hunting dog is happy-go-_____, friendly, and loves

ADJECTIVE

the company of humans and other _____.

PLURAL NOUN

Great Dane: The gentle Great Dane, famous for its _____ size, is

ADJECTIVE

also known as "the king of _____."

PLURAL NOUN

Chihuahua: This sassy little _____, often called a "purse dog," is a

NOUN

big dog in a little _____.

NOUN

MAD LIBS® is fun to play with friends, but you can also play it by yourself! To begin with, DO NOT look at the story on the page below. Fill in the blanks on this page with the words called for. Then, using the words you have selected, fill in the blank spaces in the story.

Now you've created your own hilarious MAD LIBS® game!

FAMOUS FIDOS: LASSIE

ADJECTIVE _____

ADJECTIVE _____

A PLACE _____

PERSON IN ROOM (MALE) _____

ADJECTIVE _____

ADJECTIVE _____

VERB _____

ADVERB _____

PERSON IN ROOM (MALE) _____

NOUN _____

NOUN _____

NOUN _____

ADJECTIVE _____

NOUN _____

Lassie the collie was famous for her heroics on television and the

_____ screen. On the TV show *Lassie*, the collie lived in
ADJECTIVE

a/an _____ farming community in (the) _____. Lassie
ADJECTIVE   A PLACE

belonged to an eleven-year-old boy named _____, as well as
PERSON IN ROOM (MALE)

his mother and _____ grandfather. Whenever the _____
ADJECTIVE   ADJECTIVE

boy got into trouble, Lassie would _____ to the rescue, or she would
VERB

run and find help. "BARK, BARK!" Lassie would say _____.
ADVERB

"What's that, girl?" the person would ask. "Little _____ fell
PERSON IN ROOM (MALE)

down a/an _____?" Quick as a/an _____, the trapped
NOUN   NOUN

_____ would be safe and _____. And once again, Lassie
NOUN   ADJECTIVE

saved the _____!
NOUN

MAD LIBS® is fun to play with friends, but you can also play it by yourself! To begin with, DO NOT look at the story on the page below. Fill in the blanks on this page with the words called for. Then, using the words you have selected, fill in the blank spaces in the story.

Now you've created your own hilarious MAD LIBS® game!

HAIL TO THE POOCH

PERSON IN ROOM_____

ADJECTIVE_____

ADJECTIVE_____

PLURAL NOUN_____

TYPE OF FOOD_____

NOUN_____

ADJECTIVE_____

ADJECTIVE_____

NOUN_____

NOUN_____

CELEBRITY_____

NOUN_____

MAD LIBS®
HAIL TO THE POOCH

From George Washington to _____ to Barack Obama, many
PERSON IN ROOM

United States presidents have been _____ dog lovers. Here's a list of
ADJECTIVE

_____ First Dogs:
ADJECTIVE

- **Laddie Boy:** Warren G. Harding once invited neighborhood _____
  PLURAL NOUN

  to the White House for his Airedale terrier's birthday party, where they ate

  _____ made of dog biscuits!
  TYPE OF FOOD

- **Fala:** Franklin Delano Roosevelt's beloved Scottish terrier was

  named after an Army _____ and had his own _____
  NOUN   ADJECTIVE

  secretary. Fala even starred in a/an _____ movie!
  ADJECTIVE

- **Millie:** George H. W. Bush's springer spaniel published her own book,

  ghostwritten by the First _____, which sold more copies than
  NOUN

  President Bush's _____!
  NOUN

- **Bo and Sunny:** Barack Obama received Bo the Portuguese water dog as a

  gift from _____. A few years later, the First Family got Sunny,
  CELEBRITY

  another Portuguese water _____.
  NOUN

MAD LIBS® is fun to play with friends, but you can also play it by yourself! To begin with, DO NOT look at the story on the page below. Fill in the blanks on this page with the words called for. Then, using the words you have selected, fill in the blank spaces in the story.

Now you've created your own hilarious MAD LIBS® game!

CANINE CAREERS

PLURAL NOUN _____

ADJECTIVE _____

ANIMAL (PLURAL) _____

A PLACE _____

A PLACE _____

ADJECTIVE _____

PLURAL NOUN _____

PART OF THE BODY (PLURAL) _____

PLURAL NOUN _____

PLURAL NOUN _____

ADJECTIVE _____

ADJECTIVE _____

PART OF THE BODY (PLURAL) _____

PLURAL NOUN _____

MAD LIBS®
CANINE CAREERS

Not all dogs nap and play with their toy _____ all day. Some dogs
PLURAL NOUN

have _____ jobs!
ADJECTIVE

- **Guide dogs:** Guide dogs, or Seeing Eye _____, help lead
ANIMAL (PLURAL)

the blind where they need to go, like to (the) _____ or (the)
A PLACE

_____.
A PLACE

- **Military dogs:** These dogs help troops in _____ military
ADJECTIVE

missions. They act as guard dogs, looking out for _____, and
PLURAL NOUN

they use their powerful _____ to sniff out dangerous
PART OF THE BODY (PLURAL)

_____. US Air Force dogs even jump out of flying _____
PLURAL NOUN   PLURAL NOUN

with their airmen!

- **Search-and-rescue dogs:** In a/an _____ disaster or
ADJECTIVE

in the _____ wilderness, these dogs use their powerful
ADJECTIVE

_____ to help track down missing _____.
PART OF THE BODY (PLURAL)   PLURAL NOUN

MAD LIBS® is fun to play with friends, but you can also play it by yourself! To begin with, DO NOT look at the story on the page below. Fill in the blanks on this page with the words called for. Then, using the words you have selected, fill in the blank spaces in the story.

Now you've created your own hilarious MAD LIBS® game!

DIVA DOG

ADJECTIVE _____

NOUN _____

PART OF THE BODY _____

SILLY WORD _____

SAME SILLY WORD _____

A PLACE _____

NOUN _____

NOUN _____

NOUN _____

PART OF THE BODY _____

ADJECTIVE _____

VERB ENDING IN "S" _____

ADJECTIVE _____

PART OF THE BODY _____

ADJECTIVE _____

NOUN _____

MAD LIBS®
DIVA DOG

Who's that _____ pooch with the fluffy little _____
            ADJECTIVE   NOUN

and the cute _____? Why, that's Little Miss _____!
              PART OF THE BODY   SILLY WORD

Little Miss _____ is famous throughout (the) _____.
            SAME SILLY WORD   A PLACE

Her _____ is splashed all over the Internet, and in books and
        NOUN

magazines like _____ *Weekly* and *Life &* _____. Little
                    NOUN   NOUN

Miss can't go anywhere without someone recognizing her _____!
                                                          PART OF THE BODY

Luckily, Little Miss likes attention from the _____ pup-parazzi. She
                                                  ADJECTIVE

_____ for the cameras, and greets all her _____ fans with
VERB ENDING IN "S"   ADJECTIVE

a smile on her _____. After all, without her _____ fans,
                PART OF THE BODY   ADJECTIVE

Little Miss would be just another cute face in the _____!
                                                      NOUN

MAD LIBS® is fun to play with friends, but you can also play it by yourself! To begin with, DO NOT look at the story on the page below. Fill in the blanks on this page with the words called for. Then, using the words you have selected, fill in the blank spaces in the story.

Now you've created your own hilarious MAD LIBS® game!

WHO'S THAT DOG?, PART 3

NOUN _____

ADJECTIVE _____

ANIMAL (PLURAL) _____

NOUN _____

NOUN _____

PART OF THE BODY _____

NOUN _____

PART OF THE BODY _____

NOUN _____

PLURAL NOUN _____

VERB ENDING IN "ING" _____

PLURAL NOUN _____

PART OF THE BODY _____

NOUN _____

PLURAL NOUN _____

A few more dog breeds to brighten your _____!

_____ NOUN

Yorkshire terrier: Yorkies may be small, but they are brave and _____.

_____ ADJECTIVE

Yorkies were originally bred to hunt _____ in _____

_____ ANIMAL (PLURAL) _____ NOUN

factories!

Doberman pinscher: The Doberman is a muscular _____. With

_____ NOUN

its intelligent _____ , the Doberman is often trained as a police

_____ PART OF THE BODY

_____.

NOUN

Shih tzu: The shih tzu has a long and luxurious _____. This

_____ PART OF THE BODY

playful _____ is usually friendly toward all _____.

_____ NOUN _____ PLURAL NOUN

Australian shepherd: Aussies are very energetic and require daily

_____ to be happy. They are great at herding crowds of

VERB ENDING IN "ING"

_____ on the farm.

PLURAL NOUN

Pomeranian: The Pomeranian has a big, fluffy _____ to match

_____ PART OF THE BODY

its outgoing _____. This intelligent little dog loves to please its

_____ NOUN

_____.

PLURAL NOUN

MAD LIBS® is fun to play with friends, but you can also play it by yourself! To begin with, DO NOT look at the story on the page below. Fill in the blanks on this page with the words called for. Then, using the words you have selected, fill in the blank spaces in the story.

Now you've created your own hilarious MAD LIBS® game!

POOCH PALACE

ADJECTIVE _____

ANIMAL _____

NOUN _____

TYPE OF LIQUID _____

ADJECTIVE _____

PART OF THE BODY _____

OCCUPATION _____

NOUN _____

SILLY WORD _____

PART OF THE BODY _____

A PLACE _____

PART OF THE BODY _____

NOUN _____

PLURAL NOUN _____

Welcome to the _____ Pooch Palace, the dog spa for all your

ADJECTIVE

grooming needs! Below is our spa menu. How do you want to pamper your

_____ today?

ANIMAL

- **Paw-dicure:** We'll not only trim your _____'s nails, we'll paint

NOUN

  them with a coat of _____ so your pup looks _____

TYPE OF LIQUID   ADJECTIVE

  and stylish.

- **Pup massage:** If your dog is in need of some rest and relaxation,

  a/an _____ massage might be just what the _____

PART OF THE BODY   OCCUPATION

  ordered!

- **Doggy 'do:** Is your _____ looking shaggy? Our renowned stylist,

NOUN

  Pierre _____, gives the best _____-cut this side of

SILLY WORD   PART OF THE BODY

  (the) _____.

A PLACE

- **Fur dye:** If you've ever wanted your dog's _____ to match the

PART OF THE BODY

  color of your favorite _____, look no further. The Pooch Palace

NOUN

  will make all your _____ come true!

PLURAL NOUN

MAD LIBS® is fun to play with friends, but you can also play it by yourself! To begin with, DO NOT look at the story on the page below. Fill in the blanks on this page with the words called for. Then, using the words you have selected, fill in the blank spaces in the story.

Now you've created your own hilarious MAD LIBS® game!

HOMEWARD BOUND

A PLACE _____

ADJECTIVE _____

PERSON IN ROOM (FEMALE) _____

NUMBER _____

VERB (PAST TENSE) _____

PERSON IN ROOM _____

PART OF THE BODY (PLURAL) _____

NOUN _____

ADJECTIVE _____

NOUN _____

NOUN _____

PERSON IN ROOM _____

TYPE OF LIQUID _____

ADJECTIVE _____

MAD LIBS
HOMEWARD BOUND

In (the) _____ today, one _____ family was reunited with
     A PLACE   ADJECTIVE

their beloved dog, _____, who made her way home after
                 PERSON IN ROOM (FEMALE)

being missing for _____ days. "She just showed up on our front
                NUMBER

doorstep this morning and _____," said _____. "We
                  VERB (PAST TENSE)   PERSON IN ROOM

couldn't believe our _____." The family dog disappeared
                PART OF THE BODY (PLURAL)

after leaving the family's front yard to chase after a wild _____ one
                                       NOUN

afternoon, and the family has been worried _____ ever since. They
                              ADJECTIVE

put up "lost _____" posters all over the neighborhood, and even
          NOUN

put a/an _____ in the local newspaper. "We have no idea where
          NOUN

she's been all this time," said _____. "We're just happier than
                    PERSON IN ROOM

a pig in _____ that she's home again. We can't wait to spoil her
      TYPE OF LIQUID

_____."
  ADJECTIVE

MAD LIBS® is fun to play with friends, but you can also play it by yourself! To begin with, DO NOT look at the story on the page below. Fill in the blanks on this page with the words called for. Then, using the words you have selected, fill in the blank spaces in the story.

Now you've created your own hilarious MAD LIBS® game!

WONDER DOG

VERB _____

ADJECTIVE _____

PART OF THE BODY (PLURAL) _____

ADJECTIVE _____

NOUN _____

PART OF THE BODY _____

VERB ENDING IN "ING" _____

ADJECTIVE _____

PART OF THE BODY (PLURAL) _____

ADVERB _____

NOUN _____

ADJECTIVE _____

PLURAL NOUN _____

ADJECTIVE _____

ADJECTIVE _____

ADVERB _____

VERB _____

Lots of dogs can sit, stay, and _____. But not many can do these

VERB

_____ tricks!

ADJECTIVE

- **Play dead:** When you say, "Bang! Bang!" some dogs will roll onto their

_____ and act _____. This act is sure to

PART OF THE BODY (PLURAL)   ADJECTIVE

tickle your funny _____.

NOUN

- **Dance:** Your dog may know how to wag its _____ to the beat,

PART OF THE BODY

but can it dance like nobody's _____? A dog that knows

VERB ENDING IN "ING"

this _____ trick can stand on its hind _____

ADJECTIVE   PART OF THE BODY (PLURAL)

and spin around _____!

ADVERB

- **Bring my slippers:** Feeling lazy and don't want to get out of your

comfy _____? Ask your dog to do it! If your dog knows this

NOUN

_____ trick, say, "Bring my slippers," and your dog will bring

ADJECTIVE

your _____ to you!

PLURAL NOUN

- **Jump rope:** If your dog knows this _____ trick, grab a/an

ADJECTIVE

_____ rope and a partner, swing the rope _____, and

ADJECTIVE   ADVERB

your dog will _____ over it again and again!

VERB

MAD LIBS® is fun to play with friends, but you can also play it by yourself! To begin with, DO NOT look at the story on the page below. Fill in the blanks on this page with the words called for. Then, using the words you have selected, fill in the blank spaces in the story.

Now you've created your own hilarious MAD LIBS® game!

DOG'S DELIGHT

VERB ENDING IN "S" _____

PART OF THE BODY _____

ADJECTIVE _____

PLURAL NOUN _____

ANIMAL _____

VERB _____

VERB _____

PLURAL NOUN _____

NOUN _____

PLURAL NOUN _____

NOUN _____

NOUN _____

NOUN _____

PLURAL NOUN _____

NOUN _____

ADJECTIVE _____

PART OF THE BODY _____

NOUN _____

You know your dog is happy when it _____ and wags its
_____ (VERB ENDING IN "S") back and forth. If you want your dog to be _____
(PART OF THE BODY)   (ADJECTIVE)

as a clam at all times, try any of the following _____. It's a countdown
(PLURAL NOUN)

of your _____'s favorite things!
(ANIMAL)

5. **Walks:** Though some dogs would rather stay home and _____,
(VERB)

most dogs love to go for walks to _____ on fire hydrants and sniff
(VERB)

_____.
(PLURAL NOUN)

4. **Naps:** Dogs love to curl up on a/an _____ and dream about
(NOUN)

_____—especially if they're cuddling with their favorite
(PLURAL NOUN)

_____.
(NOUN)

3. **Playtime:** Fidos love to play fetch with a/an _____ or run around
(NOUN)

chasing a/an _____. Sometimes, _____ just wanna
(NOUN)   (PLURAL NOUN)

have fun!

2. **Food:** Whether it's a can of dog _____ or _____ table
(NOUN)   (ADJECTIVE)

scraps, dogs love to eat. The way to a dog's heart is definitely through its

_____!
(PART OF THE BODY)

1. **You!:** After all, a dog is a/an _____'s best friend.
(NOUN)

MAD LIBS® is fun to play with friends, but you can also play it by yourself! To begin with, DO NOT look at the story on the page below. Fill in the blanks on this page with the words called for. Then, using the words you have selected, fill in the blank spaces in the story.

Now you've created your own hilarious MAD LIBS® game!

WHO'S THAT DOG?, PART 4

VERB _____

COLOR _____

NOUN _____

VERB ENDING IN "ING" _____

NOUN _____

PART OF THE BODY _____

VERB _____

PART OF THE BODY (PLURAL) _____

A PLACE _____

NUMBER _____

ADJECTIVE _____

VERB _____

ADJECTIVE _____

PLURAL NOUN _____

A PLACE _____

ADJECTIVE _____

A final few furry dog breeds for you to love and _____:
<u>VERB</u>

Collie: The brown and _____ collie is a friendly family _____,
<u>COLOR</u>   <u>NOUN</u>

known for its grace and elegance when _____.
<u>VERB ENDING IN "ING"</u>

Dalmatian: This black-and-white _____ is the only dog breed
<u>NOUN</u>

with spots on its _____. They have lots of energy and need to
<u>PART OF THE BODY</u>

_____ a lot.
<u>VERB</u>

Pembroke Welsh corgi: The corgi is known for its very short

_____ and stout body. The queen of (the) _____
<u>PART OF THE BODY (PLURAL)</u>   <u>A PLACE</u>

owns _____ corgis!
<u>NUMBER</u>

Miniature schnauzer: The miniature schnauzer may be small, but it is

a/an _____ guard dog, and will _____ at the sign of any
<u>ADJECTIVE</u>   <u>VERB</u>

_____ intruder.
<u>ADJECTIVE</u>

St. Bernard: The St. Bernard was originally used to hunt for _____
<u>PLURAL NOUN</u>

during snowstorms in (the) _____. They are very gentle and
<u>A PLACE</u>

_____.
<u>ADJECTIVE</u>

MAD LIBS® is fun to play with friends, but you can also play it by yourself! To begin with, DO NOT look at the story on the page below. Fill in the blanks on this page with the words called for. Then, using the words you have selected, fill in the blank spaces in the story.

Now you've created your own hilarious MAD LIBS® game!

LET'S GO FOR A RIDE!

PERSON IN ROOM _____

PART OF THE BODY (PLURAL) _____

PART OF THE BODY (PLURAL) _____

ADJECTIVE _____

NOUN _____

NOUN _____

PART OF THE BODY _____

PLURAL NOUN _____

PART OF THE BODY (PLURAL) _____

PART OF THE BODY _____

ADJECTIVE _____

ADVERB _____

NOUN _____

PERSON IN ROOM _____

EXCLAMATION _____

NOUN _____

MAD LIBS®
LET'S GO FOR A RIDE!

"_____, come!" I hear my owner call out. My _____
<u>PERSON IN ROOM</u>   <u>PART OF THE BODY (PLURAL)</u>

perk up—is that the sound of the garage door opening? Suddenly, I am excited

from my head to my _____. Can it be? Am I going
<u>PART OF THE BODY (PLURAL)</u>

for a/an _____ car ride? I bound to the door, where I see my owner
<u>ADJECTIVE</u>

getting into the car. She pats the seat. "Come on, _____!" she calls.
<u>NOUN</u>

This is the best _____ ever! I hop happily into the front seat and
<u>NOUN</u>

immediately stick my _____ out of the car window. We drive
<u>PART OF THE BODY</u>

away down the street, passing houses and mailboxes and _____.
<u>PLURAL NOUN</u>

I can feel the wind in my _____ and the sun on my
<u>PART OF THE BODY (PLURAL)</u>

_____, and everything smells _____. *Where are we*
<u>PART OF THE BODY</u>   <u>ADJECTIVE</u>

going? I wonder _____. So you can imagine my _____ as
<u>ADVERB</u>   <u>NOUN</u>

we pulled into the parking lot of Dr. _____'s office. *We're going to*
<u>PERSON IN ROOM</u>

the vet? _____! This is the worst _____ ever!
<u>EXCLAMATION</u>   <u>NOUN</u>

MAD LIBS® is fun to play with friends, but you can also play it by yourself! To begin with, DO NOT look at the story on the page below. Fill in the blanks on this page with the words called for. Then, using the words you have selected, fill in the blank spaces in the story.

Now you've created your own hilarious MAD LIBS® game!

FAMOUS FIDOS: SCOOBY-DOO

NOUN _____

NOUN _____

PERSON IN ROOM _____

FIRST NAME _____

NOUN _____

ADJECTIVE _____

PLURAL NOUN _____

PLURAL NOUN _____

SAME PLURAL NOUN _____

PLURAL NOUN _____

PLURAL NOUN _____

ADJECTIVE _____

SILLY WORD _____

MAD LIBS®
FAMOUS FIDOS: SCOOBY-DOO

Scooby-Doo is the star of the animated television _____ *Scooby-*

NOUN

Doo, Where Are You! Scooby-Doo, also known as Scooby, is a talking

_____ who solves mysteries along with four teenagers named Shaggy,

NOUN

Daphne, _____, and _____. Scooby-Doo, a

PERSON IN ROOM   FIRST NAME

Great _____, belongs to his _____ friend, Shaggy. Much

NOUN   ADJECTIVE

like Shaggy, Scooby is scared of _____ and is always hungry for

PLURAL NOUN

cookies called Scooby _____. Luckily, the prospect of eating Scooby

PLURAL NOUN

_____ and keeping his friends safe from _____ helps

SAME PLURAL NOUN   PLURAL NOUN

Scooby to be brave and stand up to scary _____. Scooby and his

PLURAL NOUN

friends always solve the _____ mystery, and Scooby always ends each

ADJECTIVE

episode by saying "_____-dooby-doo!"

SILLY WORD

MAD LIBS® is fun to play with friends, but you can also play it by yourself! To begin with, DO NOT look at the story on the page below. Fill in the blanks on this page with the words called for. Then, using the words you have selected, fill in the blank spaces in the story.

Now you've created your own hilarious MAD LIBS® game!

DOGS VERSUS CATS

ADJECTIVE _____

ADJECTIVE _____

PART OF THE BODY _____

NUMBER _____

ADJECTIVE _____

PLURAL NOUN _____

NOUN _____

PLURAL NOUN _____

PART OF THE BODY (PLURAL) _____

NOUN _____

PART OF THE BODY _____

NOUN _____

NOUN _____

NOUN _____

SAME NOUN _____

ADJECTIVE _____

NOUN _____

MAD LIBS®
DOGS VERSUS CATS

Which are better, _____ cats or _____ dogs? Anyone with
                   ADJECTIVE   ADJECTIVE

half a/an _____ knows that dogs are _____ times better
         PART OF THE BODY   NUMBER

than cats. Dogs are _____ companions, while cats only care about
                      ADJECTIVE

their own _____. Dogs are loyal to their _____, but cats
           PLURAL NOUN   NOUN

will love whoever gives them _____ to eat. Dogs like to have their
                          PLURAL NOUN

_____ rubbed, while cats will bite your _____
PART OF THE BODY (PLURAL)   NOUN

if you try to put a/an _____ on them. Most dogs love going for
                   PART OF THE BODY

rides in a/an _____, but cats just get sick all over your favorite
               NOUN

_____. Dogs love to play fetch with a/an _____, but if
     NOUN   NOUN

you throw a/an _____ for a cat, it will just look at you like you're
             SAME NOUN

_____. All in all, when it comes to dogs versus cats, only the dog is
   ADJECTIVE

truly man's best _____.
               NOUN

MAD LIBS® is fun to play with friends, but you can also play it by yourself! To begin with, DO NOT look at the story on the page below. Fill in the blanks on this page with the words called for. Then, using the words you have selected, fill in the blank spaces in the story.

Now you've created your own hilarious MAD LIBS® game!

FOREVER HOME

LAST NAME _____

NOUN _____

ADJECTIVE _____

ADJECTIVE _____

PART OF THE BODY (PLURAL) _____

COLOR _____

PART OF THE BODY _____

ADJECTIVE _____

NOUN _____

A PLACE _____

ADJECTIVE _____

PLURAL NOUN _____

ADJECTIVE _____

ADJECTIVE _____

PART OF THE BODY _____

EXCLAMATION _____

ADVERB _____

MAD LIBS
FOREVER HOME

When the _____ family went to the animal shelter,
                    LAST NAME

they never knew they'd find a/an _____ like Rex. The family
                                        NOUN

looked at all the dogs before making this very _____ decision.
                                                    ADJECTIVE

Sure, the puppies were cute and _____, but one older dog stole the
                                     ADJECTIVE

family's _____. His name was Rex, and with his fuzzy
          PART OF THE BODY (PLURAL)

_____ fur, his crooked _____, and his _____
     COLOR   PART OF THE BODY   ADJECTIVE

personality, the family knew they'd found their new _____. Plus, by
                                                          NOUN

bringing Rex back to (the) _____ with them, they saved his life. Now
                            A PLACE

Rex would have a/an _____ place to sleep, _____ to eat, and
                       ADJECTIVE   PLURAL NOUN

a/an _____ family to call his own. And Rex would more than repay
        ADJECTIVE

his family with lots of _____ wet kisses on the _____
                           ADJECTIVE   PART OF THE BODY

and unconditional love. _____! Rex had found his forever home,
                          EXCLAMATION

and they all lived _____ ever after.
                      ADVERB

MEOW LIBS

by Sarah Fabiny

MAD LIBS®

INSTRUCTIONS

MAD LIBS® is a game for people who don't like games!
It can be played by one, two, three, four, or forty.

• RIDICULOUSLY SIMPLE DIRECTIONS

In this tablet you will find stories containing blank spaces where words are left out.
One player, the READER, selects one of these stories. The READER does not tell anyone
what the story is about. Instead, he/she asks the other players, the WRITERS, to give
him/her words. These words are used to fill in the blank spaces in the story.

• TO PLAY

The READER asks each WRITER in turn to call out a word—an adjective or a noun or
whatever the space calls for—and uses them to fill in the blank spaces in the story. The
result is a MAD LIBS® game.

When the READER then reads the completed MAD LIBS® game to the other players,
they will discover that they have written a story that is fantastic, screamingly funny,
shocking, silly, crazy, or just plain dumb—depending upon which words each WRITER
called out.

• EXAMPLE (*Before* and *After*)

"_____!" he said _____
         EXCLAMATION   ADVERB

as he jumped into his convertible _____ and
                                                    NOUN

drove off with his _____ wife.
                            ADJECTIVE

"_____OUCH_____!" he said _____HAPPILY_____
         EXCLAMATION   ADVERB

as he jumped into his convertible _____CAT_____ and
                                                    NOUN

drove off with his _____BRAVE_____ wife.
                            ADJECTIVE

MAD LIBS®

QUICK REVIEW

In case you have forgotten what adjectives, adverbs, nouns, and verbs are, here is a quick review:

An ADJECTIVE describes something or somebody. *Lumpy, soft, ugly, messy,* and *short* are adjectives.

An ADVERB tells how something is done. It modifies a verb and usually ends in "ly." *Modestly, stupidly, greedily,* and *carefully* are adverbs.

A NOUN is the name of a person, place, or thing. *Sidewalk, umbrella, bridle, bathtub,* and *nose* are nouns.

A VERB is an action word. *Run, pitch, jump,* and *swim* are verbs. Put the verbs in past tense if the directions say PAST TENSE. *Ran, pitched, jumped,* and *swam* are verbs in the past tense.

When we ask for A PLACE, we mean any sort of place: a country or city *(Spain, Cleveland)* or a room *(bathroom, kitchen).*

An EXCLAMATION or SILLY WORD is any sort of funny sound, gasp, grunt, or outcry, like *Wow!, Ouch!, Whomp!, Ick!,* and *Gadzooks!*

When we ask for specific words, like a NUMBER, a COLOR, an ANIMAL, or a PART OF THE BODY, we mean a word that is one of those things, like *seven, blue, horse,* or *head.*

When we ask for a PLURAL, it means more than one. For example, *cat* pluralized is *cats.*

MAD LIBS® is fun to play with friends, but you can also play it by yourself! To begin with, DO NOT look at the story on the page below. Fill in the blanks on this page with the words called for. Then, using the words you have selected, fill in the blank spaces in the story.

Now you've created your own hilarious MAD LIBS® game!

FAMOUS CATS

ADJECTIVE _____

NOUN _____

NUMBER _____

TYPE OF FOOD _____

PLURAL NOUN _____

VERB _____

PERSON IN ROOM _____

CELEBRITY _____

PLURAL NOUN _____

NOUN _____

PART OF THE BODY _____

A PLACE _____

FIRST NAME _____

ADJECTIVE _____

ANIMAL _____

MAD LIBS
FAMOUS CATS

From cartoons to social media, cats are everywhere. Here are a few of the most famous cats:

- Morris—the cat with the _____ attitude and the posh
  ADJECTIVE

  _____ is the "spokesperson" for _____ Lives cat
  NOUN   NUMBER

  _____.
  TYPE OF FOOD

- Garfield—the famous comic-strip cat who hates _____, loves
  PLURAL NOUN

  to _____, and has no respect for _____, his
  VERB   PERSON IN ROOM

  owner's dog.

- Smelly Cat—made famous in the song sung by _____ on the
  CELEBRITY

  TV show _____.
  PLURAL NOUN

- Grumpy Cat—an Internet _____ known for her hilarious
  NOUN

  _____ expressions.
  PART OF THE BODY

- Stubbs—the mayor of (the) _____, Alaska.
  A PLACE

- Cat—the feline heroine of the movie *Breakfast at* _____'s.
  FIRST NAME

- Tom—the _____ cat that will never catch his archenemy,
  ADJECTIVE

  Jerry the _____.
  ANIMAL

MAD LIBS® is fun to play with friends, but you can also play it by yourself! To begin with, DO NOT look at the story on the page below. Fill in the blanks on this page with the words called for. Then, using the words you have selected, fill in the blank spaces in the story.

Now you've created your own hilarious MAD LIBS® game!

WHICH BREED IS RIGHT FOR YOU?

PART OF THE BODY (PLURAL) _____

ADJECTIVE _____

NOUN _____

ADJECTIVE _____

NOUN _____

NOUN _____

PART OF THE BODY (PLURAL) _____

ADJECTIVE _____

NOUN _____

SILLY WORD _____

ADJECTIVE _____

A PLACE _____

ADJECTIVE _____

PART OF THE BODY _____

COLOR _____

ADJECTIVE _____

NOUN _____

MAD LIBS
WHICH BREED IS RIGHT FOR YOU?

So you're thinking of getting a cat. Whether you prefer cats with no

_____ or _____ ears, there's a/an _____
PART OF THE BODY (PLURAL)   _ADJECTIVE_   _NOUN_

for you.

Sphynx: If you go for the _____ things in life, and don't want to
     ADJECTIVE

have to clean up cat hair, this is the _____ for you.
     NOUN

Siamese: Do you want a cat that sounds like a crying _____ and has
     NOUN

crossed _____? Well then, go get a Siamese.
     PART OF THE BODY (PLURAL)

Manx: Looking for a cat with a sweet, _____ face and no
     ADJECTIVE

_____? We suggest you get a/an _____.
   NOUN   _SILLY WORD_

Maine coon: How about a cat that's the size of a/an _____ dog? If
     ADJECTIVE

you don't mind having to brush your cat every day, it sounds like you should

get a/an _____ coon.
     A PLACE

Persian: If you love a/an _____-looking cat with a scrunched-up
     ADJECTIVE

_____, go get yourself a Persian.
PART OF THE BODY

Snowshoe: Do you love a cat with adorable _____ feet and a/an
     COLOR

_____ personality? You may want a/an _____-shoe.
ADJECTIVE   _NOUN_

From MEOW LIBS® • Copyright © 2015 by Penguin Random House LLC

MAD LIBS® is fun to play with friends, but you can also play it by yourself! To begin with, DO NOT look at the story on the page below. Fill in the blanks on this page with the words called for. Then, using the words you have selected, fill in the blank spaces in the story.

Now you've created your own hilarious MAD LIBS® game!

CAT SAYINGS

ADJECTIVE _____

PLURAL NOUN _____

PART OF THE BODY _____

NOUN _____

SILLY WORD _____

ADJECTIVE _____

VERB ENDING IN "ING" _____

ARTICLE OF CLOTHING _____

ADJECTIVE _____

NOUN _____

ANIMAL _____

NOUN _____

NOUN _____

EXCLAMATION _____

ADJECTIVE _____

ADVERB _____

ADJECTIVE _____

MAD LIBS
CAT SAYINGS

There are a lot of _____ phrases that incorporate our favorite feline
$\qquad$ ADJECTIVE

_____. Check out these sayings and their meanings:
PLURAL NOUN

- Cat got your _____?: Why aren't you talking?
  PART OF THE BODY

- You let the cat out of the _____: _____! My secret
  NOUN   SILLY WORD

  isn't so _____ anymore.
  ADJECTIVE

- It is raining cats and dogs: It is _____ like crazy.
  VERB ENDING IN "ING"

- That is the cat's _____: That is totally _____!
  ARTICLE OF CLOTHING   ADJECTIVE

- When the cat's away, the mice will play: The boss is away—let's get this

  _____ started!
  NOUN

- Curiosity killed the _____: Mind your own _____!
  ANIMAL   NOUN

- He is a fat cat: He likes to flash his _____.
  NOUN

- Looks like something the cat dragged in: _____! You look
  EXCLAMATION

  _____. What happened?!
  ADJECTIVE

- Cat on a hot tin roof: Please sit _____!
  ADVERB

- It's like herding cats: This job is totally _____!
  ADJECTIVE

MAD LIBS® is fun to play with friends, but you can also play it by yourself! To begin with, DO NOT look at the story on the page below. Fill in the blanks on this page with the words called for. Then, using the words you have selected, fill in the blank spaces in the story.

Now you've created your own hilarious MAD LIBS® game!

CAT SHOWS

ADJECTIVE _____

ADJECTIVE _____

ADJECTIVE _____

VERB _____

NOUN _____

SAME NOUN _____

NOUN _____

NOUN _____

PLURAL NOUN _____

PLURAL NOUN _____

NOUN _____

A PLACE _____

PLURAL NOUN _____

ADJECTIVE _____

NOUN _____

There are some cat owners who take their love of cats to a/an _____
ADJECTIVE

level. A/An _____ example of this: the cat show. Both _____
ADJECTIVE _ADJECTIVE_

and purebred cats are allowed to _____ in a cat show, although the
VERB

rules differ from _____ to _____. The cats are compared
NOUN _SAME NOUN_

to a breed _____, and those judged to be closest to it are awarded
NOUN

a/an _____. At the end of the year, all the _____ who
NOUN _PLURAL NOUN_

won at various shows are tallied up, and regional and national _____
PLURAL NOUN

are presented. The very first cat _____ took place in 1598 at (the)
NOUN

_____ in England. In the United States, the first cat shows were held
A PLACE

at New England country _____ in the 1860s. The most important
PLURAL NOUN

cat show in the United States is the CFA _____ Cat Show. But no
ADJECTIVE

matter which cat wins "Best in Show," every cat is a/an _____—to
NOUN

their owners, at least!

MAD LIBS® is fun to play with friends, but you can also play it by yourself! To begin with, DO NOT look at the story on the page below. Fill in the blanks on this page with the words called for. Then, using the words you have selected, fill in the blank spaces in the story.

Now you've created your own hilarious MAD LIBS® game!

CATS IN THE NEWS

PLURAL NOUN _____

ADJECTIVE _____

NOUN _____

ADJECTIVE _____

NUMBER _____

NOUN _____

NOUN _____

NOUN _____

SAME NOUN _____

ADJECTIVE _____

NOUN _____

ADJECTIVE _____

NOUN _____

VERB _____

News Anchor #1: Stay tuned, _____! After the commercial break, we
PLURAL NOUN

have a/an _____ story about a cat who saved a young _____
ADJECTIVE _NOUN_

from a/an _____ dog.
ADJECTIVE

News Anchor #2: That reminds me of the story about the cat that dialed

_____-1-1 after its owner fell out of his _____.
NUMBER _NOUN_

News Anchor #1: And how about that kitten that survived the deadly

_____ in Taiwan?
NOUN

News Anchor #2: Have you heard about the kitten that was saved from a/an

_____ by a/an _____-fighter with _____ water
NOUN _SAME NOUN_ _ADJECTIVE_

and a/an _____ full of oxygen?
NOUN

News Anchor #1: And who could forget that _____ story about a
ADJECTIVE

cat that took a/an _____ on the London Underground?
NOUN

News Anchor #2: Well, I guess he had to _____ to work just like
VERB

everyone else!

MAD LIBS® is fun to play with friends, but you can also play it by yourself! To begin with, DO NOT look at the story on the page below. Fill in the blanks on this page with the words called for. Then, using the words you have selected, fill in the blank spaces in the story.

Now you've created your own hilarious MAD LIBS® game!

HISTORY OF CATS

VERB ENDING IN "ING" _____

NUMBER _____

ADJECTIVE _____

ANIMAL (PLURAL) _____

SAME ANIMAL (PLURAL) _____

ADJECTIVE _____

PLURAL NOUN _____

ADJECTIVE _____

PART OF THE BODY _____

ADJECTIVE _____

OCCUPATION (PLURAL) _____

VERB (PAST TENSE) _____

ADJECTIVE _____

ADJECTIVE _____

NUMBER _____

ADJECTIVE _____

MAD LIBS
HISTORY OF CATS

Cats have been _____ with—or at least tolerating—people for
VERB ENDING IN "ING"

over _____ years. Cats first became a part of our _____ lives
NUMBER   ADJECTIVE

when people started to grow grain. The grain attracted _____,
ANIMAL (PLURAL)

and the cats preyed on the _____. Cats soon became
SAME ANIMAL (PLURAL)

a/an _____ fixture in peoples' _____ and were even
ADJECTIVE   PLURAL NOUN

worshipped in _____ Egypt. There was even an Egyptian goddess
ADJECTIVE

who had the _____ of a cat! However, in the _____
PART OF THE BODY   ADJECTIVE

Ages, cats came to be demonized and were thought to be affiliated with evil

_____. Many cats were _____ to ward off evil. In
OCCUPATION (PLURAL)   VERB (PAST TENSE)

the 1600s, the cat's _____ reputation was restored, and today cats
ADJECTIVE

are _____ stars and live in _____ percent of American
ADJECTIVE   NUMBER

households. Talk about a long and _____ history!
ADJECTIVE

MAD LIBS® is fun to play with friends, but you can also play it by yourself! To begin with, DO NOT look at the story on the page below. Fill in the blanks on this page with the words called for. Then, using the words you have selected, fill in the blank spaces in the story.

Now you've created your own hilarious MAD LIBS® game!

I AM A CAT LADY

ADJECTIVE _____

ADJECTIVE _____

PLURAL NOUN _____

NUMBER _____

ADJECTIVE _____

ADJECTIVE _____

VERB _____

ADJECTIVE _____

PLURAL NOUN _____

ADVERB _____

ADVERB _____

NOUN _____

ADJECTIVE _____

ADJECTIVE _____

ADJECTIVE _____

ANIMAL _____

MAD LIBS®
I AM A CAT LADY

Dear _____ Neighbor,
          ADJECTIVE

I'm glad we have come to a/an _____ understanding about our
                                    ADJECTIVE

_____. You have come to accept my _____ cats, and
   PLURAL NOUN   NUMBER

I have come to accept your _____ dog. Yes, my _____
                                ADJECTIVE   ADJECTIVE

cats may _____ in your garden, but your _____ dog
              VERB   ADJECTIVE

digs up my _____. And I will remind you that my cats purr very
              PLURAL NOUN

_____, while your dog barks _____. To conclude, I feel
   ADVERB   ADVERB

sorry for the _____-man, who is scared of your _____
                    NOUN   ADJECTIVE

dog, while he brings treats for my _____ felines. I'm glad we have
                                        ADJECTIVE

been able to come to a/an _____ understanding on this matter.
                               ADJECTIVE

Yours truly,

The _____ Lady Next Door
          ANIMAL

MAD LIBS® is fun to play with friends, but you can also play it by yourself! To begin with, DO NOT look at the story on the page below. Fill in the blanks on this page with the words called for. Then, using the words you have selected, fill in the blank spaces in the story.

Now you've created your own hilarious MAD LIBS® game!

CATS ON CAMERA

ADJECTIVE _____

VERB ENDING IN "ING" _____

NOUN _____

SILLY WORD _____

ADJECTIVE _____

ADJECTIVE _____

NOUN _____

NOUN _____

NOUN _____

EXCLAMATION _____

VERB ENDING IN "S" _____

NOUN _____

ADJECTIVE _____

NUMBER _____

ADJECTIVE _____

PLURAL NOUN _____

MAD LIBS
CATS ON CAMERA

Cat Lover #1: Have you seen the _____ video on YouTube of the cat
                                              ADJECTIVE

_____ a/an _____?
VERB ENDING IN "ING"   NOUN

Cat Lover #2: _____! It's almost as _____ as that GIF of
                        SILLY WORD   ADJECTIVE

the _____ kitten playing with a/an _____.
        ADJECTIVE   NOUN

Cat Lover #1: And that clip of the _____ cat who pushes her own
                                              NOUN

_____ down some stairs?! _____!
        NOUN   EXCLAMATION

Cat Lover #2: How about the cat who _____ along to
                                              VERB ENDING IN "S"

a/an _____ video? Totally _____!
        NOUN   ADJECTIVE

Cat Lover #1: And there must be about _____ videos of
                                                  NUMBER

_____ cats that have gotten stuck in _____.
    ADJECTIVE   PLURAL NOUN

Cat Lover #2: Yep! And I think I've watched them all.

MAD LIBS® is fun to play with friends, but you can also play it by yourself! To begin with, DO NOT look at the story on the page below. Fill in the blanks on this page with the words called for. Then, using the words you have selected, fill in the blank spaces in the story.

Now you've created your own hilarious MAD LIBS® game!

SEVEN SIGNS YOUR CAT LOVES YOU

ADJECTIVE _____

NOUN _____

SAME NOUN _____

PLURAL NOUN _____

ADJECTIVE _____

VERB _____

NOUN _____

SAME NOUN _____

ADVERB _____

NOUN _____

ADJECTIVE _____

ANIMAL _____

A PLACE _____

ADJECTIVE _____

MAD LIBS®
SEVEN SIGNS YOUR CAT LOVES YOU

Here are seven _____ signs your cat loves you:
ADJECTIVE

- Head butting—If your boyfriend or _____ did this to you,
  NOUN

  you probably wouldn't want them as your _____ anymore.
  SAME NOUN

  But when your cat does it, they are marking you with their facial

  _____, which shows your cat trusts you.
  PLURAL NOUN

- Powerful purrs—Cats purr for all kinds of reasons, but that

  _____ body rumble is saved for expressing true love.
  ADJECTIVE

- Love bites—If your cat likes to _____ on you, it means they
  VERB

  have a serious _____ for you.
  NOUN

- Tail twitching—When the tip of a cat's _____ is twitching, it
  SAME NOUN

  means they are in total control.

- Tummy up—If your cat rolls around on the ground with its tummy

  showing, it means they trust you _____.
  ADVERB

- Kneading—No, your cat doesn't think you are _____ dough;
  NOUN

  he is reliving his _____ memories of kittenhood.
  ADJECTIVE

- Gifts—You may not want to find a dead _____ in your
  ANIMAL

  _____, but this is a/an _____ sign of friendship.
  A PLACE   ADJECTIVE

MAD LIBS® is fun to play with friends, but you can also play it by yourself! To begin with, DO NOT look at the story on the page below. Fill in the blanks on this page with the words called for. Then, using the words you have selected, fill in the blank spaces in the story.

Now you've created your own hilarious MAD LIBS® game!

SEVEN SIGNS YOUR CAT IS TRYING TO KILL YOU

ADJECTIVE _____

PLURAL NOUN _____

ADVERB _____

NOUN _____

PART OF THE BODY _____

VERB ENDING IN "ING" _____

ADJECTIVE _____

PART OF THE BODY _____

SILLY WORD _____

NOUN _____

ADVERB _____

ANIMAL _____

ADJECTIVE _____

There's a flip side to all those _____ expressions of love.
ADJECTIVE

- Head butting—Beware! Your cat is not showing you that it trusts you;

  it's telling you that your _____ are numbered!
  PLURAL NOUN

- Powerful purrs—This is not a sign of true love; it's _____ a
  ADVERB

  battle cry!

- Love bites—Not actually a/an _____ of love, but your cat
  NOUN

  tasting you to decide which bit of you to eat first. _____,
  PART OF THE BODY

  please!

- Tail twitching—The equivalent of your cat _____ a sword
  VERB ENDING IN "ING"

  at you.

- Tummy up—Do not fall for this _____ trick! As soon as
  ADJECTIVE

  you put your _____ near your cat's belly, it will scratch the
  PART OF THE BODY

  _____ out of it!
  SILLY WORD

- Kneading—This is not a/an _____ of affection; your cat is
  NOUN

  _____ checking your organs for weaknesses.
  ADVERB

- Gifts—A dead _____ is not a gift; it's a/an _____
  ANIMAL   ADJECTIVE

  warning. Didn't you see *The Godfather*?!

MAD LIBS® is fun to play with friends, but you can also play it by yourself! To begin with, DO NOT look at the story on the page below. Fill in the blanks on this page with the words called for. Then, using the words you have selected, fill in the blank spaces in the story.

Now you've created your own hilarious MAD LIBS® game!

DOGS VERSUS CATS

ADJECTIVE _____

NOUN _____

ADJECTIVE _____

ADJECTIVE _____

ADJECTIVE _____

PART OF THE BODY (PLURAL) _____

NOUN _____

VERB ENDING IN "ING" _____

NOUN _____

ANIMAL _____

NOUN _____

NOUN _____

ADJECTIVE _____

ADVERB _____

ADJECTIVE _____

MAD LIBS
DOGS VERSUS CATS

If you've ever owned both dogs and cats, you know that the differences between

the two species are _____. They are like night and _____.
    ADJECTIVE   NOUN

The argument about which pet is more _____ will continue
                                          ADJECTIVE

until the end of time, but it's easy to see why cats are _____.
                                                              ADJECTIVE

For instance, cats won't embarrass you in front of your guests by parading

around with your _____ underwear in their _____.
                    ADJECTIVE   PART OF THE BODY (PLURAL)

Cats are also funnier than dogs, even if they don't know it. And they don't

give a/an _____ if you laugh at them, because they are too busy
              NOUN

_____ their revenge. Cats are natural _____
VERB ENDING IN "ING"   NOUN

repellents—no spider, fly, or _____ stands a chance if there's
                                    ANIMAL

a cat in the _____. Cats have no interest in being hooked up to
                  NOUN

a/an _____ and going for a walk; they'd rather curl up and take
          NOUN

a/an _____ nap. And it's _____ proven that cat owners are
          ADJECTIVE   ADVERB

smarter and more _____ than dog owners. So go get yourself a cat!
                      ADJECTIVE

MAD LIBS® is fun to play with friends, but you can also play it by yourself! To begin with, DO NOT look at the story on the page below. Fill in the blanks on this page with the words called for. Then, using the words you have selected, fill in the blank spaces in the story.

Now you've created your own hilarious MAD LIBS® game!

MY HOUSE. MY RULES.

ADJECTIVE _____

NOUN _____

VERB _____

NOUN _____

SAME NOUN _____

TYPE OF LIQUID _____

VERB ENDING IN "ING" _____

PERSON IN ROOM _____

VERB _____

SAME VERB _____

ADJECTIVE _____

ADJECTIVE _____

_____ Servant,
   ADJECTIVE

It's quite obvious that you think you control me, but we all know that I am

in charge of this _____. You think I am just a simple cat, but I am
              NOUN

able to out-_____ you any day of the week. Please be aware that
       VERB

"your" house is actually mine, and I am not to be disturbed if I happen to

be sleeping on your bed or favorite piece of _____. I will scratch
                      NOUN

any piece of _____ I want. I do not want to drink _____
      SAME NOUN   TYPE OF LIQUID

from an ordinary bowl; I prefer to lap water from a/an _____
                             VERB ENDING IN "ING"

faucet or a toilet. So please remember to leave the toilet seat up—I don't care

what _____ has to say about that. Don't try to get me to
     PERSON IN ROOM

_____ during the day; you should know better than that. I prefer to
   VERB

_____ at night when you are asleep; this is much more fun. You are
  SAME VERB

a/an _____ human, but you are my human.
    ADJECTIVE

With tolerance,

Your Super-_____ Cat
       ADJECTIVE

MAD LIBS® is fun to play with friends, but you can also play it by yourself! To begin with, DO NOT look at the story on the page below. Fill in the blanks on this page with the words called for. Then, using the words you have selected, fill in the blank spaces in the story.

Now you've created your own hilarious MAD LIBS® game!

AM I IN YOUR WAY?

EXCLAMATION _____

NOUN _____

NOUN _____

ADJECTIVE _____

NOUN _____

ADJECTIVE _____

VERB ENDING IN "ING" _____

NOUN _____

VERB ENDING IN "ING" _____

NOUN _____

NOUN _____

VERB _____

NOUN _____

TYPE OF FOOD _____

PART OF THE BODY _____

MAD LIBS
AM I IN YOUR WAY?

_____! Were you trying to type? I just felt the need to lie on your
EXCLAMATION

_____ keyboard at this moment. That _____ you're trying
NOUN   NOUN

to write isn't as _____ as my nap. Oh, and did you want to read
ADJECTIVE

today's _____? Tough. It's much more _____ that I use
NOUN   ADJECTIVE

it as a place to do my _____. And I hope you aren't going to
VERB ENDING IN "ING"

do the _____ today, as I am planning on _____ in
NOUN   VERB ENDING IN "ING"

the laundry _____ all day, and I don't want to be disturbed. Let me
NOUN

know when you are going to start preparing dinner, as I can help knock things

off the _____. And when you sit down to _____, I will
NOUN   VERB

certainly expect a few pieces of food from your _____. But please,
NOUN

no _____—you know I turn my _____ up at that.
TYPE OF FOOD   PART OF THE BODY

MAD LIBS® is fun to play with friends, but you can also play it by yourself! To begin with, DO NOT look at the story on the page below. Fill in the blanks on this page with the words called for. Then, using the words you have selected, fill in the blank spaces in the story.

Now you've created your own hilarious MAD LIBS® game!

THE SEVEN HABITS OF HIGHLY EFFECTIVE KITTENS

PLURAL NOUN _____

ADJECTIVE _____

NOUN _____

VERB ENDING IN "ING" _____

PART OF THE BODY _____

ADJECTIVE _____

VERB _____

ADJECTIVE _____

ANIMAL _____

NOUN _____

ADJECTIVE _____

ANIMAL _____

NOUN _____

NOUN _____

NOUN _____

NOUN _____

VERB _____

MAD LIBS
THE SEVEN HABITS OF
HIGHLY EFFECTIVE KITTENS

All kittens know they must perfect these _____ :
PLURAL NOUN

1. Be as adorably _____ as possible at all times.
   ADJECTIVE

2. Perfect that tiny, irresistible _____. Your servants will come
   NOUN

   _____ in a/an _____-beat.
   VERB ENDING IN "ING"   PART OF THE BODY

3. Learn the ways of a/an _____ ninja; you can _____
   ADJECTIVE   VERB

   anywhere. It's all about stealth.

4. You must be _____, whether you're facing down the neighbor's
   ADJECTIVE

   _____ or jumping off the kitchen _____.
   ANIMAL   NOUN

5. You may be _____, but inside of you beats the heart of
   ADJECTIVE

   a/an _____. Honor your heritage.
   ANIMAL

6. Make use of those _____-sharp claws. Climb the living room
   NOUN

   _____ and the Christmas _____ with courage and
   NOUN   NOUN

   confidence.

7. And when you sleep, curl up in the tiniest, fluffiest _____ possible.
   NOUN

   It will make your servants _____.
   VERB

MAD LIBS® is fun to play with friends, but you can also play it by yourself! To begin with, DO NOT look at the story on the page below. Fill in the blanks on this page with the words called for. Then, using the words you have selected, fill in the blank spaces in the story.

Now you've created your own hilarious MAD LIBS® game!

YOU CALL THAT CAT FOOD?

EXCLAMATION _____

NOUN _____

ADJECTIVE _____

ANIMAL _____

ADJECTIVE _____

NOUN _____

ADJECTIVE _____

NOUN _____

ADJECTIVE _____

ADJECTIVE _____

NOUN _____

PLURAL NOUN _____

ADJECTIVE _____

NOUN _____

MAD LIBS
YOU CALL THAT CAT FOOD?

_____! What is this _____ that you put in my bowl? Do
  EXCLAMATION   NOUN

you really expect me to eat this? Have I not made it perfectly _____
                                                                  ADJECTIVE

that I prefer fresh _____ to the _____ stuff that comes
                        ANIMAL   ADJECTIVE

out of a/an _____? It looks _____ and smells like a rotting
                NOUN   ADJECTIVE

_____. And I refuse to eat something that is advertised by a cat who is
    NOUN

an embarrassment to my _____ species. Don't get so _____
                            ADJECTIVE   ADJECTIVE

when I jump onto the kitchen _____ to see what you are cooking for
                                 NOUN

yourself—I might not want any of that, either. Some of the _____
                                                              PLURAL NOUN

you make look and smell as _____ as that _____ you try
                              ADJECTIVE   NOUN

to feed me!

MAD LIBS® is fun to play with friends, but you can also play it by yourself! To begin with, DO NOT look at the story on the page below. Fill in the blanks on this page with the words called for. Then, using the words you have selected, fill in the blank spaces in the story.

Now you've created your own hilarious MAD LIBS® game!

STRANGE CAT FACTS

VERB ENDING IN "ING" _____

NOUN _____

NUMBER _____

PLURAL NOUN _____

VERB _____

PLURAL NOUN _____

NUMBER _____

NUMBER _____

NOUN _____

NOUN _____

VERB _____

PART OF THE BODY _____

COLOR _____

ADJECTIVE _____

MAD LIBS
STRANGE CAT FACTS

If you think you know cats, think again:

- On average, cats spend two-thirds of every day _____.
  <small>VERB ENDING IN "ING"</small>

- A group of cats is called a/an "_____."
  <small>NOUN</small>

- A cat can jump up to _____ times its own height in a single
  <small>NUMBER</small>
  bound.

- Cats have over twenty _____ that control their ears.
  <small>PLURAL NOUN</small>

- Cats can't _____ sweetness.
  <small>VERB</small>

- The world's longest cat measured 48.5 _____ long.
  <small>PLURAL NOUN</small>

- A cat has _____ toes on its front paws, but only _____
  <small>NUMBER</small> <small>NUMBER</small>
  toes on its back paws.

- When a cat leaves its _____ uncovered in the litter box, it is
  <small>NOUN</small>
  a/an _____ of aggression.
  <small>NOUN</small>

- Cats only _____ through their _____ pads.
  <small>VERB</small> <small>PART OF THE BODY</small>

- _____ cats are bad luck in the United States, but they are
  <small>COLOR</small>
  _____ luck in the United Kingdom and Australia.
  <small>ADJECTIVE</small>

MAD LIBS® is fun to play with friends, but you can also play it by yourself! To begin with, DO NOT look at the story on the page below. Fill in the blanks on this page with the words called for. Then, using the words you have selected, fill in the blank spaces in the story.

Now you've created your own hilarious MAD LIBS® game!

CATS IN A BOX—OR BAG

ADJECTIVE _____

VERB _____

ANIMAL (PLURAL) _____

PLURAL NOUN _____

ADJECTIVE _____

ADJECTIVE _____

ARTICLE OF CLOTHING _____

PLURAL NOUN _____

VERB _____

SAME VERB _____

ADJECTIVE _____

NOUN _____

PLURAL NOUN _____

ADJECTIVE _____

ANIMAL (PLURAL) _____

VERB _____

MAD LIBS
CATS IN A BOX—OR BAG

Don't bother buying me some _____ toy; I won't _____ with it. So
ADJECTIVE   VERB

skip the fake _____ filled with catnip and those "teasers" with
ANIMAL (PLURAL)

_____ on the ends. Just give me an old _____ box. The secret
PLURAL NOUN   ADJECTIVE

of the old _____ box is that it gives me (a/an) _____
ADJECTIVE   ARTICLE OF CLOTHING

of invisibility, enhancing my super-_____. When I am in the box,
PLURAL NOUN

I can _____ you, but you can't _____ me. If the box is
VERB   SAME VERB

_____, that's even better, as it is more fun if I can barely get myself in
ADJECTIVE

it. And it is preferable if the box has a/an _____ or _____.
NOUN   PLURAL NOUN

And if you don't have a box, a/an _____ paper bag will do. Because
ADJECTIVE

within the bag live the Bag _____. And it is my mission in life
ANIMAL (PLURAL)

to _____ them!
VERB

MAD LIBS® is fun to play with friends, but you can also play it by yourself! To begin with, DO NOT look at the story on the page below. Fill in the blanks on this page with the words called for. Then, using the words you have selected, fill in the blank spaces in the story.

Now you've created your own hilarious MAD LIBS® game!

BIG CATS

VERB _____

PLURAL NOUN _____

PLURAL NOUN _____

ADJECTIVE _____

ADJECTIVE _____

ANIMAL _____

SAME ANIMAL _____

ADJECTIVE _____

ADJECTIVE _____

VERB _____

SAME VERB _____

ADJECTIVE _____

VERB ENDING IN "ING" _____

SAME VERB ENDING IN "ING" _____

A PLACE _____

ADJECTIVE _____

NOUN _____

ADJECTIVE _____

MAD LIBS
BIG CATS

Although they don't have to _____ for their food or worry about

_____, domestic cats aren't all that different from their wild

   PLURAL NOUN

_____ and sisters. All cats, domestic and _____, are

   PLURAL NOUN   ADJECTIVE

_____ carnivores, whether they prefer to eat a can of _____

   ADJECTIVE   ANIMAL

delight or an entire raw _____. Felines around the world, from

                                SAME ANIMAL

_____ tabbies to _____ jaguars, _____ for sixteen to

   ADJECTIVE   ADJECTIVE   VERB

twenty hours a day. (However, snow leopards don't get to _____

                                                 SAME VERB

in a basket of _____ laundry.) And there's the _____

              ADJECTIVE   VERB ENDING IN "ING"

thing. You might think your cat is _____ against you

                            SAME VERB ENDING IN "ING"

because it loves you. But it's marking you, just like big cats mark their territory

in (the) _____. And even though there are _____

     A PLACE   ADJECTIVE

similarities between a house cat and a cheetah, it's much safer to have a domestic

cat in your _____—so don't get any _____ ideas!

     NOUN   ADJECTIVE

MAD LIBS® is fun to play with friends, but you can also play it by yourself! To begin with, DO NOT look at the story on the page below. Fill in the blanks on this page with the words called for. Then, using the words you have selected, fill in the blank spaces in the story.

Now you've created your own hilarious MAD LIBS® game!

CATS IN BOOKS

ADJECTIVE _____

ADJECTIVE _____

VERB ENDING IN "ING" _____

ADJECTIVE _____

PERSON IN ROOM _____

PART OF THE BODY _____

PERSON IN ROOM _____

A PLACE _____

ADJECTIVE _____

ADJECTIVE _____

PLURAL NOUN _____

PART OF THE BODY _____

ADJECTIVE _____

PLURAL NOUN _____

ADJECTIVE _____

PART OF THE BODY _____

MAD LIBS

CATS IN BOOKS

Test your knowledge about cats who have made their _____ mark in
ADJECTIVE

literature:

- The cat who seems to be _____ and can't stop
ADJECTIVE

_____ at Alice: the Cheshire Cat
VERB ENDING IN "ING"

- The _____ cat in _____ King's horror
ADJECTIVE   PERSON IN ROOM

classic: Church

- The cat with a squashed _____ who belongs to
PART OF THE BODY

_____ Potter's best friend: Crookshanks
PERSON IN ROOM

- The _____ cat who is the best friend of the _____
A PLACE   ADJECTIVE

cockroach Archy: Mehitabel

- A mysterious, _____, and small black cat capable of
ADJECTIVE

performing _____ of magic and sleight of _____:
PLURAL NOUN   PART OF THE BODY

Mr. Mistoffelees

- The story of a very _____ kitten who struggles to keep his
ADJECTIVE

_____ clean and tidy: *Tom Kitten*
PLURAL NOUN

- A/An _____ tale about a cat who wins the _____
ADJECTIVE   PART OF THE BODY

of a princess in marriage: *Puss in Boots*

MAD LIBS® is fun to play with friends, but you can also play it by yourself! To begin with, DO NOT look at the story on the page below. Fill in the blanks on this page with the words called for. Then, using the words you have selected, fill in the blank spaces in the story.

Now you've created your own hilarious MAD LIBS® game!

DRESSING YOUR CAT

ADJECTIVE _____

NOUN _____

PART OF THE BODY (PLURAL) _____

ANIMAL _____

ADJECTIVE _____

PERSON IN ROOM (MALE) _____

COLOR _____

PLURAL NOUN _____

OCCUPATION _____

NOUN _____

NOUN _____

ARTICLE OF CLOTHING _____

ADJECTIVE _____

NOUN _____

ADVERB _____

ADJECTIVE _____

MAD LIBS
DRESSING YOUR CAT

Your cat can help you celebrate your favorite holidays throughout the year. All

you need to do is dress it up in a/an _____, fun _____.
                                         ADJECTIVE   NOUN

With a pair of fuzzy _____, your cat can be transformed
                         PART OF THE BODY (PLURAL)

into the Easter _____. Or be _____ and turn your
                     ANIMAL   ADJECTIVE

cat into Uncle _____ with a little red, white, and
                   PERSON IN ROOM (MALE)

_____ suit. And there are a lot of _____ for your cat to wear
     COLOR   PLURAL NOUN

on Halloween. You can dress your cat as a/an _____ in a pink tutu,
                                                  OCCUPATION

a prehistoric _____ with spikes down its back, or a superhero like
                   NOUN

_____-man with a black cape and matching _____.
     NOUN   ARTICLE OF CLOTHING

And of course any cat can be turned into Santa Claus with a/an _____
                                                                    ADJECTIVE

red suit and a cute matching _____. Just make sure you choose
                                 NOUN

_____—you don't want to get on your cat's _____ side!
     ADVERB   ADJECTIVE

MAD LIBS® is fun to play with friends, but you can also play it by yourself! To begin with, DO NOT look at the story on the page below. Fill in the blanks on this page with the words called for. Then, using the words you have selected, fill in the blank spaces in the story.

Now you've created your own hilarious MAD LIBS® game!

NINE LIVES

NOUN _____

ADJECTIVE _____

VERB ENDING IN "ING" _____

ADJECTIVE _____

ADJECTIVE _____

ANIMAL _____

ADJECTIVE _____

NOUN _____

NUMBER _____

TYPE OF LIQUID _____

NOUN _____

VERB (PAST TENSE) _____

NOUN _____

ADJECTIVE _____

VEHICLE _____

NOUN _____

NOUN _____

ADJECTIVE _____